Values and Value Theory in Twentieth-Century America

VALUES
and Value Theory
in Twentieth-Century
America

ESSAYS IN HONOR OF

ELIZABETH FLOWER

EDITED BY

Murray G. Murphey and Ivar Berg

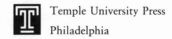

Temple University Press
Philadelphia

Temple University Press, Philadelphia 19122
Copyright © 1988 by Temple University. All rights reserved
Published 1988
Printed in the United States of America

The paper used in this publication meets the minimum
requirements of American National Standard for Information
Sciences—Permanence of Paper for Printed Library Materials,
ANSI Z39.48-1984

LIBRARY OF CONGRESS
Library of Congress Cataloging-in-Publication Data
Values and value theory in twentieth-century American : essays in honor
  of Elizabeth Flower / edited by Murray G. Murphey and Ivar Berg.
     p.   cm.
  Bibliography: p. 270
  Includes index.
  ISBN 0-87722-557-5 (alk. paper)
  1. Ethics. 2. Values. 3. Dewey, John, 1859–1952. 4. Flower,
Elizabeth. I. Flower, Elizabeth. II. Berg, Ivar E. III. Murphey, Murray G.
BJ1012.V35 1988
170—dc19   87-33675
                                                      CIP

Contents

Values and Value Theory
in Twentieth-Century America

Introduction

By all normal standards, philosophy in the twentieth century—at least in western Europe and America—has been a flourishing and vigorous discipline. Philosophy departments are so well established that it is inconceivable that there should be a major university without one. Philosophy courses are well attended, philosophers are (reasonably) well paid, philosophical journals and publications proliferate, and philosophical associations abound. But the philosophy that has interested and excited modern students and scholars is not quite the same as it was in the preceding century. Logic, epistemology, philosophy of language, and philosophy of science are the areas that have dominated our central half-century, and what may be loosely termed "analytic philosophy" has been the dominant school. It is in these fields that the great names are to be found— Russell and Gödel, Wittgenstein and Austin, Schlick and Carnap, Hempel and Quine. The nineteenth-century preoccupation with metaphysics has vanished, and no respectable philosopher now searches for the "categories." So too ethics and aesthetics, and what the Scots once called "moral philosophy," have not commanded the position in this century they had in the last. There is a deep irony in this development, for perhaps no century of human history has presented more difficult or more urgent problems concerning human life—problems of war and peace, of freedom and tyranny, of poverty and prosperity, of tradition and modernization. And yet philosophy—at least the philosophy of the dominant schools—has had little or nothing to say on these matters. Neither logic nor science, we are told, can derive an "ought" from an "is," and so in those matters that concern us most vitally we have been left to dogma or whim.

It was not always so (nor has it remained wholly so during our century). Prob- lems of virtue, right, and the good were prominent in classical philosophy, and if in postclassical times they tended to become entangled in theological doctrines, still by the eighteenth century the secular study of such issues was well advanced in Europe, England, Scotland, and America. If for Jonathan Edwards and his followers, ethics was indivisible from theology, the Scottish intellectual invasion of America led by John Witherspoon made a moral philosophy of a secular variety central to American thought. The great fluorescence of political thought that occurred between the Stamp Act and the ratification of the Constitution was profoundly indebted to French, English, and especially Scottish "moral" philosophers, and academic philosophy in America institutionalized Scottish thought, Scottish texts, and Scottish concerns. From the curious ménage à trois of Calvinism, Scottish Realism, and German Idealism that begat Pragmatism, the emphasis on the preeminent importance of the moral life was passed on to the new movement. This broadened sense of the moral life carried with it, in Pragmatism, fresh and important perspectives, especially as it tried to work out the implications of evolution: a deep appreciation of human capabilities and talents, including learning and problem-solving; the relation of knowledge to action and theory to practice; the infusion of knowledge with interest and purpose; the continuity of experience that challenges the separation of fact and value; the alignment of the moral with the more extensive concept of value and moral decision with evaluation. For James and Dewey and Lewis the moral life in this sense was always a major concern, and Dewey particularly, throughout his long life, which spanned nearly a century, never let that concern fade.

Among American philosophers of our time who have carried on this tradition, Elizabeth Flower has been one of the leaders. Her writings span the broad range of moral philosophy, including ethics, legal, political, economic, and social philosophy, and philosophy of education. Not surprisingly her interests have also been historical and have centered on the Scottish thinkers and their American followers and on the Pragmatists, particularly Dewey. During the almost forty years during which she has taught at the University of Pennsylvania, she has with unremitting candor and relentless probing forced her students to face the fact that human life in every field is irreducibly a life of moral choices—choices that are answered not by logic or by language or by science. In gathering together a selection of essays in her honor to mark her retirement from teaching, we have sought both to display something of the breadth of her work and to show the unity underlying it.

In the opening essay, Abraham Edel traces the rise of the concept of the general theory of value in the early twentieth century, demonstrating how developments within Idealism, Realism, and Naturalism all led to a focus upon the concept of value, and showing the role that that concept has played in the social sciences. Edel shows, however, that a more complex and variagated scene has emerged since World War II. Not only has value itself become an object of scientific study, but the emergence of "applied ethics" in business, medicine, law, and other fields has differentiated the content of the field, suggesting that what was joined together in the general theory of value needs to be split asunder to cope with particular contexts. With the rise of the "policy sciences" and the dawning recognition that science itself involves values, the classic fact-value distinction has begun to erode, and a new appreciation of the moral or at least the valuational character of all human action, scientific and other, has become pervasive.

Robert Schwartz picks up a different aspect of the recent history of philosophy by pointing out that, as Richard Rorty has argued, many of the assumptions that underlay modern analytic philosophy, and that until recently seemed axiomatic, have now been called into serious question. Positivist assumptions about meaning and truth, about the "given" and the certainty of knowledge, about scientific method and scientific progress, about mental states and the cognitive significance of questions about value have all come under increasing attack with the result that the analytic tradition, which lately was so dominant, is in deep trouble. But why, Schwartz asks, is this happening now, given the fact that the Pragmatists raised all of these objections eighty years ago? James and Dewey were both major figures in American philosophy and articulate spokesmen for their positions. However, Schwartz argues, for reasons not fully understood, their teachings were forgotten and have only recently been rediscovered. A partial answer to Schwartz's problem is contained in the remaining papers of this volume, which show that at least in the work of Dewey, Goodman, Flower, and others the lessons of Pragmatism were not forgotten.

It is entirely fitting, in view of Betty's own writing on Dewey and the broad range of his concerns, that Dewey should be the focus of so many of these papers. Ralph Sleeper takes up the question of Dewey's political philosophy and its relation to that of the Founding Fathers. This may seem an odd comparison to draw, for classic American political philosophy is usually seen as a product of the natural rights school, of which Dewey was a critic. But Sleeper draws here on Betty's own work on the relation of the Founding Fathers to the Scots, and particularly on her work on James Wilson, which shows that other metaphysical views besides Locke's underlay the founding of the American government. Dewey's metaphysics was of course naturalistic; for him not only was the human individual natural but so were his actions—thinking, valuing, and problem-solving. Indeed, for Dewey, cognition is evaluative and evaluation is cognitive, so no fact-value distinction is possible. Rights arise from the nature of the individual as a natural organism seeking satisfaction and are there prior to law or society. But as the human quest for satisfactions necessarily involves others, man is social by force of nature, and from cooperative actions communities arise. The consequences of individual actions, however, extend beyond the immediate community to affect other groups, and from the perception of common interests among such communities arises what Dewey calls "publics," which create states as their instrumentalities. Thus although Dewey was no believer in the classic natural law theory, his political philosophy makes individual rights prior to and a constraint upon positive government, and in rooting them in human nature itself he is thoroughly in the Scottish tradition. Democratic government is the instrument of the public to protect and advance individual rights, and the line between the proper role of government and that of individuals is one that must be established by empirical inquiry and experiment. It is just such a process of inquiry that Sleeper sees embodied in American judicial procedure, in which, on a case-by-case basis, the Congress and the courts have over the years constantly revised and redrawn that line. Thus in Sleeper's view, Dewey's political theory is entirely congruent with that of such architects of the Constitution as Wilson and serves to provide a philosophical justification for it.

In a closely related study, Peter Manicas examines Dewey's view of the relation of democracy to technological industrial society and contrasts it to that of Marx. As Manicas shows, Dewey's early democratic optimism underwent a substantial change in the 1920s when he became aware that technological society was not necessarily furthering democracy. The root of the problem, as Dewey saw it, was that technology was forcing a reorganization of society in which the public and even the communities were being undermined; impersonal relations, mass organizations, and complex interrelations made it impossible for communities and the public to recognize what their common interests were, thus destroying what Dewey understood to be the institutional basis of the democratic state. At the same time, Dewey rejected Marx's theory, even though in some respects his own analysis paralleled Marx's. He found the Marxist notion of class, which might have offered him an alternative institutional basis for democracy, unsuitable in the American context because here the workers were so divided by ethnic and religious factors that no consciousness of class existed. In Manicas's view, this left Dewey with a theory that called for a program of rational social planning but lacked the necessary institutional basis to make such a program viable.

Central to Dewey's philosophy is the theory of inquiry; indeed, Dewey's whole philosophy may be seen as growing out of his theory of inquiry. The development of cognitive psychology has brought a renewed interest in the psychological character of inquiry, and efforts have been and are being made to simulate human modes of inquiry by computer programs. Finbarr O'Connor presents a comparison of Dewey's theory with Newell and Simon's work in *Human Problem Solving*, the most rigorous attempt at such a simulation in the contemporary literature. Despite certain similarities, O'Connor finds that Newell and Simon restrict themselves to well-defined problems, whereas Dewey was primarily concerned with indeterminate ones, to problems with fixed goals, whereas Dewey regarded a change in the end-in-view as a possible outcome of inquiry, and ignore the question of problem representation that Dewey regarded as fundamental. As O'Connor notes, Newell and Simon's program is a method for searching for a fixed solution to a well-defined problem, whereas Dewey's approach is more accurately defined as an exploration of a problematic domain. Yet the notion of a "heuristic" method as developed by Newell and Simon and as elaborated by later writers represents a development that O'Connor believes Dewey would have welcomed, and cognitive psychology is likely to advance along lines marked out long before by Dewey. Areas such as problem-solving, decision theory, and the study of creativity all fall within the general domain of what Dewey called inquiry.

Given the overriding importance of inquiry for Dewey, he could scarcely not have been interested in education, and his influence in that field is greater than that of any other American. For Dewey, as John McDermott points out, experience is a transaction between the human being and nature—a transaction that is cognitive and aesthetic. It is through experience, and only through experience, that we learn and develop; "experience itself is pedagogical." Dewey had a powerful sense of the precariousness of human life, of the ever-present risk of death, defeat, and disaster, but he also understood that only by accepting such risks and by overcoming them can the individual grow. If for Dewey certainty must always elude us, satisfactions need not, provided we get from our present experience all that it holds for us. So much has been written of the future orientation of Pragmatism that we tend to forget Dewey's emphasis upon the past we carry with us and the present in which we live. In terming Dewey's pedagogy a "gamble for excellence," McDermott stresses how much Dewey attempted in both his educational theory and his educational practice to aid the individual to gain from experience the full richness it contains. Aesthetic experience is not for the elite alone but for every person who can grasp the potentialities of everyday experience. Dewey's commitment to education is a commitment to an improved quality of life for all, and his and his wife's labors at the famous Laboratory School at the University of Chicago were in attempt to realize that commitment.

The role of Darwinian science, and the religious and moral controversies it spawned, as a stimulus to the development of Pragmatism is well known. A very different response to that stimulus is provided by the work of Thorstein Veblen. An economist who refused to divorce economics from the rest of life, a social scientist who was also a philosopher, and an opponent of American capitalism who rejected the labor theory of value and the Marxist solution, Veblen stands as an interesting contrast to Dewey. In Veblen's scheme, as Murray Murphey shows, values are the basic motives of action, but they are fixed by genetic processes. Because human thought and action are teleological, there is a constant danger that teleology will be imputed to nature, which for Veblen is purely mechanical—a danger all to often realized in human history. There results a sort of dialectical struggle in which animistic modes of thought, and the institutions based upon them, such as capitalist enterprise, are pitted against mechanical modes of thought and their institutions—what Veblen calls the machine process. The outcome of this struggle remained for Veblen uncertain. His early optimism that the mechanical view was winning gave way in later years to a growing pessimism as capitalist institutions failed to succumb to the revolutionary impact of the machine.

The next two papers deal with the arts. Leon Edel picks up the challenge of C. P. Snow's famous "two cultures" thesis by asking whether art and science are the products of the same imagination. Drawing upon Freud, Edel argues that imagination is a blending of intellect and emotion and that its paradigm is found in sexual intercourse, that most fundamental of all human creative acts. If, as Freud believed, the actual process of imaginative creation lies in the unconscious, it is still possible to elucidate its relation to factors such as anxiety and illness and to illustrate its workings both in scientists and in artists. Edel grants that the scientific and artistic imaginations may require different training, but he holds that the underlying processes are the same in both cases.

Chaim Potok's paper deals with metaphor. Long a subject of major interest to literary scholars, metaphor has more recently engaged the attention of philosophers of language as it has become clear how much of our language and thought are metaphorical. As Potok shows, metaphors create new similarities rather than simply reflecting established ones; they interact with their subjects, and by serving as filters through which we know the world, they play a significant role in cognition. Metaphors are value-laden constructions that alter our conceptual schemes and so alter how we experience. The writer, Potok tells us, creates out of his own experience by a process that as Leon Edel emphasized, is usually unconscious, a mapping or scheme that he then imposes upon the world. If the mapping is both new and appropriate it creates a new insight, a new way of seeing the world and of dealing with its ambiguities.

The themes already discussed come together neatly in Lawrence Foster's discussion of the interpretation of the world views of nonliterate peoples and of their rituals. Foster presents first an illuminating comparison of the interpretations of Robin Horton and John Beattie. Horton takes the position, popular among anthropologists since Tylor, that primitive thought is not different in kind from scientific thought. Both are attempts to predict and explain experience, although the entities postulated for that purpose differ dramatically. Foster points out that Horton's earlier views of science were too positivistic and that, when modified by the more recent insights of Kuhn and Feyerabend, the proposed differentia between scientific and traditional thought dissolve. Beattie, on the contrary, argues that traditional belief is expressive and symbolic, having more in common with art than with science. But here again, Foster argues, a positivistic or neopositivistic view of art as emotive and noncognitive is in evidence. Ritual, for example, appears to be multifunctional, involving both cognitive and expressive elements. Statements literally false may be metaphorically true, and empirical considerations may bear upon both sorts of truth. Thus in challenging both Horton's and Beattie's interpretations, Foster argues that anthropology would profit from abandoning the positivist position on fact and value and urges instead a new view that holds knowledge to involve both literal statements and metaphors, both descriptions and exemplifications.

As Foster's piece illustrates the application of philosophical analysis to anthropology, so Robert Simon's illustrates its application to political science. The concept of national interest is used not only by political scientists but by political leaders and is frequently employed to justify one or another national policy. Yet the concept is a muddy one, and Simon attempts both to clarify it and to contrast it with other concepts often confused with it. Thus, he argues, the national interest must be distinguished from the interests of individual citizens of the nation and from the public interest—the latter applying chiefly to domestic political affairs, whereas the former applies chiefly to international relations. Simon opposes the so-called Realist contention that the national interest should be defined only in terms of power and security, arguing that the pursuit of national ideals and values also enters into the national interest. But the introduction of moral considerations raises difficult questions, for the "society" of nations is not strictly analogous to a society of individual persons. Yet if the international scene lacks an established moral order, it is also not quite the war of all against all; rather it seems to involve a distinct moral order in which there is a high risk of the violation of norms. Similarly, the relation of national interest to human rights does not admit of a simple solution in terms of the moral codes of individual persons, a fact that Simon brings out skillfully in his discussion of the role of the national interest in dealing with terrorism. Clearly, this is an area in which answers are wanting, but Simon succeeds in showing at least why some of the proposed answers will not do.

Ivar Berg, reflecting on nearly thirty years of efforts to give ethics a meaningful place in the training of businessmen, argues that such efforts are hopeless as long as economists and businessmen continue to believe that economics itself is value-free. Reared to believe that the individual's pursuit of self-interest must automatically serve the interests of all, and convinced that business decisions are best made on a scientific and technical basis, aspiring entrepreneurs are blind to the values underlying their own actions. To illustrate his thesis, Berg considers three cases of particular pertinence to the contemporary scene. First, he considers plant shutdowns and the attendant devastation wrought in the communities where they occur. The decision to close such plants is based typically on economic criteria only; the sociological effects are regarded as unfortunate but incidental to the dominant concerns. Second, he points to the equation drawn in American society between the educational level of an individual and his productivity. This equation, Berg notes, rests solely upon the fact that education correlates positively with income; it is assumed, without benefit of empirical evidence, that income measures productivity. Thus there is provided a putative justification for inequality, on the untested supposition that those who get more produce more. This justification is of great social importance because Americans are generally willing to accept inequality only when it can be attributed to merit. The fruits of these convictions are clear when Berg turns to his third case, structural unemployment. As he demonstrates, the whole notion of structural unemployment rests upon a mistaken conversion of a demographic description into an economic explanation, and the thesis that those who are unemployed are the least productive—the corollary from the doctrine that income measures productivity—not only has no empirical support but is directly contradicted by the dramatic accomplishments of American production during World War II. Teaching ethics to businessmen, Berg concludes, will be a waste of time until both businessmen and economists recognize the degree to which their alleged science is value-laden.

Bringing philosophy to bear on education in a manner that would have pleased Dewey, Israel Scheffler examines the current passion for introducing computers into the schools. Granting the ever-growing impact of computers on our society, it does not follow, Scheffler argues, that teaching students the computer is a proper functions for the schools. Many of the arguments used to promote such computer training are specious; few students will find jobs in computing and few will need to know the technical side of computing to deal with the machines in ordinary life. Computers may indeed be used to serve some educational ends, but Scheffler warns against the danger that fascination with the computer will lead to a narrowing of the goals of education to those for which the computer provides a means. Scheffler also stresses the impact upon our views of knowledge of metaphors borrowed from the language of computing. To think of knowledge in terms of "information," "storage," and "retrieval" is to adopt a mechanical Baconianism that omits just those questions of problem representation, definition of goals, creation of hypotheses, and creative insight that, as Dewey taught us, are central to genuine education. Here again one sees how metaphor may alter our conception of reality, in this case for the worse. The use of computers in education, Scheffler argues, must serve the purposes of education; education should not be warped to fit the capacities of the computer.

In the final paper, Joseph Margolis takes up the problem of "dirty hands," a problem that applies with particular force to our own era. The problem of dirty hands is that there appear to be real situations in which one must do what is evil in order to achieve what is good. Margolis considers the efforts of Walzer and Nagel to resolve this dilemma and points out that they fail to do so precisely because they seek solutions in terms of consistent principled conduct that defines the problem away. Instead, Margolis argues, we must proceed on a case-by-case basis, for no resolution of a conflict of principles is likely to be achieved on the basis of principles. It may in fact be rational in certain cases to act in a way that is not justified by moral principles, and it may not be *un*principled to do so.

Taken together, these essays—many of them inspired by Betty's writing or by her teaching—testify to the centrality of value in the history of philosophy in America, in aesthetic and moral decisions, in the human sciences, and in education. Through them all, concepts such as metaphor and interest, and problems such as the nature of inquiry, the relation of the factual and the evaluative, the possibilities of education, the character of knowledge, and the resolution of conflicting demands run as common threads. These essays are more than a tribute to a distinguished philosopher; they are part of the legacy she has left to the world.

I | The Concept of Value and Its Travels in Twentieth-Century America

Abraham Edel

The concept of value has traveled far in twentieth-century America. Today talk of values comes lightly to the man in the street and the man in the White House alike; it passes readily among philosophers and scientists, literary critics and political ideologists. Few realize that this was not always so. At the beginning of the century the concept of value started from a limited base. The several disciplines that it soon sought to unify, whether in federation or empire, had each its own conceptual apparatus: ethics the good and the right, aesthetics beauty, religion the holy, economics success and the functioning of the economy, politics peace and order, social life generally the key motifs of its many institutions. A new movement was launched—the "general theory of value"—to provide the super-theory. There followed widespread controversy over the nature of value. Yet by midcentury, when the lines of controversy were already fixed but no resolution was in sight, a writer in a cooperative volume that sought some agreement on the meaning of value could begin: "The time will come, I think, when the present hubbub over value will be hard even for students of the history of ideas to understand."[1] At the same time, however, a social scientist later wrote, a movement was under way in social science "to come out in the open with an explicit presentation of values."[2] Clearly the story cannot be told in one field alone, nor without tracing connections to the problems—sociocultural, intellectual, historical—to which general concepts are addressed, to the changing milieu in which they operate. These dynamic sources pay little heed to the neat classification of disciplines and the neat partition of concepts. But they can help us see the dynamism of the concepts themselves in human affairs.

The present paper takes preliminary steps toward understanding the "hubbub over value." It starts with precursor moves toward generality in the history of ethics and how they smoothed the path for the general idea of value. It notes how the American Philosophical Association in its 1913 meeting directed attention to the topic, how the nature of value was debated in the next three decades. It offers hypotheses about the underlying problems and functions of this development. It follows the awakening to the problem of values in the social sciences and the stages through which it passed. It outlines the culmination—closer to our own day—in which the sharp dichotomy of fact and value that had long been a linchpin in both moral philosophy and social science gave way, and how seeds planted by an earlier Pragmatism, dating back to Peirce's epistemology and James's psychology a century ago, blossomed in a view of the interpenetration, indeed the unity, of fact and value in experience. The revolution was not confined to moral philosophy and social science; it broke out in epistemology and the philosophy of science as well. It was propelled by a changing world and a changing society. Today it opens new doors and imposes new intellectual tasks, felt but not always articulated, and on the whole still to be faced.

I

"In the main, therefore, it is possible that the current philosophy of value is essentially new; with the wine of adventure in its veins. Value *may* prove to be the key that will eventually release all the human sciences from their present position of pathetic, if dignified futility." So wrote the Scottish philosopher John Laird, in a full-length study (1929) of approaches to the idea of value in the history of moral thought.[3] But he also hesitates and reminds himself (and us) that in the Humean tradition inquiry into "moral matters" already had the broad meaning of an inquiry into *mores*; hence general value theory may be but the recovery and development of an older idea rather than a fresh invention. Howard O. Eaton, in

The Austrian Philosophy of Values (1930), had no such qualms. He speaks of "the gestation and birth of an entirely new and independent philosophical discipline" and sees it as philosophy aspiring to become a social science.[4]

The idea of the *worth* or *value* of something had always been around in the common language, but it had rarely been made the subject of philosophical analysis and controversy. Aristotle, who analyzes thoroughly the terminology of ethics, simply uses its Greek 'equivalent casually. The nearest he comes to our contemporary problems of value is (in his *Topics*) to give a few criteria for estimating what is *better*. Bentham, in his *Introduction to the Principles of Morals and Legislation* (1789), entitles a chapter "Value of a Lot of Pleasure, how to be measured." In this, value would seem to indicate simply the effort to measure the utility of a course of action in the hedonic quest.

If we look for precursors in the history of ethics, increasing generality can be found in those theories in which the idea of the good is given a full structured basis in the picture of human life. A teleogical ethics assigns a directional purpose in life: the good becomes a certain kind of whole life. Eighteenth-century approval theories of ethics, such as Hume's, deal with virtue (the good of character) in terms of a basic sentiment of sympathy that runs through one's response to all human action. Modern Utilitarian ethics, with its hedonistic assumptions, yields the same breadth. Self-realization ethics finds a unity of the good by interpreting all striving as the maturing and making of a self.

In the first decade of the twentieth century, the *good* of traditional ethics is stretched to the utmost. In *Principia Ethica* (1903), G. E. Moore not only defines all other moral concepts directly in terms of *good* but equates good itself with *intrinsic value*. And this idea begins to absorb concepts in other fields: for example, the beautiful is defined as that whose admiring contemplation is an intrinsically valuable whole. Moreover, the central tenor of the work is the separation of value from fact; Moore insists that good or intrinsic value cannot be defined in terms of any scientific or metaphysical or religious states of affairs, but is independent and intuitively ascertainable. Ralph Barton Perry (*The Moral Economy*, 1909), thoroughly naturalistic in his approach, defines good in terms of interest and sees the moral problem as simply finding an organization of life that most secures human living and advances human interests. Because no area of life is exempt from this critique, morality has a general or overarching role. It is a total-life enterprise. Perry's *The Moral Economy* deserves special attention as the precursor of his *General Theory of Value* two decades later.

The self-conscious formulation of a general theory of value as a new project, however, is found in Wilbur Marshall Urban's comprehensive *Valuation, Its*

Nature and Laws, Being an Introduction to the General Theory of Value (1909). The unity of the inquiry is already taken for granted in Hugo Münsterberg's *The Eternal Values* (1909). In both, the new discipline is tied to a philosophical idealism. This was soon to be followed by naturalistic answers and by pragmatic answers. But answers are to questions, and these merit prior attention.

In 1913 the Executive Committee of the American Philosophical Association set the problem of values for discussion at the association's December meetings.[5] It recognized that there were already various points of view involved. The questions framed by a subcommittee asked whether value is something ultimate that attaches itself to "things" apart from consciousness or the desires and aversions of an organic being; whether a theory of the nature of things can be successfully developed without referring to a theory of value, and vice versa; how the respective existences and values or theories of these would be related and how that could be established; whether the various positions offered a single fundamental standard of values.

Looking back from the near twenty-first century, we can see that in America these questions set the agenda for twentieth-century philosophical debate, which in turn was not without some influence on social science: a debate over whether values have some place in the inventory of the real world (whether metaphysical or scientific fact) or whether values are rather human responses to such reality or fact; a debate over how theories of reality and of value could be developed—increasingly interpreted as the difference between judgments of fact and judgments of value and whether they are established in the same way or different ways; about whether standards of value are uniform or relative.

Although these questions about the nature of value, its status in the order of reality, and the methods for handling it obviously met with different answers, all the answers tacitly assume that value is a single general concept about which such questions can be asked. We have therefore to examine where in the different kinds of answers we find a source for this assumption of unity. For this purpose, let us take as brief samples the philosophies of idealism, naturalism, and pragmatism.

II

The idealist philosophers see an emerging consciousness of a world of values as a new side of reality. Urban says: "Far from being a mere fact among other facts, that which we mean by our evaluation of objects is something independent of this world, and so little merely a part of it that it is rather the whole world seen from a special point of view. Over against a world of facts is set a world of values."[6] Münsterberg finds an ultimate value character in our imposition of order on experience: "We seek the identity of experience. That is the one fundamental act which secures for us a world."[7] This act of will ensures that the world is an order, gives value to truth, and thus signifies the values of consistency, unity, connection, and the rest. The ladder of value climbs to achievement and culminates, for Münsterberg, in holiness. To build up such a world is the common task of mankind. Urban reaches beyond the will as a basis for value and offers a richer psychology: "In general, then, we may conclude that feeling of value is the feeling aspect of conative process, as distinguished from the feeling-tone of simple presentations. And by conative process we understand the total process of development by which affective-volitional meaning is acquired, the total process including actual and dispositional moments." He defines *worth* or *value* as "the funded meaning of the object for the subject in different attitudes, or as predetermined by different dispositions and interests."[8] Underlying these analyses is the sharper identification of the spiritual in man and its place in the world as a whole. Münsterberg thinks that only by recognizing that there resides in the world something valuable in itself can the challenge of relativism and skepticism be met.

The naturalistic philosophies, on the contrary, fix as their starting point the human raw materials out of which values are fashioned and that enter into value processes. They appeal not only, as the Utilitarians had done, to the phenomena of pleasure and pain, but to the more propulsive notions of appetite, impulse, desire, purpose, demand, or, in Perry's case, the general idea of *interest* seen in its sense of selective action. The term is geared to characterize all life, animal as well as man. For at the basis of the unity that Perry finds in value is an evolutionary outlook: the vast array of interests that constitute the values is the proliferation from rudimentary selective acts originally bent on survival.

Perry too finds a unity in value that sets it off distinctively. At the beginning of *General Theory of Value* (1926) he argues the need for a general theory by pointing to "the radical difference between observing, noting, remarking, measuring, on the one hand; and loving, hating, approving, condemning, on the other hand; and would seek to understand the different attitudes comprised within the second set as variations of one attitude." This is "the study of a peculiar kind of act", but we can also carry on the study of a peculiar kind of predicate, for example when we think of "happiness, preciousness, blessedness, envy, craft, guile"; the difference is between the act of *valuing* and the predicate *valuable*.[9] It is easy, says Perry, to point to a host of special sciences that study the species—economics, political science and jurisprudence, aesthetics, philosophy of religion, ethics. What is needed is a fuller study of the genus.

The generalizing move from species to genus is scarcely persuasive. Perry's argument seems to beg the question by treating the different fields as already species and so assuming that the unity is generic. Diverse uses of a term in different fields may as readily prove to be only analogical. A whole range of semantic differences lies between sheer ambiguity (as "sharp" means different things for a knife and a note) and sharing the same essential properties; among them a genus is a strong, though not perhaps the strongest kind of unity. Indeed in ancient times Plato and Aristotle differed on the unity of the good. Plato thought there was an ultimately real Form of the Good to which all aspiration was directed (whether to have children or to write poetry); Aristotle denied such generic identity and thought the human good was a form of life giving organized expression to human nature. In short, underlying a generalizing move for value there must be some justifying theory. Bentham's had been psychological; assuming all people engaged in the simple hedonistic quest, he limited the concept of value to measuring amounts and summing utility. Other theoretical bases for unity in a value concept are, of course, possible: a historical basis may find a clear line of development in human life and society; a cultural basis might find in each people a single cultural pattern that permeates all areas of life.[10]

Perhaps the strength of Perry's argument for a general concept is to be found in his evolutionary assumptions, not in his sorting of the phenomena. His attempt to sort out value and non-value phenomena embarks on the growing dichotomy of fact and value. Urban and Münsterberg reach out to the subtler value components in all knowledge.

A pragmatic approach to value theory is most fully worked out in Dewey. He had responded immediately to the invitation of the Executive Committee for refinement of issues about value.[11] Value, he says, is unnecessarily tied to the idealistic-realistic controversy; it should not become involved in the controversy over consciousness versus organism. He suggests a neutral term in analyzing value, such as selections and rejections, rather than desires. For him the important questions are whether values have an antecedent existence or depend on a valuational process (defined as "a process of reflective estimation or judgment"), how that process would modify any antecedent values, what the role of intelligence is in such modification, whether appreciation is a mode of knowing values or names their direct presence, and how it is related to criticism.

The baring of these questions is clear in the light of Dewey's mature position: an interpretation of value in terms of active reflective choice that refashions or creates outcomes for human demands, desires, satisfactions, enjoyments. The central phenomenon is the valuational process. Occasionally Dewey is tempted to allow "value" (the noun) as the product of that process, in an immediate sense of the object enjoyed or approved. Sometimes he distinguishes prizing from appraising in this sense, and assigns what is prized to value and what is appraised as undergoing the valuation process. But he generally draws back and begins to see prizing itself as having a valuating character, so that "value" is just an abstract noun without one definite object but rather the whole body of things that go through the process. Although Dewey shares Perry's philosophical naturalism, he criticizes Perry for treating interests and desires as givens. In reality a desire presupposes a problem-situation or need-situation for which a specific object is being offered as a solution; hence a prizing or a desiring is already an implicit or initial appraising. It would be a long story to trace Dewey's struggle for this active conception of valuation in the philosophical periodical literature of the second and third decade against analyses in terms of pleasure, interest, satisfaction, preference, offered by the majority of philosophers in America who tilled the field of general value theory. Its culmination was Dewey's *Theory of Valuation* (1939), but the struggle and debate did not end then.

Underlying Dewey's view of value as primarily continual evaluation is his functional view of consciousness as arising where there are hesitations in the smooth flow of habit, the occurrence of doubt and problem. Experience has thus an inherent problematic structure, and intelligence is the developed capacity for dealing with this. Because a problem situation betokens the failure of habits to provide adequate guidance, there is always an element of initiative and novelty in the solution. This gives Dewey's analysis of experience and value a forward-looking character; the analyses of induction and of value that he is criticizing impose a static character that is attentive only to the past.[12]

Perhaps Dewey's position would have been more readily understandable if linguistic chance had fastened on the term "worth" rather than "value." We do not speak of a person having worths as we do of having values—unless in specific contexts where a "man of worth" means either having wealth or being trustworthy! There would have been less temptation to make a substantive out of value and a readier attentiveness to context and process.

On the whole, then, although idealist and naturalist and pragmatist offer different theoretical bases for the unity of the concept of value, and interpret the unity in different ways, they share a generalizing of the concept. That phenomenon at that time is what accordingly requires explanation.

III

What problems beyond philosophy—sociocultural, historical, intellectual—are to be found in the early part of the twentieth century, to which the rise of the general theory of value was addressed? There is a confluence of at least three different trends.

(1) With the growth of industrialism from the eighteenth century on, a greater array of commodities was presented to the consuming public. This was only one area in which choice became both possible and necessary. In the long run various freedoms produced the same result: freedom of choice in occupation, in marriage, in residence, in mode of life, even in ideas. Choice requires comparison of alternatives and some measurement of properties. The pervasiveness of measurement in modern life is obvious. Hence the process of valuation becomes entrenched and generalized. The ordinary idea of the worth of something, always around in the common language, has to be self-consciously developed. This source for general value theory prompts a decision-model and on a broader scale finds its generalization in twentieth century decision theory.

(2) Darwinism had a powerful impact on the conception of man. On the one side it was feared; on the other, welcomed as the total naturalizing of man within the material world. The immediate consequence was to shift the basic phenomena (or values, however characterized) into scientific study rather than the arena of religion. In philosophy the lineup reaches back into the late eighteenth century, at least in Kant's attempt to separate the realm of science from the realm of religion and morality, with the first assigned to the phenomenal world and the second to the noumenal or real world. Hegel's program of tracing the unfolding of Spirit through the history of the world, natural as well as human, is an imposing reconciliation, but on the terms of Spirit. With Darwinism and its consequent intellectual ferment, the attempt to fashion a synthesis shifts to the other side: the effort is to find man's place in nature, not to find a way of exempting man from nature. Hegelian idealism uncomfortably fused with Kantian dualism provides the ammunition for the resistance.

The struggle became particularly acute after Darwin's *Descent of Man* (first edition, 1871) and its theories about the social-evolutionary origins of the moral sense. The case for a spiritual principle as necessary to morality and knowledge (and so reaching over into nature at least so far as its knowledge is concerned) is stated with great sophistication in T. H. Green's posthumously published *Prolegomena to Ethics* (1883). The complete naturalization of man will mean that morality can only be explained as fear: such natural causality admits of no free action and responsibility. A spiritual principle found in both morality and knowledge is the only way to understand human life. This provides a genuine unity in personal development, a unity evident in the development of the self. We have here a clear formulation of a self-realizationist ethic that becomes the central ethical theory of philosophical idealism in the first part of the twentieth century. It is quite evident in Münsterberg and Urban that the range of their theory is no longer a provincial ethics and that their general value approach is directed toward avoiding the consequences of a purely naturalistic view of man. To bring all the fields of value together under the banner of value is a summons to cooperate in a common front of rescuing the spirit. In Urban particularly, the Hegelian element is strong; nature is not outcast but put in its subordinate place as only a phase. Urban's *Fundamentals of Ethics* (1930) considers rising levels: at the lowest, what satisfies hunger and thirst; at the middle, what furthers or conserves life; at the upper, the development of selves and self-realization.[13]

On the naturalistic side, the attempt not to reduce spirit to nature but to find a comfortable home for the phenomena of spirit in nature is an explicit theme in Perry and Dewey. In his 1954 *Realms of Value*, Perry says that "Münsterberg would be scandalized by the liberties which have been taken with the word value since his day. For with Münsterberg and his school, 'values' possessed an exalted dignity transcending both nature and sense-perception. They have since become completely secularized, mingling with the affairs of everyday life, and consorting intimately with the vulgar facts of sense-experience."[14] Dewey early worked through Hegelian influences and parted more slowly from the self-realization ethics of Green.[15] The influence of Darwinism as setting the task of naturalizing man was explicitly recognized all along.

(3) Economics was the one social science that early talked of value. It used the concept for its own special purposes and did not at the outset offer value as a general working tool for other social sciences. But economics' own problems compelled a broadening and thinning out of the idea of value so that by the twentieth century the concept lay as a ready source for a general theory.

From at least Adam Smith on (not to go back to Aristotle) economists made a distinction between use value and exchange value. Since economics as a special modern study owed its currency to the growth and importance of markets, exchange value naturally was of special concern; use value was simply a necessary condition for an item to enter the market. Accordingly, the nature of value as a problem mean chiefly the nature of exchange value. Its treatment was no exercise in abstraction nor a study of linguistic usage; it dealt with the determinants of prices and if possible their anticipation. This brought into play an intricate web of theory. The labor theory of value in the earlier classical economists fixed on congealed labor in commodities as the crucial factor, whereas the later classical economists turned to the psychology of demand and desire. This is a familiar story. At first, relying on Benthamism, they assumed cardinal measurement for pleasures and pains and therefore the possibility of calculating the total utility of a commodity across individual valuations. (Edgworth even dreamed of a "hedonimeter" to give the individual readings.) Then ingenious ways were worked out to operate with only ordinal measurement, that is, a rank ordering of preference for each individual. Eventually, by Pareto's time, all attempts at interpersonal comparison dropped away, and total valuations had as their bedrock basis the individual's uncriticized expression of preferences and aimed at an overall maximization.

In these theoretical developments, the concept of valuation is separated from any constraint provided by the object that is being evaluated or by the process of individual valuing. Valuation is generalized to deal with the maximization of individual preferences as such. In the narrower confines of the economic market the valuation can be expressed in terms of money without any special concern about the character of the commodities other than their contribution to the maximization of money. In the broader scope of social philosophy the counters are individual will or preferential decision and social organization to foster a maximal expression and achievement of individual preferences. The generality of the value concept thus expresses the unfettered indivudualism within a community where the social aim is the maximal achievement of individual achievement.

The outcome provides a ready model for general value theory. Value, in its run-of-the-mill sense, characterizes any interest that motivates a person. As valuation, it is the measure of maximal achievement. The unquestioning acceptance of the initial interests, apart from their effect on the maximizing process, exhibits the intense individualism. But as we know, individualism had been growing over the past three centuries and invading one field after another as freedoms multiplied and liberty became the constitutive and predominant ideal. The shape of a life lived under this whole model is, of course, precisely the social philosophy of nineteenth-century liberalism.

Perry's value theory embodies this larger orientation. In *The Moral Economy* he had used the economic model deliberately: the interests are enterprises; they grow and operate in their own way toward expanded achievement; their conflicts lead to modes of social organization; the social outlook gives them a value status from the outset, to be tempered by their effect in the social process. This strong individualism is continued in *General Theory of Value*, though there are many modifications. In fact Perry turns the individualism into a specfic moral virtue of love: love, he says, is a disinterested interest in other people's interests, giving them an initial moral support. Perry's individualism is not unique in American ethical theory. Most naturalistic ethics of the twentieth century starts with interests, impulses, desires, attachments, preferences, purposes, selections, and builds theoretical schemes of integration. They differ largely according to the type of psychology that is invoked in analyzing those units.[16] The major ethical theory that cuts out a different path is that of Dewey.

IV

We may well leave the philosophical elaboration of general value theory after the fourth decade. It is rich, and its variety comes from the many angles at which it is approached. Tools are brought for its analysis from a fresh and active linguistics, a sophisticated modal logic, many psychologies (behavioral, Freudian, Gestalt).[17] Influences pour in from Europe—phenomenological, existentialist, critical.[18] Nevertheless, the questions they are answering have been largely fixed by the earlier development, and the answers correspondingly share the built-in assumptions of the very theory. Thus whether values are taken to be the expression of emotion or to have cognitive grasp, the questions are asked wholesale, for values as a whole. For example, Are values verifiable? Are values relative or absolute? For the most part, since the philosophical idealism of an earlier period has receded, the sharpest dichotomy of value and fact holds sway.[19]

Some inroads are made toward a recovery of a conceptual pluralism. To some extent Dewey's approach promotes this; since the unified aspect is process, the content can be as varied as the vast range of complexity and change allows.[20] One important linguistic-philosophical movement of the midcentury and after proved a powerful ally. This is ordinary-language (or Oxford) analysis. Concerned as it is with analyzing linguistic uses in particular contexts, it does not talk of values nor analyze value in general; rather, it examines ways in which "good,""ought," and the rest of traditional terms are used; and even of these it asks how contexts differentiate uses, moving thus to greater particularity rather than generality. For example, is there a difference in meaning according to the pronoun associated with "ought"—"I ought" (decisional), "you ought" (prescriptive), "he ought" (evaluative)? Does tense make a difference—"I ought" (present decisional), "I ought to have" (past, evaluative)? On the whole, however, this linguistic analysis, though particularistic, did not take time out to challenge the fact-value dichotomy or the generic value formulations, or deal with contexts in a broader (cultural, sociohistorical) sense than linguistic.

Meanwhile, the standardized formulations and built-in assumptions acquired free rein in the psychological and social sciences. At least three stages may be distinguished in the literature of these sciences. In the first there is little use of value language, but the sciences are beginning to discover that there is a value tinge to many of their concepts, that what they are doing is in some sense *about* values or describing the movement of values. In the second stage they set about consciously to investigate people's values. In the third, they begin to suspect that their scientific inquiry itself makes implicit valuations.

These developments were not propelled simply by the older social and intellectual movements that we suggested had operated in the rise of general value theory. For one thing, the intellectual struggle over naturalizing man had abated; the sciences of nature were far too advanced by this time for the older arguments about the relation of the living and the nonliving. The economic model had thinned out and merged into a general science of decision. The domain of choice had, it is true, broadened immeasurably; but more important, perhaps, was the recognition, after World War II, that the area of human control was becoming more and more extensive, and that decisions of a momentous character—on war and peace, on nuclear energy and its dangers, on overpopulation—could lie in human hands. This was not just a question of technological and scientific advance nor merely a mood of greater human powers. Science and technology were changing the very operations of practice, in the day-to-day provision of resources and the ways of meeting people's needs. Agriculture, for example, showed the transformation starkly. It had been a rural pursuit, isolated from the modernizing city, close to nature and at best helping it, by careful tending, by irrigation, increasingly by warding off dangers. Now the relation to industry was reversed: agriculture now depended on industry, on technology and science, for fertilizer, for seed selection, for large-scale machinery, for food processing from its products, for communication. The scope of human purposive activity in such complex organization, especially at the pace at which it was growing in the second half of the century, brought theory and practice together, strained to the breaking point older intellectual dichotomies of theory and practice, knowledge and valuation, and in general imparted an active attitude to the consideration of questions of value.

In moral philosophy, the impact of these forces came with suddenness in the 1970s, when in field after field problems of "applied ethics" were thrust upon philosophers. At present, perhaps the most vital movement in ethical theory is the attempt to draw theoretical lessons from this experience and to work out a sober relation of theory and practice. In the relation of values and social science, the transformation appears to have been more gradual, though with occasional leaps. To this we turn text.

V

Before the 1930s, psychological or social studies of moral ideas were likely to use strictly moral language and stay within the confines that language imposed. They were also likely to have a moral motivation. A notable study like Hartshorne's and May's *Studies in Deceit* (1928) deals with a moral virtue of honesty, carries out empirical surveys, and, consonant with the growing behaviorist atmosphere, concludes that there is no characterological unity in the virtue. In the 1930s and 1940s, various concepts handle what later will be considered values. Social psychology studies attitudes of groups and those that play a significant role in institutional functioning. Personality psychology makes inventories and fashions tests for character traits. Freudian theory makes a strong entry, not only with needs and instincts but also with configurational concepts like ego and superego. Psychologists now speak of ego-involvements and group norms. The concept of self, long absent from a dominantly behaviorist approach, reappears in the early 1940s.[21] Attempts to compare whole cultures rather than itemize traits had been given a strong impetus by Ruth Benedict's *Patterns of Culture* (1934). In due course these were to be seen as full-fledged value-patterns. Interestingly enough, the controversies that emerged about the book were not whether the patterns were properly to be understood as value-patterns but whether Benedict was introducing biases into scientific work by going from the diversity of patterns to a plea for tolerance, or speaking more favorably of peace than of war, of the absence of violence in personal relations than of typical aggression. Yet such an emphasis should not be surprising. The great questions of the day, in the sharp conflict of social philosophies and the milieu of impending war, and then the prosecution of the war, were matters of fundamental disagreement, questions of momentous decision. The sciences were still proclaiming their neutrality as sciences; they were not ready to consider that values were embedded throughout their regular work, although biological and physical scientists were beginning to consider value consequences in mobilizing on issues of racist theory and (later) on nuclear energy.

It is difficult today to discuss such studies without characterizing them as value studies. Only in looking back can we see that a concept of general value was supervening on or emanating from the objects of study: attitudes, personality traits, needs, motivations, involvements, institutional goals and norms, cultural patterns. The general concept, developed in philosophical theory, was there at hand, and it served as a key to open the floodgates of value study.

The gates were open and the flood came in the early 1950s. World War II was over, though fresh wars were going on or in the making. The colonial system was breaking down and nations were emerging in Asia and forseeably would in Africa. What did the mass of men (not yet women) want of the world and of their lives? Conservative voices in America were heard to say that the war had been fought to restore free enterprise throughout the world. But sober social scientists thought we ought rather to carry out empirical studies. American politicians worried whether the mass of men would opt for communism or the free world. Anthropologists and sociologists sought rather the rich texture of human wants and desires and attitudes as criteria of cultural choices. In short, they wanted to explore the values of people throughout the world. What were the kinds of values, the patterns of value, that steered people in times of unavoidable change?

The tools for such investigation had already been sharpened during the war period. Practical questions had forced inquiry: What kinds of foods would different peoples tolerate, so that we would know what packages to prepare for countries about to be liberated? (There were still memories of World War I experiences of tragic mistakes.) Should the Emperor of Japan be removed or was the institution so entrenched that surrender in that case would become a prolonged and bloody matter? More general questions of understanding arose after the turmoil of war: Why did so civilized a people as the Germans yield so readily to Hitler's ideas—was it a matter of authoritarian structure somehow embedded in deep personality structure? What had happened to peoples in the Pacific outside of the range of western civilization when their territory was swept by a million or more western soldiers? What goes on in the minds and souls of men when their parents teach them old ways and the rewards come from turning to new ways?

To name the subject-matter of so broad a range of inquiry was no easy task. A general notion of *traditions, ways of life, personality types,* even *patterns,* was not specific enough. *World-outlooks* was too broad, though it gave a sense of the systematic; *ideas* was too vague; *national character* had too psychological a slant. *Cultural configurations* conveyed simply systematic differences, but in what? Perhaps the idea of *experiments in living* would provide the proper distance and depth for study. But all these notions were submerged in presuppositions of the kind of unity that would be found. When Kroeber and Kluckholm wrote *Culture, a Critical Review of Concepts and Definitions* (1952), they found an almost endless array of different usages and different meanings in even this basic notion. What would patterns of culture then be patterns of?

The generic concept of *value* stepped into the breach. It had the appropriate generality, the appropriate openness, it could cover the appetitive and conative and desiderative and interest and—in short—preferential or selective tendencies of people in any field; it could capture habits of action and thought as well as moments of choice and decision. And it had just the right ambiguity to connote both a state of liking or prizing and criteria or evaluating. Values were the subject on which all the burgeoning inquiries now focused. Quite quickly, almost suddenly, it was respectable for American social science to deal with values as subject-matter, not of course as investigators' biases. (But even biases could now be investigated under the waxing concept of *ideology*, how investigators' or theoreticians' values crept into the work of science and distorted it.[22])

As American social scientists—particularly anthropologists and sociologists—embarked on innumerable value studies, they were intent in part too on clarifying the concept of value. But this was the lesser note. Primarily they tried to describe values in all their variety and all their transformation and in all their influence. Take, for example, the six-year Harvard Values Studies carried on in the southwest of the United States among five different cultures—Navajo, Zuni, Texas-American, Mormon, Spanish-American. They covered religious values (some elicited from responses to missionary work); land use (different patterns, relation to kinship); habits of households (ordinary habits, relations to other households, attitudes to government); attitudes to accumulation of wealth and to mutual help; values revealed in law (for example, with respect to ownership, and to different crimes); contact with other patterns (for example, veterans returning from war service); music (for example, use in ceremonial, preference and grounds); myths (typical themes and values reflected). They reported the results of psychological tests (Rorschach, Thematic Apperception, Sentence Completion) which revealed startingly different ways of seeing the world selectively.[23] For a quite different example, take the Comparative Studies in Cultures and Civilizations centered at the University of Chicago. They were oriented to international differences, with studies in Chinese thought and Islamic culture; they reached back into history and specific patterns.[24] Or again, American sociologists began to give value profiles of American society, or of segments within it.[25] Such studies in turn prompted moral philosophers to try out anthropological methods of investigation on specific moralities, with the wider field of value study reacting on the earlier parent field of ethics.[26]

As values took their place in the subject matter of social science, one might have expected the concept of value to be clarified by application. What happened was simply that the different interpretations that had characterized the general theory of value in philosophy now reappeared in the usage of the social scientists. In philosophical theories, we saw, value was often a term for any selective or preferential act or its objects (desires, interests). This was essentially descriptive of people's tendencies or habits of action. Often too, however, value referred to a criterion that operated for selection; it was judgmental or entered as a ground for decision. The usage in social science was comparably twofold: sometimes it described habits of action or selection, sometimes the criteria that governed selection or judgment. In a sample study of texts in the late 1950s, I found that the situation was complicated by the use of another concept alongside, that of *norms*. In philosophic usage, the latter suggested the normative, the judgmental; the evaluation of one's own or another's values is a normative enterprise. But in the usage of psychological or social science it appeared that the norms were rather the ways of acting that took shape as rules; hence the norms of a society or culture were the rules that operated in socialization of the growing child or in efforts to control the conduct of people. Thus although the rules were normative (in the philosophical sense) the enterprise of presenting the norms of a given society or culture was avowedly descriptive. On the other hand, "value" was often defined, in a judgmental reference, as the criteria employed for evaluation of conduct or decision or for justifying the norms. The concepts of norm and value thus turned out to have an inverse relation: where a scientist used "norms" descriptively, "value" tended to be used judgmentally for criteria of evaluation; but where "value" was used descriptively, "norm" tended to be used judgmentally.[27]

Among other social disciplines, the drift after the midcentury was dependent on closeness to practical problems. Economics, in its self-image as a pure science, continued to regard itself as free of policy values—these were a practical problem of application. It had traditionally recognized the place of value—use value and exchange value—in its subject matter and had no new discovery to make nor any need to alter the concept beyond (we have seen) what its efforts at measurement had forced. Political science, however, was hard pressed by the practical problems of national or governmental policy in a changing world. It experimented with concepts of *power* or *national interest* as constitutive of its discipline. But as these were increasingly exposed as either vague or ideological, the inner role of values in the science became threatening to its assumed purity. One experiment was to set up the separate field of policy science, which would be normative from the start, something what like political economy had been to economics. But as survey techniques expanded and technical studies occupied a large part of the field of political science, a partition took place for a time between those who found a place for values and those who denied them entry. This, however, verged on the issue we have so far postponed, whether values of investigators have a part in the science.

Some of the social disciplines do, however, have as constitutive parts some selected values, often ideals. Law and education are normative in this sense. (Occasionally, for this reason, they are removed from the roster of the sciences and turned over to the humanities. Whether a correct analysis of legal ideas and legal procedures includes a place for values (particularly social values) is an old dispute. Clearly it does for legislation, which is directly concerned with achieving goals. The goals are usually specific, and so the broad concept of values enters nowadays more appropriately for criteria of evaluation. On the other hand, the issue of selective social aims in judicial decision (over and above the general ideal of justice) is more complicated, and here it is often discussed as the place of values in decision. This becomes a shorthand for all sorts of selective grounds that enter into the determination of decision.

That the concept of values has made strides in educational theory is generally recognized. Questions of goals and ideals and social necessities and character-formation and rules and responsibilities press on the field, so that some general concept is required; value serves this well. But perhaps its penetration may be gauged from the fact that the most widespread form of moral education in the United States (now under serious attack) goes by the name of *Values Clarification*. It has given up on hopes of achieving moral development through moralizing, through persuasion and normal sanctions, through even the use of notable examples. Instead it attempts through situations and discussion to render the individual reflective about his/her preferences and choices, in the expectation that stable, publicly defended, and considered values will occupy the self. (Values clarification has been seriously criticized for its heightened individualism and for social naiveté.)

Whatever path value study has taken in the different disciplines since the midcentury, the concept of value has won a remarkable currency. We have next to look at the third stage of its progress, in which criticism of the sharp separation of fact and value made inroads in the sciences, so that each began to suspect it had investigational values within it, not just the humanities or the policy sciences.

VI

During the 1960s and 1970s the fact-value dichotomy, the umbrella under which it had long been claimed that the scientist as scientist made no value judgments and that value judgments could not be established in the factual mode of the sciences, began to crumble. This has been a long process, and the questions that were formulated in terms of the dichotomy have kept hanging on. The general value concept was an important link in the process, for by its use the realm on its side of the dichotomy was greatly extended, full of variety, and likely to come up anywhere. If the narrower domain of ethics had had to bear the burden of the controversy, the dichotomy would probably have continued with greater strength, for the True and the Good have usually been distinct and parallel.

The changes contributing to this erosion were many, and came from both the direction of science (fact) and social policy (value). The great part played by science in modern civilization (noted above) and the host of policies that rested on the work of scientists made the idea of neutrality of science as such bizarre. It appeared rather as an intimate part of the pursuit of human well-being. Of course there were disagreements about assumptions of a value sort, but there were also disagreements about fact and theory. And assumptions of all sorts admitted of further testing and correction in further experience. To draw sharp lines began to seem unwarranted. Again, the history of science itself opened the door to exploring the role of social and religious and aesthetic influences not only in the use of science but in the formulation of its problems; revolutions in science became seen as whole-world-outlook affairs, in which the factual and the valuational could not readily be unscrambled. Moreover, just as the relation of technology and pure science became more intimate, with technology being part of scientific experimentation and not just an arena of application, so the relation of science and technology to value judgments became more intimate. A striking example of this is the increasing role of ethical questions in the doing of research itself—witness the controversy over genetic research that involves possible creation of new life forms.

Many influences came from the philosophical consideration of the dichotomy. Careful linguistic analysis showed the difficulty of carrying the dichotomy through in many cases: for example, role terms (parent, policeman) already contain obligations, and terms indicating practices (for example, promising, voting) and institutions and professions (for example, the family, medicine) involve full-fledged ideals in their very definition. Of course it could be argued that these were complex notions and could be analyzed into their fact and value components. But could they? The suspicion became stronger that the question had been reversed: not atomic facts and atomic values being combined, but complex wholes being unscrambled was the natural condition of human life. This meant that the dichotomy was a *program*, not a metaphysical truth or methodological necessity. The dichotomy might very well be just an ideal impossible of accomplishment.

An excellent case of this issue—whether to compound or unscramble—is to be found in the experience of decision theory (when used in relation to practical problems), an area particularly relevant because the core of value is selectivity or decision. Older forms of decision theory wanted a preference (that is, value) scale set up separately and alongside it an ordering of the probabilities of occurrence of the alternatives between which there is to be a choice. Then these were to be combined after adopting a strategy such as greatest gain or least loss. Later forms of decision theory began instead with a set of choices and devised mathematical ways of factoring out the probabilities and the more general value order. Which serves best for the complex aims of the theory is not our present concern, but the historical episode is indicative of the character of the dichotomy: it is one possible way of trying to do things, but whether it or an alternative program is successful—and in what field, for there need be no single answer—is a matter of human experience and experimentation.

Behind these arguments was found to lie a theory of knowledge and action. The dichotomy had flourished when fact was assumed to be a complex of sense-experience (a Lockean psychology), whereas value was affective and so quite different from fact. But in the long run it became clear that the line between theory and observation was a relative and contextual one, and that affect has a strong cognitive component and purposive context. The Darwinian naturalization of man was accompanied in the pragmatic philosophers (Peirce and James initially) by a view of consciousness as arising in problematic situations of doubt, so that purpose, cognitive structuring, sensory input, and emotional affect are all aspects of a single practical situation. James particularly brought out (in *The Principles of Psychology*) the fundamentally selective character of all experience, in which among possible alternatives one is selected at a given time in the effort to meet the purposes in the particular context. Out of such habits of experience, objects and properties are classified, ideas tested and corrected, and a complex philosophy carried around with oneself. Now if the breadth given to general value in twentieth-century philosophy makes its core to lie in selectivity, then *all* ordering of experience is valuational and value is an integral aspect of fact. (In this respect Münsterberg and Urban had a richer psychology than Perry.) It remains only to note that value and fact are covering the same ground from a different perspective: if the fact is how we see things and our values depend on how we see things, then the distinction is simply the perspective of observation and that of action. Or, as Dewey pointed out in his famous paper on the reflex arc, one if from the point of view of stimulus, the other from the point of view of response.

In the social sciences, the presence of values in doing the scientific work has usually been formulated as criticism. That there is a selective element in data, methods, formulation of inquiry, definitions employed, area of theory invoked, is evident enough. But when it is revealed in criticism, it is often with the charge that biases are present or special axes are being ground. Thus the work is condemned as ideology rather than science. In more extreme contexts this may be a wise move, but in a wider sense the task is rather to recognize that there are value choices in the selectivity that is a part of all science, and that the question is always whether appropriate choices have been made, what values persistently mislead, which can properly become entrenched. But finally, the sense of values here is that of the general theory of value, not necessarily that of ethics or aesthetics or religion or social outlook.

VII

In its progress through twentieth-century theory, the general concept of value has brought some benefits and some disadvantages. The latter came from a hasty unification that insisted on general answers to general questions about value, when division of the field, patient study of many areas and their differences, and then attempts at generalization would have been more fruitful. In these respects it blocked fruitful inquiry. On the other hand, its benefits have been many, some essential and lasting, some a matter of lucky chance under very particular conditions of the time. In the latter way, the general concept of value smoothed the path to empirical study of values in the social sciences when previously this had been almost taboo, and it helped through its generality to focus on value components in science and knowledge generally. In a more lasting way it posed the problem of the fuller naturalizing of man and in the long run contributed to an understanding of the continuities of distinctive human features with the rest of the natural world. Controversy over the role of value brought out the active character of human participation in knowledge and decision, the pervasiveness of selectivity. And in its core relation to decision, it furthered immeasurably the study of valuation.

Our sketch of the career of the concept in twentieth-century America has been a hasty one. Perhaps it has shown at least that such broad categorial concepts have both intellectual and sociocultural functions, that their meaning is rarely to be found on the analytic surface or given by simple definition but requires a relation to intellectual traditions, scientific purposes, social movements. A full biography of the concept of value is obviously called for. Perhaps among the students of Betty Flower, who learned from her the importance of a rich history of moral philosophy, some may be tempted to undertake this task.

Notes

1. C. E. Ayres, "The Value Economy" in Ray Lepley (ed.), *Value: A Cooperative Inquiry* (New York: Columbia University Press, 1949), p. 42.

2. Robin M. Williams, Jr., in his article on "The Concept of Values," *International Encyclopedia of the Social Sciences* (1969), Vol. 16, pp. 283–287, quoting Mukerjee (p. 285).

3. John Laird, *The Idea of Value* (Cambridge, England: Cambridge University Press, 1929), p. 24.

4. Howard O. Eaton, *The Austrian Philosophy of Values* (Norman, Okla.: University of Oklahoma Press, 1930), pp. 15–16. Eaton studies the school that stemmed from Brentano, Ehrenfels, and Meinong, and hopes comparable studies will be done of other schools of value.

5. See *Journal of Philosophy* X (1913): 167–168.

6. Wilbur Marshall Urban, *Valuation, Its Nature and Laws, Being an Introduction to the General Theory of Value* (New York: Macmillan, 1909), p. 2.

7. Hugo Münsterberg, *The Eternal Values* (Cambridge, Mass.: Houghton Mifflin, 1909), p. 74. This work is a revised and translated version of an earlier book of his in German.

8. Urban, *Valuation*, pp. 54, 26.

9. Ralph Barton Perry, *General Theory of Value* (New York: Longmans, Green, and Co., 1926), pp. 3–4.

10. For a preliminary discussion of the need for a theoretical basis of unity in the concept of value, see Abraham Edel, "Concept of Values in Contemporary Philosophical Value Theory," *Philosophy of Science* XX (July 1953): 198–207; reprinted in Edel, *Method in Ethical Theory* (Indianapolis: Bobbs-Merrill, 1963).

11. John Dewey, *"The Problem of Values," Journal of Philosophy* X (1913): 268–269. Dewey's was not the only response. Sheldon objected to the first question as riding the old issue of reality, subjective or objective; he was not interested in that, but wanted to know what value is. Urban wrote seconding Sheldon, urging the elimination of the epistemological aspect, but this seems to be largely because he wants to study the metaphysical aspect. The 1913 volume of the *Journal of Philosophy* gives several of the papers presented at the meetings—by Harold Chapman Brown, by Perry, and by Urban. It is of special interest that all of these accept the search for a general answer to the question of what is value, give different answers, but do not question the question or seek to justify it.

12. For a comprehensive analysis of the relation of Dewey's psychology and method, see Elizabeth Flower's study in Elizabeth Flower and Murray G. Murphey, *A History of Philosophy in America* (New York: G. P. Putnam's sons, 1977; Hackett, 1979), Chap. 14.

13. Wilbur Marshall Urban, *Fundamentals of Ethics* (New York: Henry Holt, 1930), pp. 16–18.

14. Ralph Barton Perry, *Realms of Value* (Cambridge, Mass.: Harvard University Press, 1954), p. 4.

15. See Dewey's three essays on Green in *John Dewey, The Early Works*, ed. Jo Ann Boydston (Carbondale: Southern Illinois University Press). Vol. 3, pp. 14–35, 155–173 (1969); Vol. 4, pp. 42–53 (1971).

16. For example, Stephen Pepper's *The Sources of Value* (Berkeley: University of California Press, 1958) rests on E. C. Tolman's psychological analysis of purpose; DeWitt H. Parker's *The Philosophy of Value* (Ann Arbor: University of Michigan Press, 1957) utilizes a Freudian base.

17. For example: from a linguistic perspective, Everett W. Hall, *What Is Value?* (London: Routledge and Kegan Paul, 1952); from a logical perspective, C. I. Lewis, *An Analysis of Knowledge and Valuation* (Chicago: Open Court, 1946); from a Gestalt perspective, Wolfgang Köhler, *The Place of Value in a World of Facts* (New York: Liveright, 1938). Hall sees value as a categorial feature of the world, relational in character, more to be seen than defined. Lewis equates value in its basic sense with satisfaction but distinguishes it from the notion of right; the latter is imperative in character and runs through all knowledge, not the value field alone. Köhler sees value as requiredness, discernible in the phenomenological field.

18. Perhaps the most systematic works in value theory that exercised an influence from Europe are in the phenomenological tradition. See, for example, Max Scheler, *Formalism in Ethics and Non-Formal Ethics of Value*, trans. Frings and

Funk (Evanston: Northwestern University Press, 1973; original German edition, 1913–16); and Nicolai Hartmann, *Ethics,* trans. Coit (New York: Macmillan, 1932; original German edition, 1926). The most influential existentialist treatments are by Martin Heidegger and Jean-Paul Sartre.

19. All these features are particularly evident in the value theory of logical positivism, especially the emotive theory as developed by Charles L. Stevenson. See his *Facts and Values* (New Haven: Yale University Press, 1963). The state of the concept of value at the midcentury can be judged from Lepley (ed.), *Value: A Cooperative Inquiry.* The starting point was questions about value that Dewey reformulated in an article, "Some Questions about Value," *Journal of Philosophy* XLI (1944): 449–55. In the preface to the book, Lepley comments that a wide divergence emerged in the papers and that there were almost as many definitions of value terms as there were parties to the inquiry. The work, he suggests (with obvious disappointment), became a vehicle for advocacy of different philosophical views rather than a genuinely common inquiry.

20. How Dewey's ethical theory itself went through a long and complex process of change can be seen in a comparison of the 1908 edition of Dewey and Tuft's *Ethics* and the revised 1932 edition. For a sketch of the changes, see Abraham Edel and Elizabeth Flower, Introduction to the 1932 *Ethics,* Vol. 7 of *John Dewey, The Later Works,* ed. Jo Ann Boydston (Carbondale: University of Southern Illinois Press, 1985), pp. vii–xxxv. The study pays special attention to the role of the growth of the social sciences and the impact of sociohistorical events and changes in the crystallization of the mature ethical theory.

21. Ample illustration of such incipient value materials can be found in collections of papers published at that time. See, for example, Theodore M. Newcomb, Eugene L. Hartley, *et al.* (eds.), *Readings in Social Psychology* (New York: Henry Holt, 1947), prepared for the Committee on the Teaching of Social Psychology of the Society for the Psychological Study of Social Issues; Clyde Kluckholn and Henry E. Murray (eds.), *Personality in Nature, Society, and Culture* (New York: Alfred A. Knopf, 1948). See also Muzafer Sherif and Hadley Cantril, *The Psychology of Ego-Involvement: Social Attitudes and Identifications* (New York: John Wiley and Sons, 1947).

22. The concept of ideology as values imbedded in theory was given an impetus by Karl Mannheim's *Ideology and Utopia* (London: Routledge and Kegan Paul, 1936). Mannheim saw social science theories as unavoidably reflecting the social position of the theorist, whereas natural science could be objective. His only hope for a neutral social science was that intellectuals straddling classes might have a broader view. "Ideology," at first used in Marxian approaches for distorting

values, came to have a more neutral meaning as simply a value standpoint. For the possibility of dissolving ideologies and developing a science of ideology, see Abraham Edel, *Analyzing Concepts in Social Science: Science, Ideology, and Value*, Vol. I (New York: Transaction Books, 1979), Chap. 10. The forthright recognition of political and social values as inherent in social science theory, to be frankly discerned and evaluated, was of course a constant theme quite early in the century in the writings of Veblen and Myrdal and then later in those of C. Wright Mills and Irving L. Horowitz. It was, however, ignored by mainstream social science until the last third of the century, when (as we describe later) the fact-value distinction itself began to crumble.

23. The initial conception of value in the Harvard Sturdies was worked out by Kluckholn in "Values and Value-Orientations in the Theory of Action," in T. Parsons and E. A. Shils (eds.), *Towards a General Theory of Action* (Cambridge, Mass.: Harvard University Press, 1951). The particular studies are published in the Papers of the Peabody Museum of American Archaeology and Ethnology, Harvard University. See, for example: Evon Z. Vogt, *Navaho Veterans, A Study of Changing Values* (1951); Watson Smith and John M. Roberts, *Zuni Law, A Field of Values* (1954); David P. McAllester, *Enemy Way Music: A Study of Social and Aesthetic Values As Seen in Navaho Music* (1954); Richard Hobson, *Navaho Acquisitive Values* (1954); Bert Kaplan, *A Study of Rorschach Responses in Four Cultures* (1954). Attempts to work out dominant value-orientations and their variation are found in Florence Rockwood Kluckholn and Fred L. Strodbeck, *Variations in Value Orientations* (Evanston: Row, Peterson, 1961).

24. These were published as Memoirs of the American Anthropological Association, edited by Robert Redfield and Milton Singer. See, for example: Arthur F. Wright (ed.), *Studies in Chinese Thought* (1953); G. E. Von Grunebaum (ed.), *Studies in Islamic Cultural History* (1954).

25. See, for example, Robin M. Williams, Jr., *American Society* (New York: Alfred A. Knopf, 1951).

26. For example: R. B. Brandt, *Hopi Ethics* (Chicago: University of Chicago Press, 1954); John Ladd, *The Structure of A Moral Code* (Cambridge, Mass.: Harvard University Press, 1957, dealing with the Navajo); and a general study, May Edel and Abraham Edel, *Anthropology and Ethics* (Springfield, Ill.: Charles C. Thomas, 1959; New Brunswick, N.J.: Transaction Books, 1970). These dealt with ethics primarily, but a broadening sense of *the good* was converging with value theory. In fact, in this period, generic value was taking over the good, but *ought* and *right* remained specifically moral notions, often described as "moral values." Anthropological studies of value became broader in their scope. For

example, A. McBeath, *Experiments in Living* (London: Macmillan and Co., 1952), already took ethics as the mode of a whole life. John H. Barnsley's *The Social Reality of Ethics: The Comparative Analysis of Moral Codes* (London: Routledge and Kegan Paul, 1972) makes a careful distinction between the broader sense of values and the narrower sense of moral.

27. This sample study is reported in Edel, "The Concept of Levels in Social Theory," Chap. 8 in *Analyzing Concepts in Social Science.*

2 | Whatever Happened to Pragmatism?

Robert Schwartz

Perhaps the best way a teacher has to promote interest and develop understanding is to ask her students good questions. And in the various classes in ethics and in the history of philosophy that I had with Elizabeth Flower, she used to confront us with some very beautiful ones. At the same time, one of the best ways students have to help remove confusion and puzzlement is to ask their teachers questions. This is what I propose to do here, for on the topic that concerns me, I can think of no one whose thoughts I would rather hear than Flower's. But before asking my questions, I would like to recall some relatively recent history.

Whether one agrees with Richard Rorty's sweeping stories of intellectual history, or with his particular views of mind, reference, and incommensurability, or with his proposals for the future direction of philosophy, his book, *Philosophy and the Mirror of Nature*, is onto something real in its account of the changes and ferment in the field.[1] We have slowly, if not surely, been experiencing a breakdown, if not abandonment, of many of the assumptions and problematics that have occupied center stage in analytic philosophy. Even those who protest that the tradition is still quite hearty allow that the last twenty or thirty years have brought a growing appreciation that in various areas, business need not, should not, or cannot go on as usual. A brief catalog of these trends and tendencies might read as follows:

1. Language: The "museum of ideas" theory of meaning, as Quine calls it, is unacceptable. In turn, the accompanying dichotomies of the analytic versus the synthetic, truths of fact versus truths of definition, truths of reason versus empirical truths cannot be relied on to underpin significant philosophical theses. Language lies at the nexus of cognition and social interaction, and no study of language cut off from these anchoring points will prove very insightful. Furthermore, there is no apparent need nor clear place for "philosophical" or "linguistic" analyses of concepts that are not part and parcel of the formulation of empirically adequate theories for the given area under study.

2. Truth: Although Tarski has shown that it is possible to talk about truth without metaphysical embarrassment, Truth with a capital 'T' remains an illusive notion. We can, in good conscience, all admit that 'P' is true if and only if P, and that true sentences are those that say what is so. But none of this should make us sanguine about our grasp of the idea that truth is a matter of correspondence between abstract propositions and eternal ready-made facts or that we can say anything informative about just what such a relationship might be like. Nor is it obvious that the charge to "seek the truth" tells us much more about the nature of inquiry than the injunction to "do as best as you can."

3. Epistemology: Not only is the Cartesian quest for certainty dead, hopes that the techniques of modern logic can provide a basis for updating the *Rules for the Direction of the Mind* have all but vanished. It would seem unreasonable to think that we can come up with time and subject independent principles that once and for all will enable us to separate "real" knowledge from fake substitutes. Similarly, once we recognize the elusiveness of the notion of a pure "given," and further appreciate that this sort of "sensory core" is not what scientists typically turn to when testing their theories, the search for fixed empirical foundations of knowledge seems like an upromising undertaking.

Epistemology, if there is to be such a subject, must be naturalized. We have to pay attention to how organisms with the kinds of minds, resources, and interests humans actually possess go about acquiring information. Furthermore, a concept of knowledge wholly divorced from use, from human activity and practice, would hardly seem worth bothering about. But because human endeavors, both intellectual and practical, most commonly involve the problematic, the unsettled, the doubtful, and the unclear, knowledge must find its proper home in the realm of probabilities rather than in the domain of assured truths. A model of knowledge that takes the mathematically certain as its paradigm or ideal will be far removed from human decision and action, rooted as they are in the probable.

4. Science: The fact that philosophers are primarily interested in the so-called context of justification does not mean that they can afford to avoid careful study of actual scientific practice. Models of scientific method and rationality that pay no heed to the course of historical developments in science are not likely to be very satisfactory. Although it may be possible to proclaim, on *a priori* grounds, the scientific necessity of such broad principles as being objective, being open-minded, and testing one's hypotheses, what these directives amount to itself changes as science progresses. Our concepts of evidence, good reasons, appropriate use of data, etc. are not constants but are evolving notions. There can be no neutral point outside of ongoing inquiry from which we can rule on what is or is not an allowable line of argument.

We also have no grounds for thinking that science must or will come up with a single overarching theory that can meet all the goals we have in pursuing inquiry. Instead, we find in practice an assortment of theories, not readily reducible one to another, yet each representing a justified way of describing and organizing our experience. In studying scientific methodology it is thus a mistaken strategy to focus exclusively on tidied-up areas of textbook physics. The theoretical flux and empirical instability found in the social sciences may, in fact, provide even more fertile soil for philosophical investigation.

An examination of actual scientific practice also shows that the majority of workers devote their time to devising piecemeal solutions to localized problems and not to propounding grand theories. But even where the scientist's goal is of a more global nature, it is accurate to characterize the work in instrumental terms. In both cases, the attempt is to develop more elegant and more empirically adequate concepts and principles. To go on to describe science as seeking theories that copy reality, or correspond to the hidden but eternal truth, adds nothing to our understanding of the enterprise.

5. *Mind:* The proper way to study mind is to examine its place in nature. What such a study discloses is not an ethereal soul or self-contained consciousness but mind as one of the organizing forces within an adapting, socially dependent, biological organism. Mind shows itself as an evolving set of skills, enhanced perceptions, and developed learning capacities that enable the organism to deal more intelligently with its environment. Understanding the nature of mind will not result from introspective reflection on felt qualities or subjective experiences. It will depend on the careful study of how we interact, grow, and adapt to a changing world.

Mental states must, therefore, be construed *functionally*, in terms of the roles they play in organizing and integrating our activities. This stress on the functional does not mean, however, that mental life can be reduced to sets of reflexes or simple stimulus-response chains. Human response to the environment is always mediated by the developed understandings and evolving meanings given to present experience. Any attempt to explain human behavior must take into account this fuller cognitive content and the social aspects of its acquisition, elaboration, and use.

When mind is thus treated functionally, and the study of mind is placed in its appropriate biological, psychological, and social context, much of the traditional mind/body problem loses its grip. The dilemma is not so much solved as dissolved. What remains of the old dichotomy is perhaps a distinction between the kinds of vocabularies and principles that show up in astronomy, physics, and chemistry and those central to psychology, biology, and the social sciences. Although these differences are real and significant, they do little to support claims for a metaphysical or ontological gulf between the mental and the physical.

6. *Ethics and Social Philosophy:* Efforts to deny cognitive significance to questions of value, morality, and social policy, to declare talk about these issues to be merely emotive or empirically meaningless, can be sustained only by adopting theories of language, mind, and inquiry that are themselves wholly inadequate. Such disparagement can, moreover, have pernicious effects, since it tends to preclude the serious experimentation and testing of alternative modes of social, political, and economic organization, leaving us at the mercy of entrenched habits. It is also a misconception to conceive of ethics and social philosophy as *a priori* studies aimed at formulating fixed standards and rules, valid for all times and places. Enjoinders to "seek the good" or "act justly" are empty verbiage when separated from the psychological, social, and ethical contexts that give them meaning. Abstract principles gain significance when they are applied to problematic moral situations.

There is no reason then for philosophers to avoid dealing with substantive ethical issues, limiting their investigations to meta-ethical analyses. What's more, such meta-analyses will have little intrinsic interest unless they are located within and constrained by the demands and possibilities of life as it may be lived. By critically sifting accepted values, by exposing inconsistencies in settled practices, by uncovering weaknesses in political and legal institutions, and by laying bare the hidden assumptions that constrict our understanding of the nature of work, power, education, etc. the philosopher can help society clarify what it finds worthwhile and coherently articulate its goals. And by proposing, testing, and evaluating alternative institutions, social structures, and patterns of interpersonal relations, the philosopher can play a role in enabling society to pursue more perspicaciously its aspirations for human growth and flourishing.

Although it would be overstating matters to claim that nowadays everyone accepts each of these points, it is not an overstatement to say that it would be difficult to do serious philosophical work while ignoring them. One would question the adequacy of preparation of any new Ph.D. who took uncritical refuge in a meaning-fact distinction, who paid no heed to empirical evidence on the grounds that his or her analysis was "philosophical," who blithely accepted "the given," who made pronouncements about the ahistoric standards of inquiry found in all scientific practice, who identified mental life with either subjective experience or stimulus-response bonds, who simply declared aesthetic, religious, and moral discourse meaningless, or who assumed that questions of medical ethics were obviously unfit subjects for "philosophical" concern. And I believe Rorty is surely right that many of the programs and problems that have been the "hot" topics in twentieth-century analytic philosophy are beginning to look more and more like played-out, if not impossible, projects.

Now I do not find surprising that what was once considered firm has been abandoned, that many problems once thought to be "the" central topics of investigation no longer seem worth pursuing, or that important questions have not been so much resolved as dissolved. Rather, what I find surprising is that this denouement has worked its way into mainstream analytic philosophy so relatively recently. For as any student of American pragmatism knows, such shifts in approach, assumptions, emphases, and interests were what the pragmatists' revolution was all about. These ideas were not hidden beneath the surface of their work, or found only in a short phrase here or there. Nor does it require the hindsight of the 1980s to read these claims into this earlier work. The points sketchily catalogued above were just some of the main themes James, Dewey, and others labored long and hard to impress on the intellectual consciousness of their day.

This then leads me to the puzzle that I would like some help in resolving, namely, Whatever happened to pragmatism? Why were its lessons not learned? How could so much work go on assuming as rock bottom the very dualisms the pragmatists had shown to be so fragile, if not untenable? Why did so many of the traditional "problems of philosophy" still maintain their prominence in face of the pragmatists' onslaught on their essentialist presuppositions? And most puzzling of all, even if the pragmatists' tenets did not take hold and win the day, why did their work, in a comparatively short period of time, drift into philosophical oblivion?

Not only were the pragmatists' ideas and projects soon off center stage, but one could go through undergraduate and graduate training at many of the most prestigious centers of philosophy without so much as reading a single of their major works, let alone studying them in detail. To not know Russell, Moore,

Schlick, and Carnap would have been a scandal. To have run into James only as an aside in an introductory class, as the proponent of some bizarre doctrine that if it is useful to believe P, then 'P' is true, would not have been unusual. And even today, with the push to make philosophy more "relevant," I would be amazed if one out of one hundred new Ph.D.'s have read Dewey's *Democracy and Education*, in spite of the fact that the book probably had more influence and impact on our culture and institutions than any philosophical work by an American before or since.

The obliteration or disappearance of pragmatism from the philosophical scene might be more understandable had it been an esoteric movement whose ideas never gained much currency and whose proponents were obscure intellectuals working at remote universities. But nothing like this was the case. James and Dewey were recognized then, and still are, as among the best and brightest of their time; they taught at major universities, and their ideas were much discussed and debated in professional circles, as well as in the culture at large. So again my puzzle is, Whatever happened to pragmatism?

As I indicated at the start of this paper my intention has been to raise questions, not to answer them. Before concluding, however, I would like to canvass a few answers that have been suggested or may come to mind.

In "Dewey's Metaphysics," Rorty speculates that the decline of pragmatism can be

> explained if one is willing to grant that writers like Russell, Carnap, Ayer, and Black were doing a better job of showing the "psuedo-ness" of psuedo problems than Dewey had been able to do. They could do so because they had the virtue of their vices. What now seems to us . . . the dogmatism and artificiality of the logical empiricist movement was precisely what permitted this movement to criticize the tradition so sharply and so effectively. Following Kant in wishing to put philosophy upon the secure path a of science and writing as if Hegel had never lived, the logical empiricists carried assumptions of Descartes, Locke and Kant to their logical conclusion and thus reduced the traditional problematic of philosophy to absurdity.[2]

On this account, the positivists bought into the tradition. Working from within the tradition, they attempted both to criticize it and, using the tools of modern logic, put it on a more rigorous scientific basis. But under the weight of their own failures and prodded by the likes of Quine, Sellars, Wittgenstein, and Austin, it eventually became apparent that logical empiricism was not a scientifically cleaned-up version of the tradition but a reductio of it. So Rorty concludes that "the narrowness and artificiality of the dualisms which logical empiricists presupposed enabled them to do what Dewey, precisely because of his broader scope and his ability to see the tradition in perspective had not."[3]

This explanation, however, seems to me to raise as many questions as it settles. In particular, in light of the thoroughgoing critiques James and Dewey had made of "the narrowness and artificiality of the dualisms which logical empiricists presupposed," why did the positivists find it so easy to presuppose these dualisms and drag several generations of analytic philosophers along with them? And why too did the pragmatists' positive projects not attract attention, while those of the logical empiricists flourished? Scores of the ablest philosophers worked on epistemological foundations, ontological reductions, *a priori* conceptual analyses, and the demarcation of science from fiction, fact from value, and the cognitive from the aesthetic. At the same time, fewer and fewer took up the pragmatists' more substantive programs. Work on such tasks as developing adequate theories of education and educational practice, providing psychologically and biologically rooted accounts of emotion, decision, and the self, criticizing and helping to reconstruct our understandings of economic relations, political structures, and artistic appreciation all faded into the background.

Another answer to my puzzle (also a part of Rorty's answer) is that the positivists' program seemed to point the way for philosophy to escape from the never-never land of metaphysical speculation and to establish itself as a scientifically respectable discipline. But this sort of answer also strikes me as problematic. First, it still leaves unclear why and how analytic philosophy readily continued to accept the dualisms the pragmatists had so forcefully criticized. Second, this account needs fleshing out at crucial points if it is to have any explanatory value, for a major theme that runs through the pragmatists, and is especially prominent in Dewey, is just the thesis that philosophy must be approached scientifically, adopting the experimental method. The search for rational certainties, hidden essences, and *a priori* principles was a dead end. Moreover, Dewey offered detailed arguments attempting to show that philosophy had gotten into the metaphysical straights it had precisely because it had failed to deal with problems of language, mind, inquiry, and conduct in the scientific spirit. Indeed, Dewey urged the need and appropriateness of empirical study and experimentation in areas such as ethics, value theory, art, and social philosophy, areas that the positivists had turned over to the emotions and intuitions.

Finally, in accepting the dualisms of the mental versus the physical, observation

versus theory, fact versus value, the positivists found themselves laboring on many of the traditional metaphysical problems the pragmatists had sought to dissolve by a more thoroughgoing application of the experimental method. Thus, merely citing "the urge to be scientific" does not seem to me to be a satisfactory answer to my puzzle.

In conversation, Sidney Morgenbesser has suggested two other possible reasons for the decline of pragmatism. The first, surprisingly, sees C. I. Lewis as a pivotal figure. Lewis, the natural successor to the Harvard pragmatist tradition, was a most influential teacher and scholar. But although Lewis was an admirer of the pragmatists, he could never shake off his Kantian concerns for an account of warrant. He could, as he said, be pragmatic about our conceptual schemes, but he could not buy the pragmatists' account of experience. In his efforts, however, to find a fixed and firm resting place for justification, a stopping point that was more than probable, Lewis saddled us with epistemological dualisms and kept alive various research projects that would have ill-suited more orthodox followers of the pragmatists' line. Lewis also carried over his Kantian demands for unassailable sources of warrant to ethics, with much the same result.

Although I think Lewis may have been a factor in the decline of pragmatism, I do not see how he could be more than a small piece of the story. As influential as Lewis was, it is nonetheless hard to believe that such a major intellectual shift could be traced primarily to one person. Perhaps more of an answer would come from an understanding of why Lewis, so closely attuned as he was to the pragmatists, was still unable to accept their deeper claims and thus shed a larger part of the traditional metaphysical assumptions and problematic.

Another idea Morgenbesser has put forth is that the kind of work James and Dewey did, and left for their followers to pursue, was just too hard. Analytic philosophy more easily allowed for the professionalization of the field. The positivists' program enabled one to get by reading only the current standard philosophical journals, developing a narrow expertise, and applying this knowledge to solve problems internal to the specialized philosophical domain. Philosophy was doable even by the average philosopher. You could make your way showing that condition 3* should replace 3 in the analysis of concept A, by coming up with a counterexample to an explication of B, or by demonstrating that it is inconsistent to accept both C and D.

But the pragmatists were after different, often bigger game, and the game itself was to be played under different rules. The philosopher's task was to critically evaluate and clarify what was going on and try to devise better ways to understand mind, to inculcate knowledge, to develop sensitivity to art, to promote social cohesion, and to organize our political and economic institutions. The job was not only to deconstruct the past, to show where settled habits of thought and conduct had gone astray, but to take an active role in *reconstructing* the future. Philosophy is reconstruction. Furthermore, these projects were not and could not be undertaken from some neutral philosophical standpoint outside these practices. They were to be pursued from within, guided by the experimental method. On Morgenbesser's account, the problem is that if such enterprises are to be done seriously and well, they require a breadth of knowledge and depth of insight that few scholars possess. The pragmatists, then, were by and large too tough an act to follow.

How far it is possible to appeal to this latter feature to make sense of developments in twentieth-century American philosophy I am not sure. It might help explain why the pragmatists' substantive projects languished, although it does not speak to the issue of why their deconstructive lessons were not better heeded. I myself still find the whole matter something of a puzzle. That is why I should like some help with the question, Whatever happened to pragmatism?

Notes

1. Richard Rorty, *Philosophy and the Mirror of Nature* (Princeton: Princeton University Press, 1979). I have indicated where I agree and disagree with Rorty in my review of the book in *Journal of Philosophy* LXXX (January 1983): 51–67.

2. Richard Rorty, "Dewey's Metaphysics," in Rorty, *Consequences of Pragmatism* (Minneapolis: University of Minnesota Press, 1982), p. 75.

3. *Ibid.*

3 | John Dewey and the Founding Fathers

R. W. Sleeper

Conventional wisdom accords little attention and less importance to American political philosophy. As Henry Steele Commager pointed out some years ago, "It is customary, even fashionable to disparage American political thought: after all America has contributed little to formal political philosophy and boasts few political philosophers." But he goes on to say, in possible explanation: "Yet it is no exaggeration to say that over a period of a century and three-quarters American politics have been more mature and American political achievements more substantial than those of any other modern people. The contrast here between theory and practice is not really paradoxical, for in a very real sense the apparent bankruptcy of political theory is a product of the obvious prosperity of political practice.[1]

It would be easy, after the Nixon debacle, the Carter catastrophe, and the Reagan revival, to wax cynical about Commager's "exaggeration" and to expose the implicit chauvinism of his rebuttal. For what Commager refers to as "the obvious prosperity of [American] political practice" is no longer—to say the least—such as to be taken for granted. For, as is frequently pointed out, American political practice is neither widely admired nor imitated in the world arena. Gore Vidal sums up the point: "Actually, none of the hundred or so new countries that have been organized since World War II has imitated our form of government—though, to a nation, the local dictator likes to style himself the President."[2]

What then? Are *both* American political theory *and* practice, to use Commager's word, "bankrupt"? Apparently the American Taxpayers Union thinks so, for they have persuaded some thirty or so state legislatures to vote in favor of a new constitutional convention. Moreover, there is at least an even chance their effort will succeed, thus placing us in a position where we shall have to decide whether or not to replace our two-hundred-year-old Constitution by ratifying a new one. It is a breathtaking prospect, and one that is—the fact should not surprise us—very real.

It is in this context, then, that I propose to examine the relation between the political philosophy of John Dewey and the concepts that guided the work of the Founding Fathers. And I shall not confine my inquiry to the half dozen or so men who can be considered the true framers of the Constitution, or to that document alone, for, as Dewey himself pointed out,

Jeffersonian and Hamiltonian political ideas are not merely theories dwelling in the human mind remote from the facts of American political behavior. They are expressions of chosen phases and factors among those facts, but they are also something more: namely, forces which have shaped those facts and which are still contending to shape them in the future this way and that. There is more than a speculative difference between a theory of the state which regards it as an instrument in protecting individuals in the rights they already have, and one which conceives its function to be the effecting of a more equitable distribution of rights among individuals. For theories are held and applied by legislators in congress and judges on the bench and make a difference in the subsequent facts themselves.[3]

In the end, I shall argue, it is the actions of Congress and the Supreme Court, fully as much as the philosophical views of Jefferson and Hamilton and their ilk, that must be considered if we are to do justice to the political convictions of the Founding Fathers.

As I see it, there are three more or less specific areas in which Dewey's political thought is congenial to the work of the founders and which confer on that work a substantial degree of philosophical legitimacy. The first and most important is with respect to the nature of the individual—the concept of the person, if you will—and relates to the issues of rights. The second is with respect to the nature of the political institution, including the role and function of law.

And the third is in relation to method of inquiry itself, particularly in judicial procedure. As so presented, these three areas are not discrete and separable, save by abstraction, but are coalescent and interpenetrating in relationships that may be, somewhat hesitatingly, called "organic." And this is not only in Dewey's work but in that of the founders as well. It is, moreover, precisely because these three areas *are* coalescent and interpenetratinng that any investigation of them must be unabashedly metaphysical.

This last consideration, it must be confessed, presents a double difficulty. For in the conventional view, neither Dewey nor the founders are to be understood as giving pride of place to metaphysics in laying the foundations of political action. Both have been understood as "methodists" (lower case), as placing "methodology" and not "ontology" up front. For how often has Dewey been stereotyped as the "philosopher of inquiry" and as advocate of "democratic procedure" even in—heaven forbid—the classroom? Or the founders as children of the Enlightenment, of the Age of Reason and the new methods of inquiry introduced by Locke and Newton? But the facts tell against this conventional view. For both Dewey and the founders, convictions as to method and procedure in political matters are determined by antecedent considerations of metaphysical perspective.

Dewey's practice of metaphysical inquiry is empirical and denotative, designed to establish—in his happily chosen phrase—the "ground-map of the province of criticism." As such it is an investigation of those features of nature and experience that ground intelligence, making inquiry itself both possible and necessary. It is the denotation of those features, indeed, that delineates the base lines of criticism. In this practice, experience is itself seen as part and parcel of nature—it is "within" nature as participant rather than spectator—and is generated by the natural interplay of temporal processes. These processes exhibit three distinguishable but cooperating phases, roughly denotated as physiochemical, psychophysical, and human experiential. Temporal change is generated by transactional relations among these processes and phases, relations marked by "generic traits" cutting across all three. These traits—which correspond roughly to the "categories" of a more traditional metaphysics—are denotated adjectivally. Clearly the chief among these in Dewey's view are the dialectical pair precariousness and stability.[4]

In this eminently naturalistic metaphysics, it is worth noting, no *a priori* distinction between facts and values is possible. The generic and generative features that support such emergent activities as natural science provide the basis for values and valuations as well. Support is offered, or withdrawn, from factual generalizations and valuations indiscriminately. And from such considerations, metaphysics is, in Dewey's words, "bound to consider reflection itself as a natural event occurring *within* nature because of traits of the latter."[5]

By reflection, Dewey means thought and reason, inquiry and experiment—probing into the values, no less than the facts, of nature. Thinking is both a cause and an effect of changes in natural processes; it is itself a natural process, subject to both the regularities and contingencies that are among the generic traits of nature noted. It is the fact that thinking *is* among these processes of nature that make its results in knowledge both "regular" *and* "contingent" and, incidentally, accounts for Dewey's reluctance to abandon, even for the purposes of formal logic, his own criterion of "warranted assertibility" for the conventional terminology of "truth." It is from such considerations as these that Dewey's mature political thought starts out.

In his own words,

> This state of affairs suggests a definition of the role of the individual, or the self, in knowledge; namely, the redirection, or reconstruction of accepted beliefs. Every *new* idea, every conception of things differing from that authorized by current belief, must have its origin in an individual . . . Thinking is as much an individual matter as the digestion of food . . . there are variations of point of view, of appeal of objects, and mode of attack, from person to person.[6]

And yet Dewey does not isolate the individual, even conceptually, in a state of nature after the manner of Hobbes or Locke. Placed in a metaphysical perspective of dynamic tension, the individual is associated with other individuals by both chance and necessity, themes that Dewey takes up as freedom and culture. Thus, he says, "All that we can safely say is that human nature, like other forms of life, tends to differentiation, and thus moves in the direction of the distinctively individual; and that it also tends toward combination, association. . . . The problem of freedom of cooperative individualities is then a problem to be viewed in the context of culture."[7]

Viewed from this perspective, thinking is inevitably moral, and all inquiry has its moral dimension. In thinking, the precarious individual engages in transactions designed to establish equilibrium; in action he becomes political. In Dewey's words, "He becomes a social animal."[8] Thinking leads, accordingly, to the establishment of consciously intentional "communities." These communities, created from need and demand for satisfactions not otherwise obtainable, that is, to achieve "equilibrium," are limited in scope and effectiveness. A point is eventually reached when the needs of the community require the formation of the state, and it is that point when the demand for satisfaction in restoring and preserving the equilibrium exceeds the capacity of either private or community transactions. The instrumental character of the state is thus determined by the needs of the moral individual and his community of associates; its status and legitimacy are, thus, contingently related. It is "artifactual," and, like any such artifact, must be designed and modified experimentally. As Dewey warns, there is no *a priori* way of defining the powers and limitations of the state; these are matters that must be constantly under review and revision. In his words, "The line of demarcation between actions left to private initiative and management and those regulated by the state has to be discovered experimentally."[9]

In the end, Dewey rested his democratic faith on the transactions that occur in dialogue between individuals. He saw that dialogue must necessarily commence in the local community, in interpersonal face-to-face relationships; in transactions that are in unbroken continuity with the transactions that his metaphysics ascribes to existences of every kind, "everywhere and everywhen." He closes *The Public and Its Problems* with this paragraph:

> There is no limit to the liberal expansion and confirmation of limited personal endowment which may proceed from the flow of social intelligence when that circulates by word of mouth from one to another in the communications of the local community. That and that only gives reality to public opinion. We lie, as Emerson said, in the lap of an immense intelligence. But that intelligence is dormant and its communications are broken, inarticulate and faint until it possesses local community as its medium.[10]

Mention of the latter book brings us to the point at which the transition to consideration of the work of the founders should be convenient. For in *The Public and Its Problems*, Dewey addresses most directly the general question of the origin and legitimacy of the state, and of the democratic state in particular. But he does not address the work of the founders as such. Moreover, even an informed hermeneutical reading by means of which Dewey could be understood as commenting elliptically on the emergence of our nation from the Confederation through the Declaration of Independence, the activities of Congress and the Constitutional Convention of 1787, he does so in ways that seem locked in paradox.

His general account of the origin of the state runs as follows: given the moral individual as associated with others, it is a matter of fact that individual actions affect these others. This fact comprises the transactional basis of the local community and accounts for the regulatory agencies of custom and tradition. There are, however, consequences of association that escape customary and traditional regulation, consequences that affect other individuals beyond those originally associated. Given that these individuals have interests and associations of their own, these interests will be recognized as either held in common with, or as opposed to, those of the original group. The formation of "publics" with distinct interests results from such recognition, and when these publics acquire official representation states are called into being. Thus far, Dewey's general account may well accord with the transition of the separate colonies to the nascent statehood of the Articles of Confederation precedent to the Declaration and Constitutional Convention. But can it be apposite to the Constitution itself? Can it account for the origin of the democratic nation state in particular?

Dewey's generalized account turns out to be a justification of the democratic state as against all rival forms. The bottom line is that as far as any state is representative of the public interest, that state can claim legitimacy. In this argument, the central conceptual element of Dewey's theory is clearly his notion of the "public"—the identification of "interest" with the public is as redundant as the identification of "interests" with "individuals", for both identities are ontological. Insofar, then, as the concept of the public denotes something real, just so far can the state which that public calls into being through its representatives be judged legitimate. It scarcely needs saying that, for Dewey, the entire argument is cast in moral terms.

A public as conceived by Dewey is a natural entity. As William Ernest Hocking noted in his 1929 review of *The Public and Its Problems*, Dewey's public is clearly not Locke's body politic, for it requires no act of agreement or contract—explicit or implicit—for its existence.[11] Indeed, a nascent public may even be unaware of the commonality of the individual interests of which it is to be eventually comprised, the recognition of which will, as Dewey says, give it reality. This concept is a difficult one, for nowhere is Dewey's instrumentalism more closely intertwined with his historicism. The emergence of a public is a process that occurs historically; it is processive in nature and historically eventful. And paradoxical events are not excluded as consequences of the process.

Here Dewey's analysis can be seen as having a fairly specific range of reference. It was the emergence of new economic motives in the period of the mercantile and industrial revolutions that precipitated public concern with definitive rights to be accorded by law to associated individuals. Government, *nascently* democratic, becomes an instrument for the regulation and protection of commerce and industry. *Emergent* democracy is a set of devices for holding governments to their proper business as representatives of the public. Thus occurs the paradoxical event in which individual rights are recognized as inalienable while the individual, as such, is submerged by the "great impersonal concerns" of industrial capitalism. While acknowledging that the recognition of individual rights was a potent weapon in the hands of manufacturing and mercantile interests struggling against the restrictions of intrusive governments, Dewey contends at the same time that "the need of some control over these (interests) was the chief agency in making the government of these states democratic."[12]

Can this analysis be sustained? Does it fit the actual events and circumstances of revolutionary America? Is it congruent with the concepts and works of the founders? In what remains I shall argue that it is indeed, as Dewey saw, from this central paradox that democracy actually took shape in America.

Viewing it in abstraction, Hocking puts the paradox this way:

Of course if democracy is primarily a result of the struggle of the public to control the results of business, it is not primarily the result of the struggle of business to control government: and in so far as it is a result of conscious struggle at all, the instrumental ideas were weapons, and not "reflections" of conditions brought about by other forces.[13]

But the process of gestation cannot be understood in abstraction. Seen from Dewey's metaphysical perspective, the paradox resolves into tensions, conflicting demands are resolved "experimentally," and temporal "equilibrium" is achieved. Not permanently, of course; nor does this perspective, though perhaps dialectical, yield the main issue to economic determinism. No matter what the unintended consequences of history, every particular situation must be faced intelligently and intentionally. For the problem of creating a genuine democracy is, as Dewey says, "primarily and essentially an intellectual problem."[14]

That Dewey himself found the work of the founders congenial in both intelligence and intention is nowhere made more explicit than in his popular collection of 1940 called *The Living Thoughts of Thomas Jefferson*.[15] By way of introducing Jefferson to his readers, Dewey recapitulates in outline the basic analysis of *The Public and Its Problems*. He then goes on to discover Jefferson's own commitment to a processive view of government. Thus Jefferson believed that "the excellence of every government is its adaption to the state (or condition) of those to be governed by it." And on the "experimental" nature of political forms, he finds Jefferson advocating periodic revision of the Constitution (every generation) and notes Jefferson's complaint that the Constitution of 1787 makes the process of ordinary amendment too difficult. He finds Jefferson envying the New England practice of local government by town meeting and incorporating its principle into his own plan for balancing local, state, and federal authority. He finds Jefferson to be aware of the relation between culture and politics, even agreeing on the cultural relativity to which political forms must adapt themselves. He quotes Jefferson's notice of the very problem that is the central focus of *The Public and Its Problems*, that "every people have their own particular habits, ways of thinking, etc., which have grown up with them from infancy, and are part of their nature, and to which the regulations which are to make them happy must be accommodated."

It might be argued, of course, that all this is simply the "congeniality" of nostalgia, that Dewey is simply self-indulgent in finding Jefferson to support his own notions of the moral self, the basis of rights, and the legitimacy of governments, and to share his own instrumentalist view of political transactions and institutions. It might also be argued that the "congruence" noted is just accidental and incidental, that there is really no hard evidence that Jefferson shared in or anticipated Dewey's way of thinking or, as I have put it, his metaphysical perspective. For was not Jefferson, after all, a child of the English Enlightenment with all the differences in perspective that identification implies? And what about the other founders? For even if Jefferson *can* be construed as moving in the direction of an instrumentalist conception of government, his differences with the framers over the Constitution is notorious. How can it be said that he shared with them, *and* with Dewey, a common moral perspective on the role of government in promoting "the liberal expansion and confirmation of limited personal endowment," to borrow Dewey's own phrase? As at least one very recent critic has said: "There's not much evidence that many [founders] believed that government was an aid to moral development. Indeed, the men who wrote the Constitution seemed to have a much more restrictive reading of it than the generation that followed. . . . As to the Federalists, they were concerned to develop wealth and productivity, not personal endowments."[16]

This last, of course, puts the paradox to which I have already drawn attention up front. But it also contains just a hint as to the resolution of that paradox as well. For it is, indeed, precisely in the reading of the Constitution—and the other documents of the founding—that the paradox is resolved. It is central to my own argument that the reading *was* experiential in that very particular sense in which Dewey's philosophy uses that term; a sense in which the problematic situation is resolved by the adoption of procedures of inquiry and action which he does not hesitate to call "experimental." Thus Dewey stated:

> The commitment to . . . experimental procedure carries with it the idea of continuous reconstruction of the ideas of individuality and of liberty in intimate connection with changes in social relations . . . the recognition of the effect of [these changes] upon the terms on which men associate together. An experimental method is the recognition of this temporal change in ideas and policies so that the latter shall coordinate with the facts instead of being opposed to them. Any other view maintains a rigid conceptualism and implies that facts should conform to concepts that are framed independently of temporal or historical change.[17]

Taken as a way of reading the Constitution, Dewey's description applies to a central tradition in American jurisprudence. I shall turn to that tradition presently.

But first, Dewey's conception of experimental method must be clearly understood. It means "realistic study of existing conditions in their movement" and, particularly in matters of government,

> careful consideration . . . [of] leading ideas, in the form of policies for dealing with these conditions in the interest of development of increased individuality and liberty. . . . Experimental method is not just messing around nor doing a little of this and a little of that in the hope that things will improve . . . it implies a coherent body of ideas, a theory, that gives direction to effort . . . taken as methods of action tested and continuously revised by the consequences they produce in actual social conditions.[18]

That this may sound like an allusion to the doctrine of "broad construction" of the Constitution commenced by Chief Justice Marshall and supported by Hamilton in his "implied powers" thesis is not merely accidental. For although that doctrine was opposed by Jefferson and Madison when it was formulated in such decisions as *McCulloch* v. *Maryland*, that is, when Virginia's interests (read states' rights) were at stake, the issue was resolved for both parties by the decision of the Court in 1824, in *Osborn* v. *The Bank of the United States*.[19] It was in this case that the priority of individual rights over states' rights was put to the test and established as the law of the land. And it is not merely accidental that it is this doctrine that establishes a clear line from Marshall to Lincoln and the Emancipation Proclamation. That it incorporates into the founders' America both the old English and early American doctrine that the individual, as morally associated, is alone responsible for the wrongs that he inflicts, and that this should become good Jacksonian democratic philosophy is, from Dewey's perspective, only evidence of experimental intelligence at work. For although the heinous Dred Scott Decision was not avoided, it could not stand in the long run.

In *Taking Rights Seriously*, Dworkin puts the matter simply:

> The Constitution theory on which our government rests is not a simple majoritarian theory. The Constitution, and particularly the Bill of Rights, is designed to protect individual citizens and groups against certain decisions that a majority of citizens might want to make, even when that majority acts in what it takes to be the general or common interest.[20]

The basic premise of this theory is equally simple. It is that the rights of the individual are precedent to positive law and are a constraint upon it, and to the powers of government by corollary. It is this premise, explicit in the Declaration of Independence and implicit in the preamble to the Constitution, that individual rights are institutionalized by law and not created by it, that is fundamental. And it is on the hard evidence of this premise that the congruence between Dewey and the founders depends.

Clearly, Dewey argues *tout court* for rights as preexisting law. They are "natural" in Dewey's meaning of that word, but he repeatedly distinguishes them from the natural law tradition of the *philosophia perrennis* while at the same time acknowledging a debt to that tradition. Similarly Jefferson, whose actual derivation of natural rights theory is from Hutcheson and Hume, that is, from the Scottish Enlightenment, not the English Enlightenment and John Locke.[21] Even Jefferson's famous word "self-evident" is not borrowed from Locke—whence it would be merely analytic—but from Reid, through his teacher at William and Mary, Professor Small, as well as the writings of Lord Kames.[22] It is thus "communal sense" that is the ground of these "self-evident" propositions; they are "synthetic" but not *a priori*, although as Reid says, are such as are shared by both "clown and philosopher," which becomes Jefferson's "ploughman and professor."[23] And, perhaps surprisingly, Hamilton argues similarly. For in setting forth his famous "axioms of government" in *The Federalist* No. 31, Hamilton clearly views even the axioms of geometry as dependent on "the organs of perception." He rests his case for the "sciences" of ethics and politics on principles, in his words, "so agreeable to the natural and unsophisticated dictates of common-sense, that they challenge the assent of a sound and unbiased mind with a degree of force and conviction almost equally irresistible."[24]

The Federalist, in fact, argues repeatedly the popular foundation of rights that the Constitution would recognize as preexisting. And that argument looks forward, not merely to the consequences of adoption as the the law of the land, but traces the precedents back through the American Bill of Rights of 1774, to the British Bill of Rights and the earlier Petition of Right to the Magna Carta.[25] That this is an argument for the rights of what Dewey calls "the moral individual transactionally associated with others" seems clear. It is an argument for the concept that Dworkin has in mind when he argues that "men have moral rights against the state." But it is not—repeat *not*—what Aquinas, Grotius, or Pufendorf had in mind. Or Locke. There is no derivation of rights from antecedent natural law as embodied in the positive law of the state. Nor is there in Hamilton's argument any reference to rights in an original state of nature from which men are rescued by a benevolent government, so constituted as to compensate for the deficiencies of a hypothetical natural condition. *Ex hypothesi,* the English natural law theorists of the seventeenth century held to the rather self-contradictory thesis that man had certain moral rights in the natural state that nature itself frustrates. Milton and Locke, for example, held that it was the duty of the state to protect these natural rights to the point that they could not be infringed upon even in the cause of promoting the general welfare.[26] From this, of course, the tradition of "absolute" property rights is derived, and if the conventional view of Hamilton's interests is correct, it is indeed a bit odd that he failed to adopt it. What he adopted instead was an argument already familiar to the colonies.

For the colonies the paramount issue was not property; it was religious liberty. Moreover, there was in even the most Calvinist of the colonies a big difference between the Calvinism that had developed on American soil and the Calvinism of Cromwell and the "Protectorate," that is theocratic dictatorship. And although the latter was indeed exemplified in the Massachusetts ecclesiastical oligarchy of John Cotton, after the Roger Williams affair matters stood quite differently.[27] By the middle of the eighteenth century, religious liberty was itself viewed as a natural right, but not in the Lockean sense as a *legal* right. It was a *moral* right against the intrusions into the private affairs of conscience by the state. By that time the colonists had accumulated a very considerable body of experience with a variety of governmental structures in which the church was accorded varying degrees of authority over local affairs. There were widely adoped forms, and written constitutions, which established and gradually widened the separation of church and state. This, of course, required the adoption of a very different perspective from that of such believers in the establishment of churches as Winthrop and Cotton.[28]

As an instance of how different this perspective is, the *Vindication of the Government of New England Churches*, written and published by John Wise in 1717, just a few years after the Glorious Revolution in England, is sometimes cited.[29] Republished and widely circulated in 1772, this work of an Ipswich, Massachusetts, Congregationalist does comprise a clear reworking of seventeenth-century natural law theory. Wise turns it into a "powerful defense of individualism, liberty, and even democracy," in which the state is no longer covenanted with God on the Moses-on-Mount-Sinai paradigm but is the natural instrument of human creation. As such, the state is no longer a divinely sanctioned agent of God's will; it is a *convenience*, made by free individuals covenanting together in exercise of their inherent right to determine their own form of government and to alter it at will. But Wise borrows liberally from Pufendorf and sometimes sounds almost like a paraphrase of Locke. And although Wise comes out in favor of democracy as the best defense against tyranny and despotism, my own favorite source for the revised natural rights theory actually inscribed in the Constitution itself is not John Wise but James Wilson. I shall rest the case for my own thesis with a brief description of his.

As Professor Elizabeth Flower has noted, history has not been kind to Wilson, "yet this very unsung hero had a decisive hand in forming the Constitution and its philosophic grounds."[30] Born in St. Andrews, Scotland, in 1742, and having attended the university there, as well as at Glasgow and Edinburgh, Wilson was thoroughly familiar with the leading figures of the Scottish Enlightenment. He knew Kames and was at Edinburgh when David Hume was there and at Glasgow during the rectorship of Adam Smith. To quote Flower's succinct summary of his career:

> Scottish legal tradition had deep affinities with Continental thought, stemming ultimately from an idealization of Roman law. Wilson, steeped in this tradition, and equipped with the finest education in the social sciences then available, came to Philadelphia in 1765–66, just as the colonial troubles were coming to a head. He read law with John Dickinson and then served as lawyer, judge, advocate general for France, and was one of the very few who signed both the Declaration of Independence and the Constitution. Under Washington he was appointed to the first Supreme Court.[31]

Wilson started out from the commitment of the Scottish moral sense school, which he found to be "self-evident" in the sense defined by Reid. It was this that is the basis for equality, and he developed it into an explicit theory of representative democracy. More than Jefferson, although perhaps not as much as Paine in *Common Sense*, Wilson believed in common ability, the perception of common needs, and the competence of the people in self-government. The legitimate powers of government derive directly from the people, and the consent of the governed is behavioral conformity to a rule, rather than explicit or implicit agreement to a covenant or contract. Laws are merely special cases of behavioral rules to which, by common consent, the people are held obliged. Laws are not the exercise of superior powers over inferior, nor are they derived from any higher source than custom itself. Equality is not derived *from* the laws; equality is *before* the law. Flower here puts Wilson's doctrine well: "Many other colonials were driven toward a [Lockean] natural rights position; Wilson was able to rest *his* case on his doctrine of consent coupled with an empirical political behaviorism."[32]

Jefferson's phrase in the Declaration "life, liberty, and the pursuit of happiness" was an interesting departure from Locke's "life, liberty, and property," for which Wilson may well be held responsible. In an essay published in 1774, Wilson had argued that all legitimate government is founded to "increase the happiness of the governed" and that "the happiness of society is the first law of every government."[33] Together with George Mason's draft of the Virginia Bill of Rights—which states that "all men are by nature equally free and independent, and have certain inherent rights . . . namely, the enjoyment of life and liberty, with the means of acquiring and possessing property, and pursuing and obtaining happiness and safety"—one can "only conclude," as one authority puts it, "the Wilson, Mason, and Jefferson all rejected the emphasis in Locke and the common law upon the protection of property as the fundamental end of government."[34] In this, it seems, the major voice may well have been Wilson's, as far as the textual evidence is concerned. At the very least, Wilson is thoroughly consistent; Mason and Jefferson are not always so.

Wilson's role at the Constitutional Convention may also have been a decisive one, for he took a middle position between the advocates of supreme federal power over the states and those who stood firmly for states' rights against federal authority. He defended the action of the convention in drawing up a new plan of government, although it had been called merely to revise the old one, on the ground that the Constitution would not really *be* a new plan at all. It would be, rather, the codification of behavioral principles already in place. The nation, he argued, had already created itself by acting as one.[35] The "state," in any case, is but a fiction, a figure of speech that stands for the voluntary association of consenting people. He argued that there can be no irreconcilable differences of interests between the states and the nation; the several state governments and the national government are but different instruments in the service of the same people. The distribution of powers and functions between the states and the federal government should be determined by the principle of utility alone. In the end he argued for, but lost, the case for ratification of the Constitution by the people rather than by the several states.

In Wilson's view the sovereignty of the nation is just the sovereignty of the people, a view that he made most explicit in his opinion as associate justice in *Chisholm* v. *Georgia* (1793).[36] In this case Wilson, joined by John Jay, discusses at length the nature of sovereignty as it applies to the distribution of authority between the federal government and that of the several states. He concludes that, since all sovereignty is vested in the people, the distribution of authority must be determined by the nature of the people's interests and concerns. Thus, it is vested in the people of the *whole* nation "for purposes of Union," as he puts it, and in the people of the several states "for more domestic concerns." In the end, of course, even this way of deciding the matter is necessarily vague. But I think that Jefferson could have agreed that it points up the relativity of all such principles and that both Wilson and Jefferson would have appreciated John Dewey's remark when faced with a similar problem:

> In what has been said there is no attempt to lay down criteria to be applied in a predetermined way to ensure just such and such results. We are not concerned to predict the special forms which state action will take in the future. We have simply been engaged in pointing out the marks by which public action as distinct from private is characterized. Transactions between singular persons and groups bring a public into being when their indirect consequences—their effects beyond those immediately engaged in them—are of importance. Vagueness is not eliminated from the idea of importance. . . . There is no sharp and clear line which draws itself, pointing out beyond peradventure, like the line left by a receding high tide.[37]

My case however, like even the highest tide, must eventually stop. And here is as good a place as any.[38]

Notes

1. Henry Steele Commager, Introduction, to Andrew C. McLaughlin, *Foundations of American Constitutionalism* (New York: Fawcett, 1961), p. vii. For

another instance of Commager's political optimism, see Garry Wills's introduction to Lillian Hellman, *Scoundrel Time* (New York: Little Brown, 1976), p. 15. Wills quotes Commager as saying at the peak of the Cold War: "The record is perhaps unique in the history of power: the organization of the United Nations, the Truman Doctrine, the Marshall Plan, the Berlin Airlift, the organization of NATO, the defense of Korea, the development of atomic power for peaceful purposes, Point Four—these prodigious gestures are so wise and enlightened that they point the way to a new concept of the use of power." After Vietnam, Watergate, and Irangate it is tempting to add that the flaw in each of the latter "prodigious gestures" comes from the failure to appreciate the long term consequences of power as "transactional"—to use Dewey's word—in effect.

2. Gore Vidal, "The Second American Revolution?" *New York Review of Books*, February 5, 1981, p. 36.

3. John Dewey, *The Public and Its Problems* (Chicago: Swallow Press, 1954), p. 7. This edition contains the important "Afterword" of 1946, *q.v.*, and is the edition quoted *passim*.

4. The source is Dewey's *Experience and Nature*. See R. W. Sleeper, "Dewey's Metaphysical Perspective," *Journal of Philosophy* LVII (1960): 100–115. My view has changed hardly at all since this article was written, but see also R. W. Sleeper, *The Necessity of Pragmatism: John Dewey's Conception of Philosophy* (New Haven: Yale University Press, 1986), for a more detailed exposition of Dewey's "metaphysical perspective" than can be delineated here.

5. John Dewey, *Experience and Nature* (Chicago: Open Court, 1958), p. 46.

6. *Ibid.*

7. John Dewey, *Freedom and Culture* (New York: Capricorn, 1963), pp. 21, 23, 130.

8. *Ibid.* See also *The Public and Its Problems*, p. 25.

9. John Dewey, *The Public and Its Problems*, p. 64.

10. *Ibid.*

11. William Ernest Hocking, Review of *The Public and Its Problems*, reprinted in *Dewey and His Critics*, ed. S. Morgenbesser (New York: Journal of Philosophy, 1977), pp. 688–694. Quoted from p. 689.

12. Dewey, *The Public and Its Problems*, p. 98.

13. Hocking, Review, p. 691.

14. Dewey, *The Public and Its Problems*, p. 126.

15. *The Living Thoughts of Thomas Jefferson* was published originally by David McKay and reissued in paperback by Fawcett, n.d. The quotations of Jefferson that follow are from Dewey's text in the Fawcett edition.

16. Private communication from Burton Zweibach of Queens College, CUNY, and typical of the interpretation of the founders' intent by those still influenced by Beard's thesis.

17. John Dewey, "The Future of Liberalism," in *Dewey and His Critics*, p. 698.

18. *Ibid.*

19. I have used two sources for reference to Supreme Court decisions: Alfred H. Kelly and Winfred A. Harbison, *The American Constitution: Its Origins and Development* (New York: Norton, 1963), and Robert E. Cushman, *Leading Constitutional Decisions* (New York: Appleton-Century, 1963). Kelly and Harbison comment on the importance of Osborn as follows: "This principle is essential for the protection of personal liberty, for, since governments or legislatures cannot be sued for torts, the injured person's only recourse is to sue their agents" (p. 292).

20. Ronald Dworkin, *Taking Rights Seriously* (Cambridge: Harvard University Press, 1977), p. 133.

21. See Garry Wills's enthusiastic discussion of the "Scottish Enlightenment" as it influenced Jefferson, Part Four in his *Inventing America* (Garden City, N.Y.: Doubleday, 1978). A more sober discussion of the same influence is found in Elizabeth Flower and Murray G. Murphey, *A History of Philosophy in America* (New York: G. P. Putnam's Sons, 1977), Vol. 1, multiple references indexed. Of special interest is Flower's almost off-hand remark in reference to John Witherspoon, Madison's teacher at Princeton: "In countering the objection that understanding or reason must be limited to matters of truth and falsity since intelligent beings often do evil, Witherspoon maintains his integrated view of human response. Judgment must be the basis for the full range of choice and decision. Behavior generally may thus be rational in a quite modern and Deweyan sense" (p. 235).

22. The influence of Kames on Jefferson appears to have been in the period *after* the Declaration was written. Small's influence was prior, of course, and probably decisive. Small drew on Hutcheson's notion of a "communal" *moral* sense in his lectures at William and Mary. Reid, whose 1763 *An Inquiry into the Human Mind* was Small's main source in epistemological matters, departed from Hutcheson's "moral sense" by turning it into "common sense." Reid did not follow Kames—a cousin of David Hume—in turning it back into Butler's "conscience." But see also Wills's discussion in which it appears that Reid's influence may have been less than Sterne's in these matters.

23. Thomas Reid, *An Inquiry into the Human Mind*, ed. Timothy Duggan (Chicago: University of Chicago Press, 1970). Reid says, "This perception [of the

moon, from which an inference is made that the moon is spherical] is the same in the philosopher, and in the clown" (p. 211). Jefferson follows the same line of argument in the inference from simple perceptions to the "common sense" moral rules. In so doing he roughly approximates the connection that Reid himself drew between the *Inquiry* and that of the *Essays on the Intellectual and Active Powers* (Philadelphia, 1792). This volume combines in one edition two volumes separately published in Scotland: *Essays on the Intellectual Powers*, in 1785, and *Essays on the Active Powers*, in 1788. Wills says that Jefferson wrote his "ploughman-professor" argument in 1789. Thus, although Wills quotes Reid from the 1792 edition, this could not have been Jefferson's source. In any case, Jefferson's wording of the argument does ape Reid's. Wills quotes Jefferson as follows: "State a moral case to a ploughman and a professor. The former will decide it as well and often better than the latter, because he has not been led astray by artificial rules" (p. 185).

24. *The Federalist Papers*, with an Introduction by Clinton L. Rossiter (paperback; New York: Mentor, 1956), p. 193. See Rossiter's introductory remarks for a fairly sober view of the alleged "split personality" of Publius.

25. See particularly Hamilton in *The Federalist* No. 84. Hamilton here agrees with James Wilson's observation that the preamble of the Constitution "contains the essence of all Bills of rights that have been or can be devised" (quoted in Flower and Murphey, *A History of Philosophy in America*, p. 334). See also Clinton L. Rossiter, *The Political Thought of the American Revolution* (New York: Harcourt, Brace and World, 1963), Chap. 4, in which the notion of an American consensus is argued. As to the Magna Carta, see the essay by Philip B. Kurland, "Magna Carta and Constitutionalism in the United States," in Erwin N. Griswold (ed.), *The Great Charter* (New York: Mentor, paperback, 1965). Kurland's subtitle, "The Noble Lie," is indicative of his approach which approximates James Wilson's. As Wilson put it: "The boasted Magna Charta of England derives the liberties of the inhabitants . . . from the gift and grant of the King . . . But here the fee simple remains in the people, and by this Constitution they do not part with it" (Flower and Murphey, *A History of Philosophy in America*, p. 334).

26. There is abundant literature on this topic. Kelly and Harbison, *The American Constitution*, offer a serviceable bibliography and their own introduction to the topic is an excellent distillation with appropriate emphasis on the changing views on law, suffrage, and rights.

27. There is a good deal of evidence that mainstream legal thinking in America paid little attention to either the Puritan or Catholic versions of "Natural Law." See, for example, Lawrence M. Friedman's popular *A History of American Law*

(2nd edition, New York: Simon and Schuster, 1985), which is silent on the issues raised here.

28. Oddly enough some interpreters of God's law, such as Winthrop and Cotton, sometimes agree with the purely secular and utilitarian view that grounds individual human rights in the private "interests" of the person. Thus compare John Austin, *Lectures on Jurisprudence* (3rd edition; London: John Muirhead, 1869) where this appears: "[Generally] every individual person is the best possible judge of his own interests . . . Consequently, the principle of general utility imperiously demands that he commonly shall attend to his own rather than to the interests of others" (p. 162). Many colonists, like Winthrop and Cotton, disagreed with Locke's equation of rights with "property" that could be "alienated" from the individual that "possessed" it, preferring the equation of rights and "interests" that could *not* be alienated. This is not to say, of course, that Winthrop and Cotton were "utilitarians," But they do agree with Austin's premise that since rights are inherent in the private interests of the individual they are incapable of alienation. They repudiate, as Bentham and Austin later did, classic "natural rights."

29. John Wise, *A Vindication of the Government of New England Churches* (Boston: Printed by J. Allen, for N. Boone [bookseller] at the Sign of the Bible in Cornhill, 1717). Wise is often presented as a pre-Revolutionary radical, as in Sherwin L. Cook, "John Wise, the Preacher of American Insurgency," *Proceedings of the Bostonian Society*, (Concord, N.H.: Rumford Press, 1925), pp. 28–41, and G. A. Cook, *John Wise: Early American Democrat* (New York: Kings Crown Press, 1952). The later Cook builds on Clinton Rossiter's "John Wise: Colonial Democrat," *New England Quarterly*, XXII (March 1949): 3–32, but does not go quite as far as Paul S. McElroy's "John Wise: The Father of American Independence," *The Essex Institute Historical Collections*, LXXXI (1945): 201–26. Raymond P. Stearns debunks the extreme view in "John Wise of Ipswich Was No Democrat" (*The Essex Institute Historical Collections* XCVII (January 1961): page numbers not available.

30. Flower and Murphey, *A History of Philosophy in America*, p. 331.

31. *Ibid.*

32. *Ibid.*, p. 332.

33. Quoted by Kelly and Harbison, *The American Constitution*, p. 90.

34. *Ibid.*, p. 91.

35. See President Carter's phrase in his "Farewell Address": "America did not invent human rights, human rights invented America." (Quoted from my own contemporary notes.)

36. *Ibid.*, p. 191. See also Daniel Webster's brief in the Dartmouth College Case. Cushman, in *Leading Constitutional Decisions*, ranks the Dartmouth College Case (actually the *Trustees of Dartmouth College v. Woodward*) with those cases establishing important precedents for "Restrictions on the States in Behalf of Civil and Political Rights." That this case is conventionally understood as protecting the monied and propertied class is evidence of the paradox referred to earlier in this paper. The plain fact is that the decision, upholding the sanctity of private contract against the predatory actions of the State legislature, *does* protect property rights. But Marshall's opinion goes far beyond that question, discussing even the students' rights, and turns it into a doctrine of Constitutional protection for all individual rights: "The law of this case is the law of all." By the extension of "broad construction" this is an argument that derives the rights of corporate "personalities" from those of individual persons, rather than the reverse. See John Dewey's discussion of this whole matter in "The Historic Background of Corporate Legal Personality," *Yale Law Journal* XXXV (April 1926): 655–673.

37. Dewey, *The Public and Its Problems*, p. 64. It may be commented here that if, indeed, there is agreement among Jefferson, Wilson, and Dewey on these matters it is likely that they share something of Dewey's "metaphysical perspective" on the sources of both stability and precariousness in human affairs. Moreover, it may even be possible to bring Hamilton into the consensus. This might be argued as follows: the feature that distinguishes Dewey on "natural law" is precisely its *secular* naturalism, a feature not shared by Aquinas, Grotius, Pufendorf, Locke, Milton, or even John Wise and Roger Williams but one that *is* shared by Jefferson, Wilson, and Hamilton. The argument would have to show that the latter three are only, at best, *pro forma* "Deists" who placed no great philosophical (read "metaphysical") importance on the divine origin of natural law, considering its origin rather as satisfactorily grounded in nature as such, whether or not nature is divinely created. The argument would have to find Jefferson, Wilson, and Hamilton to differ from the views of such "Deists" as Voltaire, Diderot, and Rousseau (?) as well as such "Puritans" as Locke and Milton. Although the Deists and Puritans (at least as far as Locke and Milton are concerned) argued in favor of religious toleration, they also believed that natural law had a definitive divine source. Certainly Jefferson, Wilson, and Hamilton did not attach much importance to the alleged "divine source" in the development of their own views. Were an outright commitment to atheism not a severe political disability, it may be supposed, all three might have been willing to be known as such—or at least as agnostics. In any case, all three make no more actual use of God in their arguments for the natural basis of rights than could be

derived from Dewey's conception of what the term "God" means in practice; that is the "active relation between the real and the ideal" (*Common Faith* [New Haven: Yale University Press, 1934; paperback edition 1960], pp. 50–51). Although the argument must proceed by negation and could never convince the "Moral Majority," I see no reason why it could not be a convincing one. Oddly enough, if successful, the consolidated position of Jefferson, Wilson, Hamilton, and Dewey would be preciously close to that of H. L. A. Hart in *The Concept of Law* (Oxford: Clarendon Press, 1961), pp. 187–195. Hart, of course, admits only "a very attenuated version of Natural Law" and gives it only "minimal content." Nevertheless, as he also says: "This simple thought has in fact very much to do with the characteristics of both law and morals, and it can be disentangled from the more disreputable parts of the general teleological outlook in which the end or good for man appears as a specific way of life about which, in fact, men may profoundly disagree." The minimal content, which Hart conceives to be directed to human "survival," turns out, when Hart elaborates it, to include rules of "common sense" behavior, obvious "generalizations" and "indeed truisms." Such rules, for example, as would acknowledge the "vulnerability" of individuals and their need for protection as a condition of social life; "approximate equality" and "limited altruism" as well as "limited understanding and strength of will." Hart views these as having the status of "*natural necessity*" (his emphasis) and concludes that "it is in this form that we should reply to the positivist thesis that 'law may have any content.' For it is a truth of some importance that for the adequate description not only of law but of many other social institutions, a place must be reserved, besides definitions and ordinary statements of fact, for a third category of statements: those the truth of which is contingent on human beings and the world in which they live in retaining the salient characteristics which they have" (p. 195).

38. I cannot, however, stop without at least acknowledging my debt to Elizabeth Flower's chapter on Dewey (Flower and Murphey, *A History of Philosophy in America*, pp. 811–887), which, in emphasizing the influence of "Scottish Common Sense Realism" on the development of Dewey's thought, first suggested the theme of this paper. Flower's account of Reid, Stewart, and Brown, who were "preoccupied with the relation of psychology to logic" and their "enlargement of experience to include the aesthetic and the social," is indeed a preamble to the argument that I have presented here, as is her emphasis on Brown's and Stewart's interest in pursuing the role of philosophy "as a resource for directing human advance," She shows, as well, how Brown's account of "the biological basis of behavior and the organic character of human response" is surely as much a char-

acteristic of the intellectual perspective of at least some of the framers as Locke's rigidly dualistic and rationalistic perspective. In the end, according to Flower, it is as much to these "common sense" views, as to Hegel, Peirce, and the various permutations of idealism, that we must look for an understanding of John Dewey's philosophical development. Thus: "Dewey's pragmatism owes a profound debt to the hardheaded American reading of Common Sense"—which was largely due to the Scottish Enlightenment, *not* to the English (p. 821).

4 | Dewey and the Class Struggle

Peter Manicas

During John Dewey's very long life, from 1859 to 1952, immense changes occurred in the world. In his lifetime, a Civil War ended slavery and the United States went from a fragmented, provincial, and agrarian society to an industrial civilization; thence from the Great War, it became the most powerful nation on earth. With World War I, the state came to full maturity and, of course, with the Bolshevik Revolution, socialism became more than an idea. A devastating depression in the capitalist world was followed by Nazism, Fascism, and World War II. Dewey died in the early years of the Cold War after having seen the advent of the nuclear age.

In their monumental *A History of Philosophy in America*, Elizabeth Flower and Murray Murphey rightly emphasize that "Dewey's philosophy resists encapsulation" and that "the development of his views is virtually a study in philosophic ecology." As they say, Dewey was a concrete thinker, acutely perceptive that changing situations demanded reformulation of problems and refashioned conceptual tools.[1] In celebrating the work of Betty Flower, I want in this essay to pursue an aspect of this, to concentrate on Dewey's reflections on the prospects of reconstructive creative intelligence, on liberal democracy, and on American capitalism. I mean to do this against the background of Marxism. Although Dewey continued to rethink his views on these critical matters, I conclude that in fundamental ways both Dewey and the Marxists were mistaken. On one hand, the prospects for reconstructive creative intelligence within the framework of capitalist democracy are anything but good. Dewey himself might finally have agreed, but his failure to go the root of the problem gave his conservative epigones ample opportunity to deradicalize his otherwise radical thought. On the other hand, the Marxists are at least as wrong about the prospects of proletarian revolution—leaving us, in my view, with a political impasse that calls for more imagination than I can muster. My pessimism is not complete, however, because I want to see what of a positive sort can be gleaned from Dewey and from Marxism.

In *German Philosophy and Politics* (1915), Dewey's first systematic political work, Dewey traced the philosophic basis of patriotic statism in Germany and concluded that "the present situation presents the spectacle of the breakdown of the whole philosophy of Nationalism, political, racial and cultural." Dewey rejected the sufficiency of "arbitration, treaties, international judicial councils, schemes of international disarmament, peace funds and peace movements." Reminiscent of anarchist thought, he called for "more radical thinking" of the problem (*GPP*, p. 130).[2] The problem of statist politics was also present in *Democracy and Education*, published the next year. He asked: "Is it possible for an educational system to be conducted by a national state and yet the full social ends of the educative process not be restricted, constrained, and corrupted?" Dewey thought that the answer could be yes, *if*, to be sure, we were talking about education "in and for a democratic society." By 1917, in a series of articles written for the *New Republic*, Dewey attacked pacifism and suggested instead that Americans join the war effort, for he believed that it could become an opportunity to foster and secure "our" conception of democracy. Dewey was not insensitive to the limits and dangers of his position, dangers incisively pointed out Randolph Bourne, his friend and former student. For Bourne, not only was there no evidence that Dewey's "democratic desires" could be realized by being a party to imperialist war but "creative intelligence" could give way to hysteria and to a narrow instrumentalism. Bourne perceptively noted that "the young men being sucked into the councils of Washington and into war organization everywhere" had "absorbed the secret of scientific method as applied to political organization." Bourne concluded that creative intelligence could now be "lined up in the service of the war technique."[3]

The Espionage Acts of 1917 and 1918 were passed and by 1919, the Red Scare had fully ripened. Dewey's worst fears were coming true. Positive steps, of course, could be taken. With Dewey, Norman Thomas, Clarence Darrow, Roger N. Baldwin and others as founders, the American Union Against Militarism became, in 1920, the American Civil Liberties Union (ACLU). It was hardly sufficient. In 1921 Sacco and Vanzetti were tried, and in 1927 they were executed. These events surely had a profound effect on Dewey. He wrote that for him, America had been put on trial along with Sacco and Vanzetti. But if America was to be indicted, what *exactly* was the charge? Dewey recognized that in the absence of a clear answer here, any politics was doomed.

In *Democracy and Education*, democracy was already being construed by Dewey as both "a mode of associated living" and "a form of government." In that book, the two ideas went hand in hand. Education in a political democracy had as its aim "sustaining and extending" democracy as a mode of associated living, of "conjoint communicated experience." As a way of life, democracy was "the extension in space of the number of individuals who participate in an interest so that each has to refer his own action to that of others, and to consider the action of others to give point and direction to his own." "The widening of the area of shared concerns" breaks down "barriers of class, race and national territory." Such widening was not, Dewey wrote, "the product of deliberation and conscious effort." On the contrary, it was the result of "the development of modes of manufacture and commerce, travel, migration and intercommunication which flowed from the command of science over natural energy" (*D&E*, p. 87).

But by the time of his 1927 *The Public and Its Problems*, Dewey had made a remarkable about face. Not only had he developed a brilliant analysis and critique of democracy as "a form of government," but it was now clear to him that democracy as a way of life was *not* being fostered by the new interdependencies and the new capacities of technological society. On the contrary, democracy as a mode of associated living was being profoundly *undermined* by these same forces.

Turning his attention to democracy as a form of government, Dewey argued that the democratic state had emerged at a specific period in the development of the modern state for reasons largely unrelated to the goal of realizing democracy, understood as a form of association in which people collectively govern themselves. At best, political democracy "represents an effort . . . to counteract forces that so largely determined the possession of rule by accidental and irrelevant factors, and . . . an effort to counteract the tendency to employ political power to serve private instead of public ends" (*PP*, p. 83). But political democracy had failed even to realize these limited goals. "In a word," he concluded, "the new forms of combined action due to the modern economic regime controls present policies, much as dynastic interests controlled those of two centuries ago. They affect thinking and desire more than did the interests which formerly moved the state" (*PP*, p. 108).

Dewey's analysis demonstrated the depth of the problem, for it was not with the institutions of political democracy, with, for example, the machinery of elections or the existence of a free press. Moreover, there were parties that competed for the vote, and to an important degree, presumably, the rule of law prevailed in America. The problem was the public itself: "The machine age has so enormously expanded, multiplied, intensified and complicated the scope of indirect consequences, have formed such immense and consolidated unions in action, on an impersonal rather than a community basis, that the resultant public cannot identify and distinguish itself" (*PP*, p. 126). The public is "unchoate and unorganized," "lost," "eclipsed," "confused," and "bewildered." This theme is persistent in Dewey's writings of the period.

In *Individualism Old and New* (1929), Dewey spoke of "the lost individual," lost because although "persons are now caught up in a vast complex of associations, there is no harmonious and coherent reflection of the import of these connections into the imaginative and emotional outlook of life" (*ION*, pp. 85–86). In *Freedom and Culture* (1939), he spoke of a kind of "molluscan organization, soft individuals within and a hard constrictive shell without." Turning on the schools, Dewey argued:

> Schooling in literacy is no substitute for the dispositions which were formerly provided by direct experience of an education quality. The void created by lack of relevant personal experiences combines with the confusion produced by impact of multitudes of unrelated incidents to create attitudes which are responsive to organized propaganda, hammering in day after day the same few and relatively simple beliefs asseverated to be the 'truths' essential to national welfare. (*F&C*, p. 46)

Dewey did not, I think, minimize the problem. Interdependencies had created shared problems, but along with this, conditions had been created that made their identification *as shared* extremely difficult. Worse, conditions had been created that made *democratic action* nearly impossible. Indeed, "Perhaps to most, probably to many, the conclusions which have been stated as to the conditions upon which depends the emergence of a Public from its eclipse will seem close to a denial of the possibility of realizing the idea of a democratic public" (*PP.*, p. 185). Yet, if he did not minimize the problem, he was anything but clear on its *causes* and, consequently, on what ought to be our response to it. Was the eclipse of a democratic public the inevitable consequence of technology, of the emergence of the state? Did capitalism play a role in this, and if so, what role?

As if, then, to assuage the pessimists, he wrote: "One might indeed point for what it is work to the enormous obstacles with which the rise of a science of physical things was confronted a few short centuries ago, as evidence that hope need not be wholly desperate nor faith wholly blind" (*PP*, p. 185). The analogy is troublesome. Physical science liberated itself from superstition. Will cooperative intelligence in political matters do the same? But by what logic? C. Wright Mills, himself powerfully influenced by Dewey's analysis of the disintegrated Public, was indignant with Dewey's easy way out. Still, the problem was not, as H. S. Thayer, Morton White, and others have charged, that Dewey tired readers with "the importance of using scientific intelligence in political affairs without hearing him give concrete political programs." As James Campbell has demonstrated, Dewey always had practical suggestions and concrete programs, for example, the ACLU, his efforts at forming a third party.[4] More serious, did his practical proposals presuppose what his analysis had forbidden? That is, if as Campbell rightly argues, Dewey's method of social reconstruction assumes "that we live our lives in, or on the verge of clusters of democratic communities: larger and smaller, overlapping and telescoping, groups of concerned and active individuals who seek the common good in a democratic way," then doesn't this assume the existence of publics in Dewey's sense? Dewey's efforts at forming a third party failed because, *in his own analysis*, the Public was "lost," "eclipsed" and "bewildered."

I promised to view Dewey's analysis and politics against the background of Marx and Marxism. Marxism is a revolutionary philosophy, and its central political concept is the idea of class struggle. Marx himself did not, of course, rule out the possibility the the proletariat could use the institutions of political democracy to bring about a social revolution. Yet it was more likely for him and those who followed him that class struggle would erupt into class war, that the great mass of proletarians, having achieved revolutionary consciousness, would then be the agents of a dramatic and violent transformation to the new order. Marx was never uncritical about the problems of this view and by at least 1899 (the year of publication of Karl Kautsky's draft program of the Austrian Democratic Party), Marxists in general saw that although "economic development" and "class struggle" would create "the conditions for socialist production," they would not—at least directly—create a revolutionary consciousness among the workers. By 1902, Lenin could insist: " 'Everyone agrees' that it is necessary to develop the political consciousness of the working class." "The question was," he continued, "*how* that is to be done and what is required to do it?"[5] There were, of course, two main lines of answer to Lenin's famous question: Lenin's view that the proletariat needs a vanguard party of professional revolutionaries, operating conspiratorily to bring workers revolutionary consciousness "from without," and Rosa Luxemburg's view that social democracy was not "joined to the organization of the proletarian" but was "itself the proletariat."[6] In her view, although the mass strike, for example, was a valuable weapon in generating revolutionary consciousness among workers, neither Blanquism nor Jacobin organization could serve socialist revolution. Tragically, World War I and its aftermath devastated the Social Democrats of Europe. It also gave space to Lenin. The consequences of these events were, of course, monumental, although neither Dewey nor anyone else could have seen this at the time.[7]

Dewey had visited the Soviet Union in 1928. In no sense could it be said that he was an ideological anti-Marxist. He had assessed the Bolshevik Revolution as "an experiment to discover whether the familiar democratic ideals—familiar in words at least— . . . will not be most completely realized in a social regime based on voluntary cooperation, on conjoint workers' control and mangement of industry" (*C&E*, Vol. 1, p. 424). Dewey saw, it is clear, that socialism was inconceivable without democracy and that, as the foregoing suggests, democracy in its complete sense demanded socialism. Nevertheless, his analysis of the democratic state made it plain to him, although not to the Marxists, that in the United States, at least, proletarian revolution was not on the historical agenda. For him, as I shall suggest, the critical issue was the very idea of *class*. But there was a symmetry in the political postures of the Marxists and of Dewey that it is well to notice here. If, as Lenin saw, "everyone agrees" that the problem was to develop political consciousness among the *workers*, for Dewey, rejecting class analysis, the problem was, how to develop political consciousness among *the citizens*? In what follows, I want to suggest that Dewey and the Marxists made complementary errors and that they could have learned very much from one another.

The workers were not to be agents of social change. It was not that there was not oppression and inequality in America, that workers were not exploited, nor that they were happy with their lot. One didn't hear their "angry voices," Dewey wrote, but that was *not* because they were drowned out by "shouts of eagerness for adventurous opportunity." Rather, "the murmurs of discontent are drowned" by "the murmurs of lost opportunities, along with the din of machinery, motor cars and speakeasies" (*ION*, p. 78–79.). This metaphor, suggestive of the writings of Marcuse of Foucault, was employed in the context of Dewey's brilliant analysis of American individualism. It was not roast beef, but "repressive needs," "normalization," and "atomization" that had disintegrated class consciousness. As Poulantzas was to put it in the 1970s, in the liberal democracies everything happens as if the class struggle did not exist.[8]

On the other hand, Marxism had just what Dewey lacked: an adequate theory of capitalist society, a theory that gives us a way to see opportunities and to take advantage of them appropriately, a theory that can inform our direct experience and thereby make it educative, a theory that identifies common goods and the causes of common evils, a theory that, because it goes to the root of our problems, is able to address concrete problems in terms of an inclusive goal.

There are, of course, "Deweyans" who would deny that one needs such a theory, especially one that envisions some inclusive social goal. For them, Dewey's "experimentalism" is "piecemeal" and "ameliorative" just because it rejects even the possibility of such a theory. I for one do not think that such an interpretation can be sustained. In *Individualism Old and New* and *Liberalism and Social Action*, Dewey explicitly affirms the need for an inclusive view. Of course, Dewey's style of presentation, his rejection of totalizing generalization, arid abstraction, and of "fixed and final goods" is easily assimilated—wrongly—to what C. Wright Mills scornfully titled "liberal practicality."

In fact, it is more than disconcerting to notice that much of the time at least, Dewey is very close to a Marxism. This might be developed in some detail, but for present purposes, look only at *Individualism Old and New*. In that critical text, Dewey argued that the issue that Marx had raised, "the relation of the economic structure to political operations—is one that actively persists." "Indeed," he continues, "it forms the only basis of present political questions" (p. 103). In the pages that follow, Dewey gives a straightforward account of the crisis, similar to that on the third volume of *Capital*. He writes:

> There are now, it is estimated, eight billions of surplus savings a year, and the amount is increasing. Where is this capital to find its outlet? Diversion into the stock market gives temporary relief, but the resulting inflation is a 'cure' which creates a new disease. If it goes into the expansion of industrial plants, how long will it be before they, too, "overproduce"? (*ION*, p. 109)

There is even a clear reference to the upshot of the Marxian labor theory of value: "That the total earnings of eight million wage workers should be only four times the amount of what the income-tax returns frankly call the 'unearned' income of . . . eleven thousand millionaires goes almost without notice" (*ION*, p. 107). Perhaps even more Marxist sounding is his claim that "large and basic economic currents cannot be ignored for any length of time, and they are working in one direction." Indeed, "economic determinism is now a fact, not a theory"

(p. 119). His excellent account concludes with a text that could have been written by Engels:

> There is a difference and a choice between a blind, chaotic and unplanned determinism, issuing from business conducted for pecuniary profit—the anarchy of capitalist production—and the determination of socially planned and ordered development. It is the difference and the choice between a socialism that is public and one that is capitalistic. (*ION*, pp. 119–120)

Finally, Dewey also sees the relation between this theoretically informed analysis and the problem of the "lost individual." "We live," he writes, "politically from hand to mouth." "The various expressions of public control . . . have taken place sporadically and in response to the pressure of distressed groups so large that their voting power demanded attention. They have been improvised to meet special occasions. They have not been adopted as parts of any general social policy" (*ION*, p. 115). It is clear enough why this is the case. Under present arrangements, "financial and industrial power, corporately organized, can deflect economic consequences away from the advantage of the many to serve the privilege of the few" (*ION*, p. 115). The political parties themselves, the ostensible vehicles of mobilization for change, "have been eager accomplices in maintaining confusion and unreality" (*ION*, p. 114).

This analysis, as pertinent today as when it was offered, is not untypical of Dewey. It suggests that Dewey's understanding of the political possibilities of democratic politics in capitalist America was anything but naive, and that, in important ways, it was close to Marxism. But for all this, he seems persistently to lose sight of the critical issue. An instance is the book that some have taken to be one of Dewey's more radical political tracts, *Liberalism and Social Action*, written in 1935.

As is well known, Dewey there insisted that "Liberalism must become radical, meaning by 'radical' preception of the necessity of thorough-going changes in the set-up of institutions and corresponding activity to bring changes to pass" (*LSA*, p. 62). Dewey emphatically rejected reform that dealt with but "this abuse and now that without having a social goal based on an inclusive plan," but he was less clear what that goal and plan was. One thing was clear: Dewey rejected Marxism, especially "the idea of a struggle between classes, culminating in open and violent warfare as being the method for production of radical social change" (*LSA*, p. 78).

Dewey, of course, had a clear and adequate instrumentalist view of violence.

In another place he had written that "what is justly objected to as violence or undue coercion is a reliance upon wasteful or destructful means of accomplishing results." In *Liberalism and Social Action*, similarly, it was not violence *as such* that was the issue. To his credit, he recognized, with the Marxists, that "force, rather than intelligence is built into the procedures of the existing social system" (*LSA*, p. 63) and that even free expression will be tolerated only "as long as it does not seem to menace in any way the status quo of society" (*LSA*, p. 65). When it does, he wrote, the state will be quick to use official violence in the name of protecting "the general welfare." Dewey had learned from his experience with Palmer raids and the tragedy of Sacco and Vanzetti.

What then was his objection to the class war notion of the Marxists? Dewey might have argued, although he did not, that the Marxist analysis was substantially correct but that, for good historical reasons, the idea of struggle between classes culminating in open welfare had to be rejected. The argument for this conclusion would be complicated, but it would be fully consistent with Dewey's own analysis of the democratic state. In a nutshell, because of changes in the last eighty years or so in the development of capitalist societies, but especially in America where race and ethnic division loomed so large, class solidarity was inevitably undermined. Put simply, "workers" was no longer a useful *political* category, and still less the idea, already put in doubt by Marxists, that the workers would be a *revolutionary* class.

Yet I would insist that this does not make Marxism politically irrelevant. The issue is complicated but I must be brief. "Class" in Marxism is a *theoretical* concept, grounded in the central concept of mode of production. Classes are not defined by a set of empirically given characteristics, for example, income, social status, or occupation. Marx's *Capital*, which in my view remains indispensable for an understanding of capitalism, provides a theoretical and abstract account of the capitalist mode of production. Abstractly considered, there are but two classes, the owners of the means of production and the producers of surplus value, the proletariat. But of course the real world is not *just* a mode of production. It is a society with a mode of production. It has state structures, churches, gender and racial conflicts, schools and mass media, "professionals," and all sorts of "workers" who are not proletarians—defined as producers of surplus value. In the nineteenth century, it was still possible to keep things simple by identifying the growing class of industrial workers with a growing and increasingly organized proletariat, to suppose, as *The Communist Manifesto* had it, that "the small tradespeople, shopkeepers, and retired tradesmen generally, the handicraftsmen and peasants—all these sink gradually into the proletariat." "The workers," now "the immense majority," now "organized," would become a revolutionary class. But close as that had come to being prophetic, just before World War I, that time had now passed.

This was not, in any case, the line of argument that Dewey took. Instead, he rejected *in toto* the central core of Marxian analysis, replaced it with a vague technological determinism and then recurred to a conception that had been a favorite of his for many years, the idea that experimental methods had to be applied to politics.

Dewey observed, rightly, that "according to the Marxians . . . the economic foundations of society consist of two things, the forces of production on one side and, on the other side, the social relations of production." Further, for Marxians, scientific technology is part of the forces of production. It is dynamic while the social relations are static; they "lag behind." Dewey was ready to admit that "what was happening socially is the result of the combination of these two factors," but he insisted that it was but "a truism" to call this combination "capitalism" and to say, accordingly, "that capitalism is the 'cause' of all the important changes that have occurred" (*LSA*, p. 81). In his view,

> Colossal increase in productivity, the bringing together of men in cities and large factories, the elimination of distance, the accumulation of capital, fixed and liquid—these things would have come about, at a certain stage, no matter what the established institutional system. They are the consequences of the new means of technological production. (*LSA*, p. 92)

Dewey has not been alone in this contention, of course. It has been a theme of technological determinists of all sorts, but especially more recent prophets of "industrial society," Marxists and non-Marxists alike. In this view, at a certain point in the development of scientific technology, because technology directly defines the labor process and through this, the wider social relations as well, capitalism and socialism "converge."

Dewey's concrete approach should have put him on guard. Although he often succumbs to the high abstraction "industrial society," he seems also to have seen that *the way* changes occurred in the West, the *particular* application of technologies and the *particular* distribution of wealth and resources, was fundamentally shaped by the motive, logic, and consequences of the accumulation of capital; had *this* been different, technological production could surely have been different. Putting the matter as briefly as possible, insofar as the relations of private property define "the accumulation of captial," the state is preferably *liberal.* This means not just that private and public are bifurcated but that government will be predictably limited in addressing problems thrown up by the process of capital accumulation. At the very least, it must be constrained to activities consistent with the maintenance of the system of private accumulation.

Dewey's claim that "the release of productivity is the product of cooperatively organized intelligence" is correct. As Marxists point out, production is socialized in capitalism. Moreover, if one wants the productivity associated with industrial societies, there is no alternative to that. But Dewey's idea that "coercion and oppression on a large scale exist" because "of the perpetuation of old institutions and patterns not touched by scientific method" is patently fallacious. Indeed, in the text already quoted from *Individualism Old and New*, he had it right: "There is a difference and a choice between a blind, chaotic and unplanned determinism, issuing from business conducted for pecuniary profit, and the determination of a socially planned and ordered development," between "a socialism that is public and one that is capitalistic" (*ION*, pp. 119–120.)

Once Dewey lost touch with the root of the problem, he could no longer offer plausible solutions. He offered:

> The question is whether force or intelligence is to be the method upon which we consistently rely and to whose promotion we devote our energies. Insistence that the use of force is inevitable limits the use of available intelligence. . . .

> There is an undoubted objective clash of interests between finance-capitalism that controls the means of production and whose profit is served by maintaining relative scarcity, and idle workers and hungry consumers. But what generates violent strife is failure to bring the conflict into the light of intelligence where the conflicting interests can be adjudicated in behalf of the interests of the great majority. (*ION*, pp. 79–80)

The argument is a bad one for at least three reasons. First, Dewey's absolutist either/or, either force or intelligence, is unwarranted. No serious revolutionary, not Marx, not Lenin, not even Bakunin, so tied his hands in the way that Dewey suggests, even if for them violence was inevitable. One would have supposed that Dewey's fine understanding of the use of violence by the state in defense of the status quo would have led him to the conclusion that as regards radical social change, some violence would, at some point, be necessary.

Second, whatever difficulties class analysis faces, Marxists were not so foolish as to suppose that the lions, the finance capitalists, would sit down with the lambs and "adjudicate" away their privileged power. The "objective clash of interests," which Dewey rightly acknowledged, was neither temporary nor negotiable. Rooted in the capitalist system as such, it left the parties locked "in a death clutch."

Third, Dewey here does presuppose that publics exist, for it is only then, as he here implies, the "cooperative intelligence" can be a mode of social reconstruction. Immediately after he condemns Marxists for "a rigid logic," he says: "The 'experimentalist' is one who would see to it that the method depended upon by all in some degree *in a democratic community* can be followed through to completion" (*ION*, p. 80, my emphasis).

It will not be easy to explain Dewey's continuing optimism that creative intelligence can be effective even where it so patently lacks institutions. It is easier to explain his decisive turn against Marxism. By 1928 at least, Dewey had given up on the Socialist party. By this time, the Soviets had already severely abused, perhaps irreparably, the idea of "socialism." They would, in the years coming, disillusion still more. Dewey's notion of Marxism was essentially the Marxism of the Second International, a Marxism flawed in more ways than one. Still, there was a consensus by all who called themselves Marxists that if one wants to understand anything that happens in the modern world, one had best grasp the logic of capitalist accumulation. To be sure, Marxists had all too often argued that capitalism was the *only* evil and that therefore, once rid of it, all would be lovely. One would have thought that the thirties proved otherwise.

In his 1939 *Freedom and Culture*, Dewey attacked Marxism as unscientific on grounds that it had "a monistic block-universe theory of social causation" (*F&C*, p. 88). The charge was not unfair to the Marxism of the day. The monistic theory of history, Plekhanov's contribution to the Marxism of the Second International, was a disaster. Social causation was plural and reciprocal. Moreover, the actual course of history was the cluttered product of contingencies that no theory could assimilate. On the other hand, Dewey had never himself been clear on the causal question regarding capitalism, industrial society, and the modern state. Indeed, he shared with the Marxists a tendency toward technological determinism. Similarly, he was fully correct to charge that no one was less scientific than the "scientific" Soviet Marxists: "Scientific method in operating with working hypotheses instead of with fixed and final Truth is not forced to have an Inner Council to declare just what is the Truth" (*F&C*, p. 97). Still, after acknowledging that "much of our political democracy is more formal than substantial," Dewey could now defend what he took to be a characteristic American "looseness of cohesion and indefiniteness in direction of action":

We take for granted the action of a number of diverse factors in producing any social result. There are temporary waves of insistence upon this and that particular measure and aim. But there is enough democracy so that in time any one tendency gets averaged up in interplay with other tendencies. (F&C, p. 94)

Had Dewey forgotten what he had written but ten years previously? Or is it merely that America *without* a Public was still a better place than the existing alternatives? He wrote, "As compared with the fanaticism generated by monistic ideas when they are put into operation, the averaging of tendencies, a movement toward the mean, is an achievement of splendor" (F&C, p. 94). To be sure, one doesn't need a very good society to compare well with Nazism and Stalinism. But why, in Dewey's own analysis, should we assent to the idea that in America, public policy *ever* reflects "an averaging of tendencies"? Why isn't it *always* in the interest of "financial and industrial power, corporately organized"—just as he had said in 1927 and 1929?

Lenin was, I think, correct when in 1902 he argued that "the *only* choice is—either bourgeois or socialist ideology. There is no middle course (for mankind has not created a 'third' ideology)." Dewey tried, perhaps, to create a "third" ideology and a method to go with it. The socialist and anarchist radical traditions, reflective of their nineteenth-century roots have always been revolutionary in the sense that radical social change was seen to involve a mass insurrection against the prevailing order of things. Mesmerized by the French Revolution, radicals had the idea that socialist revolution was inevitable, and that it would be popular and insurrectionary. But of course no socialist revolution has occurred in any of the advanced capitalist liberal democracies. Dewey saw that the prospects for such were dim, that this idea was finally a fatal illusion. But if Dewey did not succeed in creating a third ideology, neither bourgeois nor Marxist, he left an instructive legacy. It can hardly be doubted that the Public, "eclipsed" in 1927, has not been found and that Dewey was correct to insist that finding it was the primary imperative of a politics. But how to do this? His answer might go as follows: Try, by taking advantage of any opportunity that presents itself, to bring into existence Publics; try to give direct experience and educative quality by informing it; try to create from our atomized relations incipient communities that can be fostered and enlarged, and try to do this by identifying common goods that can call for active support and participation. Of course, this is not to say much, even if, as I think, it is true and important. Still, armed with a Marxist *understanding* of what is happening to us and why, it may be possible to take advantage of opportunities and to try, as Dewey offered, to build some incipiently but progressively growing democractic Publics.

Notes

1. See Elizabeth Flower and Murray G. Murphey, *A History of Philosophy in America* (New York: G. P. Putnam's Sons, 1977), Vol. 2, pp. 811–812.

2. I have examined Dewey's political philosophy from the vantage point of anarchism and argue that in critical ways, Dewey shared much with anarchists, especially in their respective quarrels with Marxism. See P. T. Manicas, "John Dewey, Anarchism and the Political State," *Transactions of the Charles S. Peirce Society* XVIII (1982): 133–158. References to Dewey's writings will be indicated with abbreviations, where necessary, and page numbers within parentheses. Bibliography and abbreviations follow the notes.

3. See Randolph Bourne, "The Twilight of the Idols" (1917); reprinted in his *Untimely Papers* (New York: Huebsch, 1919); Morton White, *Social Thought in America* (Boston: Beacon Press, 1957), Chap. 11.

4. See James Campbell, "Dewey's Method of Social Reconstruction," *Transactions of the Charles S. Peirce Society* XX (1984): 363–393.

5. See "What Is to Be Done?" *Essential Works of Lenin*, ed. H. M. Christman (New York: Bantam, 1966).

6. See Rosa Luxemburg, "Organizational Questions of the Russian Social Democracy," (*Die Neue Zeit* [Stuttgart], July 22, 1903/4, Zweiter Band; I: S.482–492; II:S.592–535), mistitled "Leninism or Marxism" in the best-known edition. See also Bertram D. Wolfe (ed.), *The Russian Revolution and Leninism or Marxism?* (Ann Arbor: University of Michigan Press, 1961).

7. It is difficult, but essential, to try to avoid anachronism here. The "failures" of the Bolshevik Revolution, Stalinism, and the subsequent identification of socialism with "totalitarianism" were not the concern of Dewey in the twenties and early thirties. His 1939 *Freedom and Culture* marks a shift. See below. By the 1940s, of course, Dewey was vigorously attacking totalitarian attempts, Fascist and Marxist, to reconstruct society. See, for example, *The Problems of Men* (New York: Philosophical Library, 1946), pp. 138–139.

8. I mean to suggest that a great deal of recent western Marxist thought has moved in the direction of Dewey on this critical point. Demonstrating

this, however, requires another essay. For an overview, see Perry Anderson, *Considerations on Western Marxism* (London: NLB, 1976).

Dewey's writings cited:

GPP   *German Philosophy and Politics*. New York: Henry Holt, 1915.

D&E   *Democracy and Education*. New York: The Free Press, 1966.

PP   *The Public and Its Problems*. Chicago: Swallow Press, 1954.

C&E   *Characters and Events*. Edited by Joseph Ratner. Two volumes. New York: Henry Holt, 1929.

LSA   *Liberalism and Social Action*. New York: Capricorn, 1963.

ION   *Individualism Old and New*. New York: Capricorn, 1962.

F&C   *Freedom and Culture*. New York: Capricorn, 1963.

5 | Dewey, Inquiry, and Problem-Solving

Finbarr W. O'Connor

Dewey is seldom as exasperating as he is in his formulation of the theory of inquiry. One would be hard put to find a less perspicuous definition of a central concept in a major theory than "Inquiry is the controlled or directed transformation of an indeterminate situation into one that is so determinate in its constituent distinctions and relations as to convert the elements of the original situation into a unified whole."[1] He might perhaps have done better, but it is not surprising that he should have found an intuitively clear definition out of his grasp when one considers what he hopes to achieve from it. It gathers together the various strands of his views on psychology, epistemology, metaphysics, ethics, aesthetics. He hopes by it to give an account of how human beings think, but in a way that makes no suggestion of dualism (hence there is not to be a distinction between subject and object) or of mentalistic states, that describes what ordinary people do when they reflect on the most ordinary of experiences and still covers the elements of the most selfconsciously sophisticated scientific methodology, that encompasses both the role of biological needs in stimulating thought and the place for formal logical forms, that finds a place both for what motivates thought and criteria of evaluation, that finds a place for novelty and the unique while also providing for how funded experience is funded and contributes to future projects. He argues that there is a common pattern to inquiry (to all inquiries), but he is

8 2

insistent that no element of this pattern can be considered fixed, nor may any be considered in isolation from the others. Although offering a theory by which thought is identified with problem solving, he stubbornly refuses to give solutions.

Given these aims, it is unreasonable to expect a short, accurate, but immediately accessible summary definition. Further, even when expounded at length, one might reasonably expect a complex theory. In truth, Dewey's theory is subtle rather than complex. The counters of the theory are few—*situation, problematic, suggestion, idea*—and not on their face technical terms, but their interaction in the theory yields a subtle reinterpretation of what they mean. Dewey's account of the pattern of inquiry in Chapter Seven of *Logic: The Theory of Inquiry* can be read in a way that makes it accessible and relatively easy to take. Inquiry begins when we encounter an indeterminate situation, a case that is confusing or perplexing and that causes us to doubt. Indeed, who could disagree? We then try to understand the problem we are facing. We examine it, turn it over, explore various aspects of it and reach a preliminary understanding of why it is a problem for us. Again, one might say, perfectly straightforward, even truistic. We then consider what might solve it, examine our resources, carry out experiments if indicated. We select among various alternative solutions that which seems most plausible and act on it. If it works, we proceed with our lives; if it does not work, we return to some earlier stage in the process and try again.

The simplicity of this is deceptive. Ask some questions and the trap doors open. Is this account descriptive or prescriptive—is it of how we behave or how we ought to behave? Both, says Dewey, or, rather, within its terms the difference between thinking and good thinking can be registered, just like the difference between good farming and bad farming (p. 103). The choice of example is weighty here: an example that strongly suggests the distinction between good and bad thinking should be thought of not in terms of some categorial and principled change of kind between an *ought* and an *is*, but rather in terms of characteristics that pervade pedestrian human practices. Whatever it is that makes for "good" thinking, it is not an exclusive property of some few people (the "intelligent"), nor is it to be observed on some few occasions or in some few contexts that will then be held up as an ideal model to be followed. The spectacular achievements of a Newton or an Einstein exemplify inquiry, indeed, but we should not overlook inquiry as it is displayed by the uneducated artisan who figures out a way to achieve the objective by a novel use of the tools at hand.

Again, on first reading, Dewey's account of the indeterminate situation is easily digested. We have all experienced the feeling of being puzzled, the feeling that something is missing that should be there, the feeling of uncertainty on how to proceed, the sense of frustration on encountering an obstacle. And we have all experienced how such feelings incite reflection. "Indeterminacy" serves to cover many more specific characterizations: "A variety of names serves to characterize indeterminate situations. They are disturbed, troubled, ambiguous, confused, full of conflicting tendencies, obscure, etc." (p. 105). But then the trap door opens, for Dewey goes on:

> It is the *situation* that has these traits. *We* are doubtful because the situation is inherently doubtful. Personal states of doubt that are not evoked by and are not relative to some existential situation are pathological; when they are extreme they constitute the mania of doubting. Consequently, situations that are disturbed, troubled, confused or obscure, cannot be straightened out, cleared up and put in order, by manipulation of our personal states of mind. (pp. 105–106)

How can situations, as opposed to human beings, be doubtful, and inherently so? We do indeed want to distinguish, in his example, among cases of doubt those that are pathological from others; but is the distinction properly drawn by whether doubt is attributed to the situation? Is the distinction not to be made on the basis of characteristics in the situation that give rise to doubt in the mind of the human observer? Or is the distinction he is drawing, say in the case of perplexity, that between a situation's being perplex*ing* and a person's being perplex*ed*? I am perplexed by a friendly greeting from one whom I thought an enemy; the greeting, I conceive, is perplexing. The perplexity is resolved by an explanation of the greeting, and the resolution lies in a change in me, not in the greeting. Obviously there is more here than meets the eye. In fact, this very initial encounter with Dewey's view illustrates the question: we (the reader) are presented with an indeterminate situation: we are confused. Is it because Dewey (the text) is confused, or confusing? In Dewey's theory we are now on the way to formulating a problematic situation and are well into inquiry.

My object here is to explore some of the subtleties of Dewey's view of inquiry. My strategy will be to juxtapose it and an influential modern theory of problem-solving and ask how Dewey's view matches this more contemporary version. The strengths and difficulties in each may offer illumination in both directions.

I. Problem-Solving as Heuristic Search

The theory in question arises from an intersection between the information processing approach in cognitive psychology and of computer science.[2] Its central tenets were formulated in Newell's and Simon's monumental *Human Problem Solving*.[3] In this work Newell and Simon set out to simulate on the computer human problem-solving in three specific areas of problem—theorems of elementary propositional calculus, chess and cryparithmetic (for example, the famous DON-ALD + GERALD = ROBERT)—and presented a computer program (called *General Problem Solver*) that had the required capacity. The book introduced a distinctive conceptual apparatus to describe problem solving. The setting of a problem is the *task environment*, which refers to "an environment coupled with a goal, problem, or task. . . . It is the task that defines a point of view about the environment, and that, in fact, allows an environment to be delimited" (p. 55). Problem-solving is initiated by the perception of a gap between an *initial state* and a *goal state*: "A man is confronted with a problem when he wants something and does not know immediately what series of actions he can perform to get it." To solve a problem is conceived of as a *search* through some *problem space*. This is the problem solver's *representation* of the task environment and includes "the initial situation presented to him, the desired goal situation, various intermediate states, imagined or experienced, as well as any concepts he uses to describe these situations to himself" (p. 59).

> To have a problem implies (at least) that certain information is given to the problem solver: information about what is desired, under what conditions, by means of what tools and operations, starting with what initial information, and with access to what resources. The problem solver has an interpretation of this information—exactly that interpretation which lets us label some part of it as *goal*, another part as *side conditions*, and so on. (p. 73)

The problem space can be partially represented as having the structure of a tree, the root being the initial state (for example, the starting configuration of chess pieces on the board), the nodes being other states (other possible configurations of the chess pieces), the branches being moves by which one state is transformed into another. The branches terminate with the goal state (or states). To search through the tree requires that a program have the capacity to generate states and to recognize a terminal state.

In these terms, the most obvious way to solve a problem is to generate all possible paths and then check to see which contains the goal state. Thus, in proving a theorem from an axiom set, one might generate all possible theorems derivable in one step from the axiom set, then check to see if it contains the desired theorem; if not, one generates all possible theorems derivable in one step from the set of axioms conjoined with the theorems already derived, and again checks to see if the resulting set contains the desired theorem, and so on until it appears. The great achievement of *Human Problem Solving* was to recognize that this mode of search is inefficient and impractical. Further, an exhaustive search is often impossible. It runs afoul of what has come to be called the "combinatorial explosion," or the extraordinarily rapid increase in the number of possibilities.[4] Consequently the search method must be *heuristic*.

The notion of a heuristic is fundamental to modern problem-solving theory. In the context of the "search" language of *Human Problem Solving*, a heuristic method is selective rather than exhaustive. It selects a likely path to begin with and in its subsequent moves selects on the basis of the information gained from previous moves. The behavior the distinction is intended to mark is familiar. If we are dealing with a lost book, we do not map out all the possible places it might be and search them systematically, looking on the table, the chair, under the bed, and so on blindly. Our search may still be planned and methodical but guided by considerations such as which locations are most likely (for example, if we remember where we last used the book) or convenience (since I am looking in the car trunk—where I remember seeing it—I might as well check the interior of the car too). Again, in attempting to prove that some expression is derivable from a set of premises, we use "rule of thumb" as a guide to which rule to apply. Thus it is a rule of thumb in logic that if the desired expression is a conditional, and its antecedent appears as an antecedent of a conditional among the premises while its consequent appears among the premises as a consequent of a conditional, one looks for an application of the Hypothetical Syllogism rule. Logic textbooks now commonly offer lists of guides like this.

The emphasis in *Human Problem Solving* is on the capacity of a heuristic method to be selective and to be sensitive to the results of past moves. The model proposed offers a general heuristic, called *means-end analysis*, by which problems in the domains studied could be solved. Essentially the method involves comparing the current state of the problem space with the goal state, noting the differences between them, and then making a move that will reduce the differences. The method can be crudely illustrated as it might apply to solving the "hobbits and orcs" puzzle. You are given (initial state) three hobbits and three orcs on the left bank of a river. The object (goal state) is to get them on the right bank. But you must do it using a boat with a capacity of two and in such a way that you never permit a combination on either bank in which the number of orcs exceeds the number of hobbits (side condition). There are five possible first moves (HH, OO, HO, H, O). Of these, two (HH, H) are impermissible by the side condition. Which of the other three moves is "best"? Means-ends analysis will select either OO or HO over O, since taking two across the river reduces the difference between initial state and goal state by a greater amount than taking one across would. This illustrates selectivity. The significance of the capacity to be guided by the results of past moves is illustrated from a later stage in the puzzle. The configuration after the fourth move is: HHHO on the left bank and OO on the right. Reducing the difference maximally dictates that you move HH to the right bank, yielding the configuration HO on the left and HHOO on the right. With the boat on the right bank there are five possible moves, HH, OO, HO, H and O, and of these OO, H, and O are impermissible, leaving either HH or HO. Both involve moving in a direction apparently away from the goal state, for each reduces the number of the right bank from four to two. Hence, reducing the difference will not select which move should be made. HH, however, has been the immediately preceding move, and so should you select HH the result will be to return to a configuration already achieved. Hence, a heuristic that remembers previous configurations will select HO. This in fact turns out to be the critical step in solving the puzzle (in the sense that when people fail to solve it, it is normally due to an inability to "see" this move).

To conclude this brief exposition of the theory, one further aspect needs to be stressed. Newell and Simon regard the theory as empirical, and indeed, in a sense, experimental:

> Computer science is an empirical discipline. We would have called it an experimental science, but like astronomy, economics, and geology, some of its unique forms of observation and experience do not fit a narrow stereotype of the experimental method. Nevertheless, they are experiments. Each new machine that is built is an experiment. . . . Each new program that is built is an experiment. It poses a question to nature, and its behavior offers a clue to an answer.[5]

Beyond this, the programs designed are intended not just to solve problems but to do so in a way that matches human problem-solving. The methodology as a whole therefore also involves observing human beings engaged in solving problems, and the hypotheses (particularly about what heuristic procedures are applicable to given problems) are tested in both computer and human behavior. Human observations are carried out in *protocol analyses.*[6] A protocol attempts to describe what is going on when people solve problems. In a verbal protocol the subject is asked to "think aloud," to say everything he or she thinks while working through a task. A special case of protocol analysis is "expert-novice" research, which involves contrasting the performance of people who are experts with respect to the problem at hand with that of nonexperts and constructing testable hypotheses to account for the differences. What is learned from these protocols is then tested in the form of a program; what is learned from the program behavior informs future protocols.

II. Inquiry and Heuristic Search

To what extent does the theory of inquiry match that of heuristic search? There are significant similarities to be found. Both stress the goal-directedness in human thinking; both stress planning, and for both thinking is sequential. The relationship between "task environment" and "problem space" in one theory is partially translatable into the relationship between "indeterminate situation" and "problematic situation" in the other theory. Both theories purport to give an account for problem-solving of any kind. In Deweyan language, inquiries in one field differ from those of another, but the pattern of inquiry will be the same; in Newell's and Simon's language, any problem-solving can be described as a search of the problem space by heuristic methods, although the specific heuristics may differ from field to field (for example, there are heuristics specific to bridge). And both share the conviction that the specific form that inquiry (heuristics) will take from field to field is to be discovered in experience.[7] Lastly, the cybernetic setting of the modern theory should also prove congenial as a translation device for inquiry. It has often been observed that Dewey's early view of "reflex arc" was an attempt to express the relationship of feedback among components of a system.[8] It is now characteristic of models of problem-solving to establish throughout feedback loops among the components of the process.

There are also differences. The two theories differ explicitly in the scope of the problem-solving activity they address. *Human Problem Solving* quite explicitly excludes consideration of factors that for Dewey enter the indeterminate situation, and it also omits the whole question of how problems get represented in the first instance. In these two respects one may say that heuristic search is narrower than inquiry. On the first omission, *Human Problem Solving* excludes the sensory and the motor as well as issues of motivation and personality (p. 8). Issues of what motivates the process are by-passed by having the problems studied be the choice of the researcher rather than of the subject. From this it follows that the notion of "task environment" cannot be equated with "indeterminate situation." Thus, to the extent that there is difficulty in understanding what Dewey has in mind when he speaks of the indeterminate situation as being "doubtful" or "confused" or "conflicting," one cannot expect illumination from Newell's and Simon's theory. Similarly, and again explicitly, Newell and Simon see the task of problem representation as distinct from the task of "problem solving within a given representation." Problem-solving theory as a whole includes both as parts, but

> The theory to be presented in this book has much more to say about methods and executive organizations than about creating new representations or shifting from one representation to another. This emphasis turns out to be consonant with the kinds of problem solving we have studied, where our human subjects do not in fact change or modify their representations appreciably during the course of their problem solving.(p. 90)

In Deweyan language, this means that the *construction* of the problematic situation is left untouched. The important first stage of inquiry is assumed to have already taken place.

These differences are differences rather than disagreements. Newell and Simon do not deny the importance of problem representation. Indeed, Dewey's remark "a problem well put is half-solved" (*Inquiry*, p. 108) finds an echo in Newell's and Simon's "some problems do exist in which the whole difficulty of solution resides in finding the right representation. Once that representation has been discovered, solving the problem becomes a trivial matter" (p. 90). More recently, they have said that

> The whole process of moving from one representation to another, and of discovering and evaluating representations, is largely unexplored territory in the domain of problem-solving research. The laws of qualitative structure governing representations remain to be discovered. The search for them is almost sure to receive considerable attention in the coming decade.[9]

Still, underlying the issue of problem representation may be a fundamental disagreement between inquiry and heuristic search. One way to state the possible conflict is to suggest that from Dewey's point of view to conceptualize inquiry as *search* is unduly narrow. Although *Human Problem Solving* does not deal with problem representation, one is left with the clear impression that this task is also conceptualized as a search, in this case for the appropriate problem representation, and this search will have its own heuristic methods. Thus, the general model of heuristic search will be extended from problem-solving within a representation to choosing a representation. This is not to imply that the choice of representation is fixed or final, because (as the quotation given above makes clear) representations may be changed and revised as a result of what is learned from attempting to solve the problem under those representations. What does seem fixed is that problem-solving for Newell and Simon must be directed by some representation or other.

To think of problem-solving as search works well for the kinds of problems studied in *Human Problem Solving*. In the language of the theory itself, any problem can be characterized by three components: its initial state, its goal state, and its operators (the operations that are permissible within that problem space). A problem is *well-defined* if all three are completely specified; otherwise it is *ill-defined*.[10] The problems of *Human Problem Solving* are well-defined. In each case the subject knows the starting point, the goal, and what moves are permissible. But is search the appropriate way to think of what is done in the case of ill-defined problems? Since each of the three components can be specified or unspecified independently of the others, many types of ill-defined problems are possible—a problem might have a completely specified goal, but be unspecified with respect to the other two: the goal is clear, but not how to reach it nor where you are starting from (for example, you want to go home, but do not know where you are or what resources you have to draw upon). Or, a problem might be specified with regard to states but not with regard to operators: for example, you know you are on one bank of a river and want to get to the other, but do not know what the range of possible actions is.

Dewey is clearly interested primarily in how to deal with ill-defined problems. And he insists over and over again that no element of inquiry can be considered fixed. Inquiry, he says, is indeterminate in two ways—the evoking situation is indeterminate and the issue is indeterminate; that is, we cannot be sure in advance of what the solution will turn out to be. But in a well-defined problem, although we may not know which exact route we should take (which branch of the tree most efficiently leads to the goal) we do not in the midst of the process question the goal. In Dewey's terms, this means the goal state for the problem is fixed. Another way to view this is through Dewey's notion of *end-in-view*. The sense in which inquiry is goal-directed for Dewey is that it is controlled by ends-in-view (as distinct from actual outcome). In some respects what Dewey says about ends echoes Newell and Simon on how goal states function: " 'Learning from experience' . . . takes place chiefly on the basis of careful observation of differences found between desired and proposed ends (*ends-in-view*) and attained ends or actual consequences."[11] In Newell's and Simon's language, it is the goal state as *represented* that guides actions. The critical difference between the two models is that in heuristic search the match of actual state to goal state is performed in order to assess only whether the solver is nearer or farther from the goal. In inquiry, on the other hand, the match of actual end to end-in-view may lead to a revision of the end-in-view. Means-ends analysis certainly permits the pursuit of and construction of subgoals. If the goal state itself is to be reconstructed, however, and the goal state is part of the problem representation, then we need to find a way to permit a re-representation of the problem. If so, then the issue of formulating a problem representation is not just a matter of filling in some stage of the process earlier than problem-solving under a representation but an ingredient of the latter. Representation is not just a condition of problem-solving, but a possible outcome of it.

Whereas Newell and Simon adopt as their paradigm case of problem-solving that of solving well-defined problems, it appears that Dewey would take as the paradigm a problem ill-defined in all three dimensions. In order to engage in problem-solving, the heuristic search model implies at least some goal state, some definite object of search. Consider by contrast this early account by Dewey of how thinking arises:

> A child begins very early to explore and test the things and people about him. He is curious. He handles, tastes, looks, listens, and things get meanings. He finds obstacles and is forced to contrive a way to do or get what he wants. When a child in a hunting tribe begins to hunt he must study the ways of wild animals. If he is to get his living from the soil or the sea he will watch the sky, and try to forecast the weather. He will wonder at the movements of sun, moon, and stars. If he becomes a trader he must decide what goods to carry, and will match wits with his customers. All these problems call for *thinking*, that is, for making use of something which he has seen, or known, or known about, before in order to help in meeting this new situation.[12]

These cases show a distinct lack of emphasis on goal direction or purposefulness. They contrast sharply with paradigmatic cases of search, such as looking for lost keys, or (to take a longer term project) the planning involved in finding a way to enter a career. The emphasis is rather on the situation itself and its demands. Goals or aims arise from the situation rather than are brought to it. Thus, Dewey's description suggests, the fisherman may not set out to watch the sky *in order* to predict the weather; rather, in watching the sky and noticing its changes and associations, it occurs to him that he has a goal that more controlled observation of the sky will further. The formulation of the goal may occur late in the practice.

If we need a metaphor to contrast with "search" and to express inquiry more adequately, it is "exploration," as Dewey uses it above of the child. Exploring some terrain suggests a practice much more open-ended, much more "indeterminate," than searching in the terrain for something. A searcher knows in advance what counts as a "successful solution." A searcher may change goals in the midst of the search—you may set out to search for silver and turn instead to searching for gold. Explorers may begin with a vague sense of what they are likely to find, and may as a result of what they find transform the exploration into search, but they do not know in advance the direction of the inquiry. Finding a sea route to India is a search; opening the New World is an exploration. Finding the murderer of Inspector Jones is a search; eliminating poverty is an exploration. Fixing a car that won't start is a search; deciding whether you need a car is an exploration. Solving an equation is a search; writing an essay is an exploration.

The nub of the matter is this. If problem-solving is to be modeled on search, then the difference between finding the murderer of Inspector Jones and eliminating poverty (apart from subject matter) is that one has a clearly defined goal and the other does not. We know what counts as finding the murderer; we do not know what counts as eliminating poverty. Hence one can say that the representation of the latter problem is a poorer representation than that of the former. That in turn means that we are farther back in the problem-solving process with regard to the poverty problem than we are with regard to the murderer problem. Formulate the poverty problem with a clearly defined goal, and then we can search among alternative paths for a solution to it. The Dewey position, as I interpret it, is that we do not come to a consideration of the poverty problem equipped with a set of antecedent representations (including possible goals) of it from which we select one. For Dewey, the framing of the problem is an act of construction rather than a selection. We are indeed equipped with some resources upon which we draw to understand the problem, and among these resources are past interpretations of similar situations; however, if the problem framing is to be merely a selection from these, we have become bound to the past and innovation is excluded. More fundamentally, if we see problem-framing as more creative (in that we encourage new interpretations to compete with old) but still a matter of selecting among representations, then we may not be open to learning from the results of acting on the selected interpretation. Since constructing an interpretation has the effect of "transforming" the situation, as does acting on this interpretation, ends-in-view may emerge quite different from any of those among which we originally made a selection.

As a final illustration, consider two ways in which we write. In one, we know what we want to say from the beginning, and we concentrate on finding an effective means to say it. This seems appropriately analyzable as a matter of search. In the other, we do not know what we want to say; we write in order to find it out. Here we may not finally decide what we want to say until the writing is done, and only then are we in a position to formulate, so to speak, the "goal" of the writing. It seems to me that Newell and Simon have the first in mind as the paradigm case of problem-solving and would regard the latter as the effect of a poorly represented problem. Dewey, on the other hand, sees the second as the paradigm of inquiry, and the first as a special case in which the weight of the problem is not so much on problem formulation as on implementation.

III. Inquiry and Problem-Solving Heuristics

Newell's and Simons's theory might be regarded as the most rigorous version of problem-solving in the contemporary literature, and the last section above argued that there is a deep difference in how it regards problem-solving and how Dewey regards inquiry. Beyond the rigorous theory of *Human Problem Solving* there is a vast body of literature on problem-solving, some of it deeply influenced by the heuristic search model but less constrained by what is possible in computer simulation. Two features stand out in this literature. One is the use of the notion of *heuristic,* but with a sense other than that used in *Human Problem Solving* and one that may prove helpful in Dewey's broader conception of inquiry; the other is an attention paid to process or phases, and along the lines of Dewey's analysis.

In *Human Problem Solving* a heuristic method is nonexhaustive and used to aid in deciding what step next to select. In the broader literature, "heuristic" has taken on a somewhat different meaning. It has become common to contrast heuristic with an *algorithm,* an algorithm being a rule such that its correct application guarantees successful solution (for example, rules of addition in arithmetic), while a heuristic is a rule such that its application makes success more likely but does not guarantee it. In poker, "a full house beats a straight" is algorithmic, since by its correct application one can always decide which of two (relevant) hands wins. On the other hand, "never draw to an inside straight" is heuristic—it serves to guide decision but in some cases will lead to a wrong decision. A common position is that problem-solving is identified with using heuristics, although with some disagreement over whether heuristics should be general[13] and over whether they should be used in domains where algorithms are available.[14] Examples of such heuristics include: work backwards, draw a diagram, build a model, simplify the problem, look for an equivalent problem, identify the unknowns, generalize or specialize, use analogies or metaphors, change representation (verbal, symbolic or visual), assume the solution and determine its properties. A fundamental issue in formulating or teaching heuristic methods is how general they should be, which involves trading off scope for power—the more general the greater the scope (for example, draw a diagram), the more specific they are, the more direction they provide but with narrower applicability (for example, draw a Venn diagram).

The second striking feature of this literature is a pervasive use of models by which the process of solving a problem or making a decision is broken up into steps or phases. The ancestor of all this is, of course, Dewey's model in *How We Think*. In addition to his the two most famous are Graham Wallas's and Polya's. Wallas's—offered as a model of creativity—has these steps:

1. Preparation

2. Incubation

3. Illumination

4. Verification[15]

Polya's, offered as a model of mathematical problem-solving, has these:

1. Understand the problem

2. Devise a plan

3. Carry out the plan

4. Look back[16]

To illustrate the range of such models in recent writing: In management, Simon himself proposes three "phases of decision making," *intelligence, design,* and *choice:*

1. Search for problems and data

2. Generate and analyze alternatives

3. Select the best alternative[17]

Drucker has a five-step model for management decision-making:

1. Define the problem

2. Analyze the problem

3. Develop alternative solutions

4. Select the best solution

5. Convert the decision into effective action[18]

As a problem-solving model, John R. Hayes offers:

1. Finding the Problem

2. Representing the Problem

3. Planning the Solution

4. Carrying out the Plan

5. Evaluating the Solution

6. Consolidating the Gains[19]

In decision-making, there is a Janis's and Mann's:

1. Appraising the Challenge

2. Survey the alternatives

3. Weigh the alternatives

4. Deliberate about commitment

5. Adhering despite negative feedback.[20]

In creativity studies there is Parnes's:

1. Looking at the "Mess" to find problem

2. finding a "fuzzy" problem

3. Fact Finding

4. Problem Finding

5. Idea Finding

6. Solution Finding

7. Acceptance finding[21]

And in systems design there is van Gigch's:

1. Define the problem

2. Identify systems boundaries, the suprasystem, and relevant environmental systems.

3. Establish systems objectives

4. Search for and generate alternatives

5. Identify outputs of the alternatives

6. Evaluate alternatives by comparing outputs with objectives

7. Choose the best alternative

8. Implement the decision[22]

The language among these models differs, and some have unique emphases (for example, Wallas's *incubation*, Hayes's *consolidation*, Janis's and Mann's *adhering despite negative feedback*, Parnes's *fuzzy problem*), among them there is considerable agreement on the "joints." Also notable is that these models attempt to deal with just those aspects of problem-finding and problem-representation that we found lacking in the heuristic search model. Indeed, as these models might suggest, the domain of study that Dewey set out as inquiry has grown into three related but distinct bodies of literature: problem-solving, decision-making, and creativity. For issues of motivation and of the circumstances under which a person becomes aware of a problem, one goes to the decision-making literature. For help on formulating the problematic situation one goes to the literature on creativity.[23]

Much of this literature is oriented to pedagogy; it is concerned with how to teach problem-solving, decision-making, or creative thinking. This allows us to draw the various strands of this paper together around the practical question of whether or how inquiry is to be taught. A standard response to Dewey's theory, particularly by teachers, is to ask how it can be put into practice; they are often disappointed by what they find in it. The lesson of *Democracy and Education* centers on distinguishing between a "real" problem—"the experience of a personal thing of such a nature as inherently to stimulate and direct observation of the connections involved, and to lead to inference and its testing"—and a problem imposed by the teacher.[24] Only from the former, Dewey suggests, can we expect ideas. This implies a heavy responsibility on the teacher to choose rich but personally motivating problems, to design situations in which confusion or perplexity or indeterminacy will arise—enough to motivate inquiry but not so much as to frustrate. Many teachers find this impossibly "idealistic."

The modern use of heuristics offers a way out. When a teacher asks what to do when a student just does not have any ideas, or thinks in a cliched way about a problem, there are heuristics designed to do just this. And heuristics are often matched to particular stages in the process—heuristics to generate ideas, to represent problems, to evaluate solutions, and so on.[25] Ever sensitive to the dangers of blocking innovation, Dewey was resolutely hostile to rules of thought. But he did distinguish between principles and rules in a way that makes principles remarkably like the modern conception of heuristic: "A principle evolves in connection with the course of experience, being a generalized statement of what sort of consequences and values tend to be realized in certain kinds of situation; a rule is taken as something ready-made and fixed."[26] By a principle the lessons of experience can be conveyed in a way that does not "deaden thought." A principle, he says, is a tool or aid that guides but does not impose a solution.

Of course concentrating on heuristics risks transforming them into rules, if we believe this is the only way to deal with problems. Even so, I believe the notion of heuristic is a genuine addition to inquiry. Choices of particular heuristics and decisions about how general or specific they should be are matters to be evaluated in experience, and indeed a considerable degree of experimental work is devoted to their evaluation.[27] To the degree to which we can maintain their character as tools rather than rules, and to the degree that we can maintain an attitude of skepticism as to their utility, I think Dewey would be pleased by the developments.

Notes

1. John Dewey, *Logic: The Theory of Inquiry* (New York: Irvington Publishers, 1982; original edition 1938), pp. 104–105. Page numbers in parentheses refer to the 1982 edition.

2. For a general classification of differences in cognitive psychology, see Stephen E. Palmer and Ruth Kimchi, "The Information Processing Approach to Cognition," in T. J. Knapp and L. C. Robertson (eds.), *Approaches to Cognition* (Hillsdale, N.J.: Lawrence Erlbaum, 1986), pp. 37–77.

3. A Newell and H. A. Simon, *Human Problem Solving* (Englewood Cliffs, N.J.: Prentice-Hall, 1972). I also draw on John R. Anderson, *Cognitive Psychology and Its Implications* (San Francisco: W. H. Freeman, 1980); K. J. Gilhooly, *Thinking: Directed, Undirected and Creative* (New York: Academic Press, 1982); and John R. Hayes, *The Complete Problem Solver* (Philadelphia: Franklin Institute Press, 1981).

4. To generate all proofs in Chapter Two of *Principia Mathematica* requires generating more than 10^{1000} proofs (Newell and Simon, *Human Problem Solving*, p. 109). John Haugeland estimates that a game of chess involving forty moves would require 10^{120} combinations (*Artificial Intelligence* [Cambridge, Mass.: MIT Press, 1986], p. 178).

5. Allen Newell and Herbert A. Simon, "Computer Science as Empirical Inquiry: Symbols and Search," in John Haugeland (ed.), *Mind Design* (Cambridge, Mass.: MIT Press, 1985), pp. 35–36.

6. See Hayes, *The Complete Problem Solver*, pp. 51–69. For Hayes, protocol analysis is "cognitive psychology's most powerful tool for describing psychological processes" (p. 51).

7. Indeed, in *How We Think* (Boston: D. C. Health and Co., 1910), Dewey's "analysis of the process of thinking into its steps or elementary constituents" might be regarded as based on a proto-protocol analysis, since he introduces it as based on descriptions of four cases, "taken, almost verbatim, from the class papers of students" (p. 68).

8. See Elizabeth Flower and Murray G. Murphey, *A History of Philosophy In America* (New York: G. P. Putnam's Sons, 1977), Vol. 2, p. 830. Perhaps the clearest expression of Dewey's connection with modern cognitive psychology is G. A. Miller, E. Galanter, and K. Pribham, *Plans and the Structure of Behavior* (New York: Holt, Rinehart, and Winston, 1960), Chap. 2, in which Dewey is explicitly associated with "the cybernetic hypothesis."

9. Newell and Simon, "Computer Science as Empirical Inquiry," in Haugeland (ed.), *Mind Design*, pp. 63–64.

10. The distinction between "well-defined" and "ill-defined" problems is most carefully worked out by Walter R. Reitman, "Heuristic Decision Procedures, Open Constraints, and the Structure of Ill-Defined Problems," in Maynard W. Shelly II and Glenn L. Bryan (eds.), *Human Judgments and Optimality* (New York: John Wiley and Sons, 1964). Defining a problem by these three features is the most commonly accepted usage among psychologists. Hayes adds as a fourth dimension that of "constraints," or conditions, which may not be violated by the solution. Thus, for Hayes the general form of a well-defined problem is: "Move from I (initial state) to G (goal state) by O (operators) but without violating C (constraints)." A particular advantage of this type of definition is that it makes no suggestion that problems are "bad" or out of the ordinary. But ordinary usage may have just this implication—which is captured by K. F. Jackson's view that problems are characterized by two features: an objective and an obstacle (or obstacles). See *The Art of Problem Solving* (New York: St. Martin's Press, 1975).

11. John Dewey, *Theory of Valuation* (Chicago: University of Chicago Press, 1939), p. 30. Note also that his description of the process sounds very much like means-ends analysis.

12. John Dewey and James Tufts, *Ethics* (Revised ed.; New York: Henry Holt, 1932), pp. 37–38.

13. A heuristic is "a general suggestion or strategy, independent of subject matter, that helps problem solvers approach, understand, and/or efficiently marshall their resources in solving problems" (Alan H. Schoenfeld, "Can Heuristics be Taught?" in Jack Lockhead and John Clements [eds.], *Cognitive Process Instruction* [Philadelphia: Franklin Institute Press, 1979], p. 315).

14. "A proceeding whose aim is the obtaining of [justified beliefs without

recourse to testimony or authority] is called an *inquiry*; the special type of inquiry in which no automatic way of finding an answer is known is called *problem solving*" (Max Black, *Critical Thinking* [2nd ed.; Englewood Cliffs, N.J.: Prentice-Hall, 1952], p. 285). By contrast, Anderson distinguishes between *creative problem-solving* and *routine problem-solving*, the former requiring the development of new procedures while the latter involves the application of existing procedures. These procedures can be heuristic or algorithmic (*Cognitive Psychology and Its Implications*, pp. 257, 268).

15. Graham Wallas, *The Art of Thought* (London: Jonathan Cape, 1926).

16. G. Polya, *How To Solve It* (Princeton: Princeton University Press, 1945).

17. Herbert A. Simon, *The New Science of Management Decision* (New York: Harper and Row, 1960).

18. Peter F. Drucker, *The Practice of Management* (New York: Harper and Row, 1954).

19. Hayes, *The Complete Problem Solver*. Among all the models Hayes's consolidation step seems to stand out as a unique one.

20. Irving G. Janis and Leon R. Mann, *Decision Making: A Psychological Analysis of Conflict, Choice and Commitment* (New York: The Free Press, 1977).

21. J. Parnes, *Creative Behavior Guidebook* (New York: Charles Scribner's Sons, 1967).

22. John P. van Gigch, *Applied General Systems Theory* (New York: Harper and Row, 1978).

23. In Hayes, *The Complete Problem Solver*, Anderson, *Cognitive Psychology and Its Implications*, Diane F. Halpern, *Thought and Knowledge* (Hillsdale, N.J.: Lawrence Erlbaum, 1984), and Barry F. Anderson, *The Complete Thinker* (Englewood Cliffs, N.J.: Prentice-Hall, 1980), all four intended as textbooks, problem-solving is distinguished from decision-making and creativity.

24. John Dewey, *Democracy and Education* (New York: Macmillan, 1916), p. 155.

25. A very complete listing (seventy in all) is given in Arthur B. Van Gundy, *Techniques of Structured Problem Solving* (New York: Van Nostrand Reinhold Co., 1981). Also see T. Rickards, *Problem Solving Through Creative Analysis* (Essex, U.K.: Gower Press, 1974).

26. Dewey and Tufts, *Ethics*, pp. 304–305.

27. For a skeptical review of the evidence of the utility of various heuristics see D. N. Perkins, "General Cognitive Skills: Why Not?" in S. Chipman, J. Segal, and R. Glaser (eds.), *Thinking and Learning Skills* (Hillsdale, N.J.: Lawrence Erlbaum, 1982), Vol. 2, pp. 339–363.

6 | The Gamble for Excellence: John Dewey's Pedagogy of Experience

John J. McDermott

What the best and wisest parent wants for his [her] child, that must the community want for all of its children.

John Dewey,
School and Society

In 1977, Elizabeth Flower and Murray G. Murphey published a stunning work of historical exposition and commentary on the development of American philosophy. The task of writing the long, detailed chapter on the thought of John Dewey fell to Elizabeth Flower, who for decades has been celebrated in philosophical circles for her analytic acumen, capacity for trenchant critique, and wise, informed grasp of the swirling currents in American thought. (Parenthetically, I recall, vividly, some years ago, her brilliant defense of the St. Louis Hegelians against some wags who knew nothing of their importance or the seriousness of their endeavor.)

The chapter on the philosophy of John Dewey by Elizabeth Flower is a masterpiece of intellectual scrutiny. She weaves the tapestry of Dewey's early thought, isolating for clarity and then reintegrating the many themes, strands, and influences that fed the complexity and subtlety that he carried into his mature work. On the thorny issues of the relationship between means and ends, the difference between truth and warranted assertions, the theory of inquiry and the ethical context of Dewey's thought, she is unfailingly accurate and perceptive. Frequently Flower offers us a line or a cameo version of Dewey's philosophy, which provides us with a quick, startling insight to his work. For example, of Dewey she writes that "the environment is changing progressively as the activity progresses." And, "after all, we live in a network of affections; the qualities of virtue are the qualities which help us feel and assign worth in such a network."[1]

Although Flower concentrates on the epistemological and methodological facets of Dewey's work, she is ever alert to the enduring social and educational matrix that is riven throughout all of his thought. She states that "growth or development of selves, not attainments, is the primary educational goal, although of course education is not confined to formal schooling."[2] Indeed not, especially in a democratic society where all of the apertures of insight are called upon to teach us how to be human.

At the end of her chapter on Dewey, Flower points us in the direction of the next step, Dewey's philosophy of education. She cites Dewey as follows: "If we are willing to conceive education as the process of forming fundamental dispositions, intellectual and emotional, toward nature and fellow-men, philosophy may even be defined *as the general theory of education*."[3]

With considerable modesty and some trepidation, I offer the following pages as a personal perspective on Dewey's philosophy of education, set in our contemporary situation and in honor of the bequest of our colleague, the philosopher Elizabeth Flower.

Entropy, the loss of energy in a closed physical system, is now regarded as an eschatological cosmic threat. For those of us who think closer to home, say in decades, the entropic character of American society with regard to the education of its children is no less a threat, given our values in a democratic society. I do not think it hyperbolic to state that a dismal cloud of systemic lethargy has settled over the American educational process, one that seems to have weaned both imagination and energy from the process of inquiry. The reasons for this development are no doubt both complex and many. One reason is certainly the self-aggrandizing and soulless mills known as colleges of education and their political ties to the nefarious and self-perpetuating sources of mediocrity, state accrediting agencies. Another reason is the drab school curriculum with its multiple daily interruptions and the omnipresence of the weary but oracular pronouncements of the social sciences, ever out of date and always cast in a prose that no one ever has occasion to use again.[4] A third reason is the extraordinary dilution of intellectual sophistication and accrued wisdom in our teachers. Having been taught nothing, except how to "manage," they know nothing. Although this is dramatically true of most teaching in the elementary and secondary schools, it has permeated colleges and universities as well. No doubt that there are exceptions to the above jeremiad. Ms. X, Mr. Y, and Professor Z dot the landscape of our schools, colleges, and universities. They are heroic, brilliant, embattled, and often excoriated exceptions to my judgment. But they are precisely that, exceptions.

Lest you think that I speak from some intellectual ivory tower, allow me to assure you that my remarks are based on experience and not from a jaundice generated by distance. I have taught students for more than thirty-five years, inclusive of preschools and kindergartens, secondary schools, community colleges private colleges, city and state universities, labor colleges, the handicapped, prison students, and adult education extension students. As a member of the National Humanities Faculty, I have visited many classrooms throughout the United States. My students number more than twenty thousand, from all walks of life and with a range of values, needs and ambitions that mirrors our nation in the last four decades. Their message to me, in an increasing crescendo especially in the last decade, was in a variant of verbal and prose forms of articulation, but it always came to a muted, embarrassed, yet forthright complaint that the vast majority of their educational experiences were repetitive, dull, insouciant, and paradigmatically *boring*. Should we wonder why an inner city school district in a major city in California can have more than 60 percent daily absenteeism or why just recently the New York City public school system can announce concern about the fact that more than 40 percent of their students are not finishing secondary school, dropouts to personal and economic oblivion. Must it be so? I think not.

I recently returned from an assignment in Budapest, Hungary. While there, I volunteered to teach two seminars in contemporary American civilization to the students in Eötvös Lorand University, the major academic institution in Budapest. The building was ancient and decrepit. The halls and the stairwells were jammed. The classrooms were funky, tiny, dirty, and victims of socialist craftmanship, complete with splattered paint, dead windows, a blackboard from 1890, and a dirty cloth for an eraser. The students, members of a select number of eight hundred students in the English language program, jammed into the room, elbow by knee, crowded, alert, burning with the fire of inquiry, and hungry for new stuff, new ideas, new names, and another way to build themselves into a wider world.

I felt the pressure on me to be enormous. I could not let them down; I could not disappoint them. I had to deliver. What to say? How to say it? I did my best, finally hitting on pluralism as a key to contemporary America, its history, its present, and its best future. I left time for questions. Shyness pervaded at first until a young woman student looked right at me and said in beautiful English: so far, so good for American pluralism, but how then do you make a decision if everyone has a right to their point of view? She wanted to understand the meaning of consensus. Off we went, into constitutional issues, abortion, school busing, food stamps, nuclear deterrence. It was exhilarating. After the second seminar, a young male student asked me why did they kill Malcolm X? In the conversation, he also cited an article from *Der Spiegel* on James Baldwin and the exilic propensity of American writers. Could I explain that phenomenon to him, he gently asked; that is, why Henry James, Ernest Hemingway, Gertrude Stein, the countless painters and poets, James Baldwin, all were seeking America away from America?

During this heady experience, I kept thinking of my own students past and present. I thought of the brilliant students, mostly Jewish, at Queens College in the 1950s. The best of them devotees of psychoanalysis, they were headed for law at Harvard, medicine at Hopkins, and philosophy at Yale. Their social conscience was trapped in the narcissistic mirror of Dostoevsky's "Underground Man." I thought of the Roman Catholic intellectual high rollers and the Jesuits I taught at Fordham University Graduate School in the 1960s, brilliant, accomplished, multilingual, and experientially repressed. I thought of my Queens College students in the late 1960s, hopheads, acidheads, movement cretins, sensitive, and woefully uninformed. I thought of my Queens College students in the middle 1970s, well-meaning, dull, plodding, spiritless. I thought of my labor college students, mostly Black and Hispanic of the late 1970s, and found a flame in their eyes kindred to my Budapest guests. Finally, I thought of my Texas A & M students of the past decade. They are smart, national merit smart, and they are the cream of this wounded crop coming from our best secondary schools. Unfortunately, they have no symbolic bank. They cannot convert the literal to the symbolical. Let me tell a story.

A few years ago at Texas A & M University, I taught a seminar course entitled The Philosophy of Literature. The gathering theme was that of the family, and the readings were appropriate to that theme. Among them were: Aeschylus's *Agamemnon*; Sophocles's *Oedipus Rex*; O'Neill's *Long Day's Journey into Night*;

Baldwin's *Go Tell It on the Mountain*; Plath's *The Bell Jar*; McCuller's *The Heart Is a Lonely Hunter*; Roth's *Call It Sleep*; Dostoevsky's *Brothers Karamazov*; and other readings from Ellison, Camus, and Kafka. On the way to class one morning I met one of my students. He was a white male, intelligent, and a graduating senior in mining engineering. He had only one three-credit elective and by virtue of a happenstance student grapevine conversation, he enrolled in my course. He had lined up a position after graduation, making more than $30,000 a year to start. I asked him how he was doing. He became very agitated and blurted out, terrible. He said it was my fault or someone's fault but this course had knocked his socks off, blitzed him. He was up every night, all night, reading the books, avoiding his engineering obligations. He was appalled at how little he knew about other cultures, about the way in which the world gets itself on through the endless varieties of attitudes, values, fears, and foibles. He asked me why no one had ever introduced him to this literature, and he realized that it happened for him serendipitously. Finally, he commented that the family name, Tyrone, in *Long Day's Journey* was misnamed, for it should have had his own family name. The play was for this young man a rendition of family autobiography.

Poignant though the story may be, our young man is not an exception. In the thousands of student semester-long journals that I have read, the most constant theme is the "shock of recognition" upon first facing great philosophy and literature. Due to the extreme emphasis on preprofessional education within the last decade, the woeful character of our students' grasp of the historicity and complexity of life has heightened considerably. I am aware that this conflict between getting things done and speculation is not new to our generation. It is found in the first book of Aristotle's *Metaphysics*, and the dispute has periodic refrains in the history of western education. John Henry Newman phrased this conflict as the unawareness that not everything useful is good but that everything good is useful. In "Discourse VII" of his classic work *The Idea of a University*, Newman considers "Knowledge Viewed in Relation to Professional Skill."

> This process of training, by which the intellect, instead of being formed or sacrificed to some particular or accidental purpose, some specific trade or profession, or study or science, is disciplined for its own sake, for the perception of its own proper object, and for its own highest culture, is called Liberal Education; . . .

> And to set forth the right standard, and to train according to it, and to help forward all students towards it according to their various capacities, this I conceive to be the business of a University.

Now this is what some great men are very slow to allow; they insist that Education should be confined to some particular and narrow end, and should issue in some definite work, which can be weighed and measured. They argue as if every thing, as well as every person, had its price; and that where there has been a great outlay, they have a right to expect a return in kind. This they call making Education and Instruction "useful," and "Utility" becomes their watchword. . . .

"Good" indeed means one thing, and "useful" means another; but I lay it down as a principle, which will save us a great deal of anxiety, that, though the useful is not always good, the good is always useful.[5]

Newman represents a different century and a different cultural context, but his vision is telling and it still faces the same kind of opposition, one that has no awareness of the ambience of all human activity and of the necessity to integrate our hands with our affections. Closer to our own necessity to integrate our hands with our affections. Closer to our own time and clime, the version of John Dewey, an understanding of which is our task in this essay, is different but comes to the same result. For Dewey, the cardinal sin is the separation of percepts from concepts, that is, the separation of pedogogy from lived experience. Being a quintessential American, in a way that was not characteristic of William James, who was a Europhile and did not understand America as a society, Dewey turned Newman's ideal back on itself. With Dewey, the everyday carried with it pregnant possibilities that would emerge and occasionally explode, if attention, that is, "creative intelligence," were brought to bear. The tradition of the arts, the humanities, and the sciences become horizons rather than fixed ends and sources of elitism or academic patronizing, such that all experience vibrates with potential insight. This is not only the goal of a university, as in Newman, but it is the ideal for all pedagogy, for children, for adults, young and old, and for outcasts. To bring this off, nothing less than a systemic revamping of present national policy is necessary, a salutary and worthy goal, a gamble for excellence. In order for us to grasp this position of Dewey, it would be necessary to retrack all of his writing and his life. No such opportunity is available in the present setting, so we provide only benchmarks and highlights before turning to the upshot of Dewey's thought for our contemporary situation.[6]

In both his undergraduate education at the University of Vermont and his graduate education at Johns Hopkins, Dewey came under the sway of disciples of continental idealism, especially the Hegelian variety. In this, he was like most of his peers in late-nineteenth-century American philosophy, with the notable exceptions of William James and C. S. Peirce. Dewey took a logic course with the beleaguered and fractious Peirce at Hopkins although he did not realize its significance until many decades later.

While teaching at the University of Michigan, Dewey began to undergo deep changes in personal, religious, and philosophical outlook, much of which was initiated by his alert, modern, and socially conscious young wife, Alice Chipman Dewey. Suffice to say that Dewey began to break from the abstractions of neo-Hegelian idealism, a development that was consummated by his reading of William James's *Principles of Psychology*, published in 1890.[7] Yet, in an important way, Dewey retained the thought of Hegel as "a permanent deposit" in his thinking.[8] The character of that deposit was to separate him from his pragmatist companions, James and Peirce, for Dewey maintained an abiding awareness of the social and institutional context in all of his thinking, a characteristic that was to be central to the development of his subsequent philosophy of education. Dewey soon began to follow the route laid out by James, one that was to lead to his naturalistic metaphysics as a bedrock for his pedagogy and his aesthetics. In 1905, Dewey joins the fray in an effort to make experience the major metaphor in an understanding of how we find ourselves in the world.

> The criticisms made upon that vital but still unformed movement variously termed radical empiricism, pragmatism, humanism, functionalism, according as one or another aspect of it is uppermost, have left me with a conviction that the *fundamental* difference is not so much in matters overtly discussed as in a presupposition that remains tacit: a presupposition as to what experience is and means. . . .
>
> Immediate empiricism postulates that things—anything, everything, in the ordinary or non-technical use of the term "thing"—are what they are experienced as.[9]

To be "experienced as" is to realize, following James, that "life is in the transition," that "experience itself, taken at large, can grow by its edges" and "in the simplest and completest cases the experiences are cognitive of another."[10] *Experience, itself, is, pedagogical.* Dewey states this in the following passage:

> Generalizing from the instance, we get the following definition: An experience is a knowledge, if in its quale there is an experienced distinction and connection of two elements of the following sort: *one means or intends the presence of the other in the same fashion in which itself is already*

present, while the other is that which, while not present in the same fashion, must become so present if the meaning or intention of its companion or yoke-fellow is to be fulfilled through the operation it sets up.[11]

Now what does this sortie into the denizens of epistemology and metaphysics come to so far as our effort to present Dewey's philosophy of eduction? The answer is that such an awareness of Dewey's position is the linchpin necessary to understanding his aesthetics and consequently his pedagogy. The reason for this judgment is simple and straightforward. Unless one knows how Dewey diagnoses experience, then his approach to education takes on an obviousness, so castigated by the legions of casual commentators and critics who have never read his work in the round.

Allow me to be explicit and direct. There are many thinkers who believe that to be in the world is to be a spectator to a picture or an actor upon a stage. Neither James nor Dewey believe this to be so. There are many thinkers who believe that knowledge is an affair of concepts, definitions, and proper nouns. Neither James nor Dewey believe this to be so. There are many thinkers for whom experience is mute, rendered only articulate by the language of mental activity. Neither James nor Dewey believe this to be so.[12] What then does Dewey hold to be so insofar as we have experiences? I put this in my own words with an attempted textually informed editorial license on behalf of the position of John Dewey.

The human organism, strikingly akin to other advanced organisms, transacts with the affairs of nature. The human organism, however, is paradoxical in that it knows whereof, whereat, and whereby this transaction takes place; in short, the human organism is aggressively self-conscious.[13] This transaction between the human organism and nature is experience. The transaction is ever striated not only with problems, knots, but with the problematic as an ontological condition of being in and of and about the world. To be human is to be constantly, ineluctably, irreducibly faced with the problematic.

For Dewey, one can make one's way through this network of difficulties, although attempted resolutions inevitably generate new difficulties. Life has *no final perch*. Many years ago Dewey described this viewpoint to a lay audience. An elderly woman approached Dewey after the lecture and said to him as follows: 'Mr. Dewey, you describe life as though one climbed a mountain to the top and then descended, only to climb another mountain to the top. Mr. Dewey, what happens when there are no more mountains to climb?' Dewey answered in properly laconic Yankee form and true to his metaphysics, 'You die, Madam!'

Make no mistake, we have a major difficulty spelled out in Dewey's version of the human quest, namely, the absence of closure, of ultimate certitude, and of transcendent meaning. In short, there is no immortality. Yet, equivalently, make no mistake, we do not have nihilism.

Dewey accepts the claim of James that experiences are indeed cognitive of one another, so that the transaction is not without a guide, a source, a leaning, a hint, a hunch, an Indian head watch. Keep your eye on the ball, it speaks. Listen to the wind, it speaks. Hear the murmurs, read the gestures, mark the gait, catch the tone, eye the color, reach and keep one foot on the ground.

Formal education teaches us that experience can be denoted. The brilliant phyla of Aristotle is a masterpiece of local organization. Modern molecular science has shown that the makeup of nature can be put differently, although still in a conceptual structure. It is Dewey's wisdom to insist that experience is also connotative. More, as Dewey stresses, all inquiry, that is, all reflective experience of nature, has an experimental potential. Inquiry is not limited to naming and placing, for it can forge, shift, and reconstruct the way in which our experiences come at firsthand. At an intitial glance this seems to make considerable sense as a description of our basic transaction with the world. Alas, the description turns out to be far more ideal that characteristic.

Two major obstacles loom in the way of our capacity to enter into an experimental, resolving, healing, and future-oriented transaction with the world as it comes to us. First, as Dewey stresses over and over, we tend not to trust our own experience to be significant, leading, warning, and revealing. In fact, we have been taught to either deride the importance of our own experience, and therefore enter an incommunicative shell, or from insecurity and a hesitant sense of the true worth of our experiences, we rattle on in a monologue as self-aggrandizing as it is empty. Second, in our confrontation with our own experience, we are all too often severely hobbled by the trappings of our own education, informal and formal, especially the latter. Although the world as experienced speaks in dulcet, loud, peremptory, cajoling, and symbolic ways, it is rare that we hear anything. Although the world as experienced struts its colors, carried by blossom, bird, and sky, it is rare that we see anything. Although the world as experienced preens its scents, floated by sea, cave, animal, and cuisine, it is rare that we smell anything. Although the world flaunts its texture by bristle, horsehair, cactus, and spider web, it is rare that we feel anything by touch. It is not as Yeats warned, that the center does not hold; rather, it is that the senses do not grasp, do not reach, for they have become captives of the denotative mind rather than extensions of our bodies.

Given the riot of possibilities in the ancient world, who can fault Aristotle for putting "things" and "species" in order, according to his own light. Before Aristotle, in the writings of Plato, and from Aristotle to this day, the poets have been struggling to free our experience from the clutches of definition and the roster of self-defining names, which have rendered our experience more of the inert than of the symbolical. No one says this more perceptively than Dewey's mentor, Ralph Waldo Emerson.

> We learn nothing rightly until we learn the symbolical character of life. Day creeps after day, each full of facts, dull, strange, despised things, that we cannot enough despise,—call heavy, prosaic and desert. The time we seek to kill: the attention it is elegant to divert from things around us. And presently the aroused intellect finds gold and gems in one of these scorned facts,—then finds that the day of facts is a rock of diamonds; that a fact is an Epiphany of God.[14]

Granted that Dewey does not use the theological imagery of Emerson, he is nonetheless in complete accord with Emerson's belief in the epiphanic character of reality. Such a belief is rooted in the ancient Stoics and finds subsequent articulation in the thought of Augustine, Scotus Erigena, the Franciscans of the High Middle Ages, and Jonathan Edwards. The tradition is quickly caught in the lines of the poet Gerard Manley Hopkins.

> And for all this, nature is never spent;
> There lives the dearest freshness deep down things.[15]

With the exception of the Stoics, these are alien bedfellows for the thought of John Dewey. Yet the tradition comes to him through Emerson and is reenforced by the richness of the American landscape and by the puritan Yankee tradition by which nature is refractory and speaks directly to us, for better or for worse.

> Man finds himself living in an aleatory world; his existence involves, to put it baldly, a gamble. The world is a scene of risk; it is uncertain, unstable, uncannily unstable. Its dangers are irregular, inconstant, not to be counted upon as to their times and seasons. Although persistent, they are sporadic, episodic. It is darkest just before dawn; pride goes before a fall; the moment of greatest prosperity is the moment most charged with ill-omen, most opportune for the evil eye. Plague, famine, failure of crops, disease, death, defeat in battle, are always just around the corner, and so are abundance,

strength, victory, festival and song. Luck is proverbially both good and bad in its distributions. The sacred and the accursed are potentialities of the same situation; and there is no category of things which has not embodied the sacred and accursed: persons, words, places, times, directions in space, stones, winds, animals, stars.[16]

Dewey writes this text in a chapter called "Existence as Precarious and as Stable." He had an uncanny sense of the rhythms at work in the transaction between ourselves and nature. Like James, Dewey never lost his fidelity to the organic, to physiological as the source of major metaphors to describe our comings and goings, our ups and downs, our systolic and diastolic binding to the flow of our experiences as they articulate the personal way in which each one of us has the world. Yes, our experiences are articulate, for just as nature speaks to us, so too by our experiencing of nature do we speak to ourselves. How we experience the world, that is, how we speak to ourselves, is the script of our personal consciousness. I am not a person who experiences the world as sheerly other. My experiencing the world is who I am. The task is to grow, to mature by virtue of insight, affection, and, notably for Dewey, setback. In *Art as Experience*, Dewey describes this rhythm of our transaction with nature as constitutive of our "career and destiny."

No creatures lives merely under its skin; its subcutaneous organs are means of connection with what lies beyond its bodily frame, and to which, in order to live, it must adjust itself, by accommodation and defense but also by conquest. At every moment, the living creature is exposed to dangers from its surroundings, and at every moment, it must draw upon something in its surroundings to satisfy its needs. The career and destiny of a living being are bound up with its interchanges with its environment, not externally but in the most intimate way.[17]

Dewey then proceeds to claim that setback and even "temporary alienation" are *necessary* if the human organism is to grow. Failure, disappointment, missing when reaching are as constitutive of our person as is fructification.

Life itself consists of phases in which the organism falls out of step with the march of surrounding things and then recovers unison with it—either through effort or by some happy chance. And, in a growing life, the recovery is never mere return to a prior state, for it is enriched by the state of disparity and resistance through which it has successfully passed. If the gap between organism and environment is too wide, the creature dies. If its activity is not enhanced by the temporary alienation, it merely subsists. Life grows when a temporary falling out is a transition to a more extensive balance of the energies of the organism with those of the conditions under which it lives.[18]

Given this setting, in which our transactions are fundamentally aesthetic, Dewey deplores the tendency of education to divide our activities between high and low culture or between the fine and the useful arts. He is not attempting to level the world of art to some form of proletarian socialist realism; rather, he is pointing to the extraordinary potentialities of the ordinary, if we would learn how to diagnose the rhythm of our own experiences. For Dewey, so-called high art and culture act more like a beacon light, a luminous cloud, a dawn, a sylvan path through the great pines, a symbolic jolt to our constant tendency toward habituation than as an arbiter of acceptable experiences as bathed in condescension. The best of art and culture casts light, not stones, at our everyday experience, although the light often focuses on the murky, the dangerous, the evil that seem to inevitably accompany our human journey. He insists on the continuity between our artistic activities, our crafts, and the texture of our ordinary experience.

When artistic objects are separated from both conditions of origin and operation in experience, a wall is built around them that renders almost opaque their general significance, with which esthetic theory deals. Art is remitted to a separate realm, where it is cut off from the association with the materials and aims of every other form of human effort, undergoing, and achievement. A primary task is thus imposed upon one who undertakes to write upon the philosophy of the fine arts. This task is to restore continuity between the refined and intensified forms of experience that are works of art and the everyday events, doings, and sufferings that are universally recognized to constitute experience.[19]

The separation of art from the everyday "deeply affects the practice of living, driving away esthetic perceptions that are necessary ingredients of happiness, or reducing them to the level of compensating transient pleasurable excitations."[20] We find here Dewey's profound concern for the quality of the life lived by the average person, those millions who flocked to America in the immigrant decades from the late nineteenth century until well into the twentieth century. Consequently, just as his pedagogy is informed by the central importance of the aesthetic, so too does it have a political bite.

The political side to Dewey's lamentation about the separation of art from the everyday is his concern for what he calls "the lost individual," that person who has been cut adrift by the erosion of the classical loyalties that permeated previous societies in Europe and previous generations in America. Writing in 1930, Dewey provides a text that has the eerie ring of contemporaneity.

It would be difficult to find in history an epoch as lacking in solid and assured objects of belief and approved ends of action as is the present. Stability of individuality is dependent upon stable objects to which allegiance firmly attaches itself. There are, of course, those who are still militantly fundamentalist in religious and social creed. But their very clamor is evidence that the tide is set against them. For the others, traditional objects of loyalty have become hollow or are openly repudiated, and they drift without sure anchorage. Individuals vibrate between a past that is intellectually too empty to give stability and a present that is too diversely crowded and chaotic to afford balance or direction to ideas and emotion.[21]

The attempted resolution of this anomie by a revival of evangelical selfrighteousness or by the separation of American society into stratified classes as identified by aesthetic taste and by educational opportunity appalls Dewey, for whom neither "dogmatic fundamentalism," nor "esoteric occultism," nor "private estheticism" can cultivate the social binding necessary to ensure a creative human life for all.[22]

Despite Dewey's lifelong commitment to egalitarian education, we find nothing of the Pollyanna attitude in his views. He has a firm grasp on the obstacles that face any attempt to achieve educational equity, and he wants that equity to be not only of opportunity but of remediation as well. Dewey has no patience with a simply external qualification for opportunity, as found in the standardized tests of our time. On the contrary, he sees it as the responsibility of society to prepare our children sufficiently so that equal opportunity will not become a hollow promise or a door opening to a corridor that leads to the back door and the junk heap of failed expectation. Dewey believes, as I do, in the educability of all persons, each to the full realization of the limits of their capacities. He regards the realization of these potentialities as a primary obligation of the community, spelled out as you and me.

Equality does not signify that kind of mathematical or physical equivalence in virtue of which any one element may be substituted for another. It denotes effective regard for whatever is distinctive and unique in each, irrespective of physical and psychological inequalities. It is not a natural possession but is a fruit of the community when its action is directed by its character as a community.[23]

One of the obstacles confronting us is naïveté about the corporate world and its ties to the political process. Dewey has no illusions that a gathering of scholars and educators can do any more than fingernail scratch a sheet of aluminum. We make a grievous mistake, he warns us, if we think that stentorian rhetoric and plea-bargaining for equity will effect a sufficient change in what is an essentially arrogant and unconcerned echelon of self-centered entrepreneurs, sustained and funded by bureaucratic hacks. In 1935, Dewey's *Liberalism and Social Action* was an attack on American society, worthy of Marx, although without the self-defeating specter of revolutionary intent. His diagnosis is revealing.

The conditions that generate insecurity for the many no longer spring from nature. They are found in institutions and arrangements that are within deliberate human control. Surely this change marks one of the greatest revolutions that has taken place in all human history. Because of it, insecurity is not now the motive to work and sacrifice but to despair.[24]

In his own way, Dewey had developed an analysis of American society which paralleled that of Marx's critique of European society in the *Economic and Philosophic Manuscripts of 1844*.[25] Dewey, however, was not prone to emulate the inflammatory prose of the American Marxists of the 1930s, for he believed that the transformation of institutions, especially the schools, was possible without resorting to a violent overthrow of an elected government. Still, Dewey realized that good intentions and affectionate rhetoric on behalf of the American *Lumpenproletariat* was insufficient and, in fact, may have simply been used by the power elite, to quote the phrase of C. Wright Mills, an epigone of Dewey, to co-opt those who thought that they were making headway in the transformation of American society, when actually all was business as usual.[26] Dewey knew that the rhetoric on behalf of the schools had to be accompanied by political power such as to effect institutional values, goals, and priorities.

The educational task cannot be accomplished merely by working upon men's minds, without action that effects actual change in institutions. The idea that dispositions and attitudes can be altered by merely "moral" means conceived of as something that goes on wholly inside of persons is itself one of the old patterns that has to be changed. Thought, desire and purpose exist in a constant give and take of interaction with environing conditions. But resolute thought is the first step in that change of action that will itself carry further the needed change in patterns of mind and character.[27]

More, much, much more needs to be said about Dewey's metaphysics, epistemology, aesthetics, and politics if we seek to obtain a true grasp of his pedagogy, for all his endeavors are of a piece, quiltlike, none of them fully intelligible without each of the others as a backup, a refrain, or a continuation. Nonetheless, in this cramped setting we are forced to push on and thus we take a look at Dewey's pedagogy itself.

In the midst of Dewey's voluminous writings, four works stand out as directly significant for his pedagogy and as having extensive influence. The first two were published at the turn of the century, *School and Society* and *The Child and the Curriculum*.[28] As is obvious, these works represent an integrated quadrant of concerns, no one of which can function successfully without a satisfactory relationship with the remaining three areas of consideration. Dewey wrote these works while in the midst of his ten-year tenure as administrator of the Laboratory School at the University of Chicago, the first such program in experimental education in the United States. With his wife, Alice Chipman Dewey, who was the bellwether of the program, Dewey developed a pedagogy that was child-centered and that did not treat children as small adults. Before the powerful and incisive work of Maria Montessori in Italy, the Deweys had discovered the extraordinary capacity of children to learn when there was continuity between the educational program and their own experiences.[29] From their work in the Laboratory School, the Deweys developed the famous "project method," by which children both design and respond to scenarios in which the context for learning is that of actual situations. This approach is in keeping with the process metaphysics and the pragmatic epistemology that Dewey was constructing at that time. Dewey writes that "development does not mean just getting something out of the mind. It is a development of experience and into experience that is really wanted.[30] The burden is clearly on the teacher to provide a pedagogical situation both geared to the needs of the child and that will open horizons for growth and a richer experience of the future.

In 1916, Dewey published *Democracy and Education*, his most famous book in the precincts of professional educators, although most of them read it independently of his wider philosophical enterprise and therefore approach the book unintelligently. The pervading theme of this book is Dewey's emphasis on the importance of human growth.

> Taken absolutely, instead of comparatively, immaturity designates a posi-tive force or ability, —the *power* to grow. We do not have to draw out or educe positive activities from a child, as some educational doctrines would have it. Where there is life, there are already eager and impassioned activ-ities. Growth is not something done to them; it is something they do.[31]

The "doing" is central to Dewey's view of how children become educated. He is opposed to all forms of rote learning unless they can be integrated with an ongoing project, as in the learning of mathematics or a language. Growth is not a casual word for Dewey, for its absence denotes dying, as when children, by virtue of the pedagogical ennui which so often envelops them, become dead unto themselves. In our time, they escape into varieties of electronic media, a hyped-up version of the comic books and Saturday movie serials of Dewey's time. He sees serious social and political results in the estrangement of children from formal learning. In our contemporary language, Dewey foresees a creeping narcissism, sure to begat either anomic drifters or Yuppies who have no compassion for the underclass: "Only gradually and with a widening of the area of vision through a growth of social sympathies does thinking develop to include what lies beyond our direct interests: a fact of great significance for education."[32]

How do we widen "social sympathies," such that our children assume the mantle of the egalitarian and democratic ethos? Dewey is very explicit on this matter, invoking the possibilities and risks attendant on the radically empirical process metaphysics sketched above. Like James, Dewey is not naive that all will go well. I have made it clear that he has a heightened sense of the pervasive disasters that await us in our journey. Nonetheless, Dewey has a trust that experience, whatever may be its constant travail, provides its own potential source of healing.

> To "learn from experience" is to make a backward and forward connection between what we do to things and what we enjoy or suffer from things in consequence. Under such conditions, doing becomes a trying; an experiment with the world to find out what it is like; the undergoing becomes instruction—discovery of the connection of things.[33]

Unfortunately, the followers of the thought of John Dewey lacked his depth of understanding relative to the complex question of how one has experience, does experience, and receives experience. His opponents, still afflicted with the diseases of metaphysical foundationalism, a penchant for the *a priori* or assorted conceptual schemes, self-verifying, mocked his emphasis on anything so homely, so prosaic as experience. The first camp, under the banner of progressive education turned his thought into an endorsement of education as a circus, free of restraint, unstructured, and socially irresponsible. The second camp plodded on, teaching fewer things to fewer people until the decade of the 1960s, when the watchword was to tune in and drop out, often fueled by cerebral acid in response to the wailing cry of Grace Slick and the Jefferson Airplane, to feed your head.

In 1938, approaching the age of eighty, Dewey struck back in a small but trenchant book entitled *Experience and Education*. He attacked the either/or options just sketched and then proceeded to revivify his own meaning of what is meant by experience as central to a liberating and *effective* pedagogy. He immediately makes clear that "it is not enough to insist upon the necessity of experience, nor even of activity in experience. Everything depends upon the *quality* of the experience which is had."[34] Such quality does not emerge casually. The child must be assisted to diagnose his or her own experiences, as they take place, in time and in space. The traditional approach to education that stresses preparation for a future that may or may not happen, strikes Dewey as deadly and counterproductive to the needs of the child.

> What, then, is the true meaning of preparation in the educational scheme? In the first place, it means that a person, young or old, gets out of his present experience all that there is in it for him at the time in which he has it. When preparation is made the controlling end, then the potentialities of the present are sacrificed to a supposititious future. When this happens, the actual preparation for the future is missed or distorted. The ideal of using the present simply to get ready for the future contradicts itself. It omits, and even shuts out, the very conditions by which a person can be prepared for his future. We always live at the time we live and not at some other time, and only by extracting at each present time the full meaning of each present experience are we prepared for doing the same thing in the future. This is the only preparation which in the long run amounts to anything.[35]

If Dewey is right, as I believe, that we live only at the time we live and at no other time, then our present approach to education is caught between an insufficient sense of the necessary past we must carry and an emphasis on a future which most likely will not happen. To the contrary, we must find a way to assist and convince our children and those adults who seek to renew themselves that it is necessary to constantly diagnose the messages of their own experiences while at the same time submitting these messages to the supporting and countervailing responses of their peers. Further, they must build into their diagnosis the experiences and insights of those who have gone before them, making allowance for the shift in historical context while still remaining open to wisdom from another setting.

I do not suggest that Dewey's approach to pedagogy is a panacea, any more than I would endorse a competing viewpoint. In our pluralistic society, it is impossible to have any single version of the educational process become able to account for all needs, all situations and all desires. Still, Dewey's emphasis on the centrality of experience carries with it enormous good sense, empirical sustenance, and a capacity to involve our attention to the past, the present, and a future that is experientially linked to our present. I am not unaware that to cast one's education into the vagaries of experience has a treacherous aspect to it, for experience, despite its obviousness as the philosopher Charles Sanders Peirce holds, is that which "takes place by a series of surprises."[36] The enemy, however, is the humdrum, the habitual, the routine. Better to love and be crushed than not to love at all.

My awareness of the dangers that lurk in opening ourselves to experience as the source of pedagogy prompted the title of this essay, for in fact we must gamble for excellence. We must take a chance that if we cast off the chains of the obvious and ride with the flow, we may very well drown. Then again, we may not drown. We may cavort, play, suck air, and rise again. Better to drown in the water of life than to be suffocated in the rote of obviousness.

Notes

Acknowledgment: For critical consideration of the above material, I am grateful to the participants in a Conference on Education at Risk: Directions for the Future From the Wisdom of the Past as sponsored by Rockford College, Rockford, Illinois.

1. Elizabeth Flower and Murray G. Murphey, *A History of Philosophy in America* (New York: G. P. Putnam's Sons, 1977), Vol. 2, pp. 848, 865.

2. *Ibid.*, Vol. 2, p. 866.

3. John Dewey, *Democracy and Education, The Middle Works* (Carbondale: Southern Illinois University Press, 1980), Vol. 9, p. 338.

4. See John J. McDermott, "Cultural Literacy: A Time for a New Curriculum," in McDermott, *Streams of Experience: Reflections on the History and Philosophy of American Culture* (Amherst: University of Massachusetts Press, 1986), pp. 180–195.

5. John Henry Newman, *The Idea of a University* (New York: Longmans, Green, and Co., 1896), pp. 152–153, 164.

6. For a systematic and chronological representative selection of Dewey's writings, see John J. McDermott (ed.), *The Philosophy of John Dewey*, 2 vols. (Chicago: University of Chicago Press, 1981). The entire corpus of Dewey's writings is being edited in a critical edition by Jo Ann Boydston. *The Early Works*, 5 vols., 1882–1898; *The Middle Works*, 15 vols., 1899–1924, have been published by Southern Illinois University Press. Eight of sixteen volumes of *The Later Works*, 1925–1953, have thus far been published. See also Jo Ann Boydston (ed.), *Guide to the Works of John Dewey* (Carbondale: Southern Illinois University Press, 1970), which is a detailed analysis of Dewey's writings and a bibliographical checklist by subject. Thus far, the only thorough biography extant is George Dykhuizen, *The Life and Mind of John Dewey* (Carbondale: Southern Illinois University Press, 1973). An excellent starting point for the study of Dewey's thought is the above mentioned chapter by Elizabeth Flower.

7. See John Dewey, "From Absolutism to Experimentalism," in McDermott (ed.), *The Philosophy of John Dewey*, Vol. 1, pp. 1–13.

8. *Ibid.*, p. 8.

9. John Dewey, "The Postulate of Immediate Empiricism," *The Middle Works*, Vol. 3 (1977), p. 158.

10. William James, *Essays in Radical Empiricism: The Works of William James*, ed. Frederick Burkhardt (Cambridge, Mass: Harvard University Press, 1976), p. 42.

11. John Dewey, "The Experimental Theory of Knowledge," *The Middle Works*, Vol. 3 (1977), pp. 114–115.

12. In fact, for James, the reverse position is on specific record. See William James, "The Stream of Consciousness," *Psychology: Briefer Course* (Cambridge, Mass.: Harvard University Press, 1984). "It is, the reader will see, the reinstatement of the vague and inarticulate to its proper place in our mental life which I am so anxious to press on the attention" (p. 150). (Parenthetically, I spend many comparatively fruitless hours trying to teach this to my students in the College of Medicine.)

13. I do not preclude other creatures from this power. I simply do not know. Evidence seems to suggest that some organisms such as chimpanzees and dolphins

have a nascent capacity for such awareness. So be it. The fact is that human organisms are obviously, treacherously, and delightfully self-conscious. Such is a fact of our situation.

14. Ralph Waldo Emerson, *The Complete Works of Ralph Waldo Emerson* (Cambridge, Mass.: Houghton Mifflin, 1903–1904), Vol. 4, p. 132. See also Emerson, "Works and Days," *ibid.*, Vol. 7, pp. 155–185. For the influence of Emerson on the Classical American philosophers, inclusive of John Dewey, see John J. McDermott, "Spires of Influence: The Importance of Emerson for Classical American Philosophy," in McDermott, *Streams of Experience*, pp. 29–43.

15. Gerard Manley Hopkins, "God's Grandeur," *Poems* (New York: Oxford University Press, 1948), p. 70.

16. John Dewey, *Experience and Nature, The Later Works*, Vol. 1 (1981), p. 43.

17. John Dewey, "The Live Creature," in McDermott (ed.), *The Philosophy of John Dewey*, Vol. 2, p. 535.

18. *Ibid.*, p. 535.

19. *Ibid.*, p. 526.

20. *Ibid.*, p. 532.

21. John Dewey, "The Lost Individual," in McDermott (ed.), *The Philosophy of John Dewey*, Vol. 2, p. 599.

22. *Ibid.*, p. 604.

23. John Dewey, *The Public and Its Problems, The Later Works*, Vol. 2 (1984), pp. 329–330.

24. John Dewey, "Renascent Liberalism," in McDermott (ed.), *The Philosophy of John Dewey*, Vol. 2, p. 646.

25. Karl Marx, *The Economic and Philosophic Manuscripts of 1844* (Moscow: Foreign Languages Publishing House, n.d.). See also T. B. Bottomore (ed.), *Karl Marx: Early Writings* (New York: McGraw-Hill Book Co., 1963).

26. See C. Wright Mills, *Sociology and Pragmatism* (New York: Paine-Whitman Publishers, 1964), pp. 277–463.

27. John Dewey, "Renascent Liberalism," in McDermott (ed.), *The Philosophy of John Dewey*, Vol. 2, p. 647.

28. John Dewey, *School and Society, The Middle Works*, Vol. 1 (1976), pp. 3–109; John Dewey, *The Child and the Curriculum, The Middle Works*, Vol. 2 (1976), pp. 273–291.

29. See Maria Montessori, *The Montessori Method* (New York: Schocken Books, 1921).

30. Dewey, *The Child and the Curriculum*, p. 282.

31. Dewey, *Democracy and Education*, p. 47.

32. *Ibid.*, p. 155.

33. *Ibid.*, p. 147.

34. John Dewey, "The Need for a Theory of Experience," in McDermott (ed.), *The Philosophy of John Dewey*, Vol. 2, p. 508.

35. John Dewey, "Criteria of Experience," in McDermott (ed.), *The Philosophy of John Dewey*, Vol. 2, p. 523.

36. Charles Sanders Peirce, *Collected Papers*, ed. Charles Hartshorne and Paul Weiss, vol. 5 (Cambridge, Mass.: Harvard University Press, 1934), Sec. 51, p. 37. Peirce also says, "But without beating longer round the bush, let us come to close quarters. Experience is our only teacher" (Sec. 50, p. 37).

7 | Thorstein Veblen: Instinctive Values and Evolutionary Science

Murray G. Murphey

Thorstein Veblen occupies a curious place in American intellectual history. He was a member of that extraordinary generation that bloomed between the Civil War and World War I and whose work altered permanently the American intellectual scene. His writings have been much read and are well known; nevertheless, his own contributions have proven very difficult to assess. Although he is often classed with James and Dewey among the prophets of democratic liberalism,[1] his kinship with this group is at least dubious and is usually asserted more on the basis of what he was against than of what he was for. His *Theory of the Leisure Class* has become a classic of American satire and his terms "conspicuous consumption," "conspicuous leisure," and "conspicuous waste" have become part of the liberal vocabulary, yet it is not at all clear that Veblen saw himself as a satirist, and great uncertainty prevails as to just what his positive doctrines were. My purpose here is first to examine the premises underlying Veblen's thought, and second to show how an understanding of the premises leads to an understanding of certain of his major claims in economics. Thus it is hoped we may come closer to understanding this "man from Mars."[2]

Veblen received a Ph.D. in philosophy from Yale in 1884. Not being a minister, or even orthodox, he failed to get a job teaching philosophy, and in 1891 he went to Cornell to study economics. Economists were not required to be men of God and Veblen did manage to get work at the University of Chicago in 1892.[3] Given this background, it is not surprising that Veblen should have approached economics from a different point of view than most, and his philosophic views are crucial to an understanding of his economics. But the only explicitly philosophical piece he wrote that has survived was an article on Kant's *Critique of Judgment*, which was published in the *Journal of Speculative Philosophy* in 1887.[4] This article, however, gives some important insights into Veblen's position.

Veblen opens the article by setting the *Critique of Judgment* in the context of the other critiques. The first critique, he says, established "the notion of strict determinism, according to natural law, in the world"; the second established "the notion of freedom in the person."[5] Given the division between the phenomenal and noumenal realms, freedom and determinism may not conflict, but for freedom to play any role in the world the free person must be able to act as an efficient cause in nature. If such action is to be rational, it must be based upon a knowledge of the effects that will follow upon the actions taken, and the individual must therefore be capable of establishing empirical generalizations that hold for the future. This is possible only through induction, and according to Veblen the purpose of the third critique is to explain and justify inductive reasoning.

Veblen notes Kant's distinction between the determinative judgment, by which universal rules are applied to particular cases, and the reflective judgment, by which the universal rule is found once the particular cases are given. The problem of the reflective judgment is then the problem of induction—of inferring empirical generalizations on the basis of particulars. What justifies such an inference? Only if the reflective judgment is guided by an *a priori* principle will such an activity be legitimate, for as "the result aimed at lies beyond experience, the principle according to which it is to proceed cannot be given by experience."[6] It also cannot come from outside the reflective judgment, because that would make the judgment determinative, and it must therefore come from the reflective judgment itself. This *a priori* principle of the reflective judgment is, Veblen says, the principle of the "adaptation of the part of the object to the laws of the activity of our faculties of knowledge."[7] Thus induction will be legitimate only if nature forms an orderly logical system of the sort the human mind seeks to create out of its experience and knowledge. Kant regarded this as equivalent to saying that we must view nature as if it was the product of an intelligent creator who has purposely structured it to fit the needs of the human mind. The stress should fall on the *as if*, for Kant held this principle to be subjective only. We must accept such a principle as a regulative principle for the operation of the reflective judgment, but Kant held that it could not be proven true of the world. It is therefore a maxim that guides inquiry—a presupposition of inductive investigations—but subjective rather than objective because the reality of such an intelligent creator lies beyond the possibility of proof. Nevertheless, the principle is crucial, for it functions as a foundation for induction. Only if the world is taken to be systematically ordered and free from chance will induction yield true results.[8]

The test of the correctness of an induction, Veblen holds, is a feeling of gratification. This is so because "whenever the intellect finds the object of its knowledge to be such as to admit of the unhampered activity of the faculties employed about them, there results a gratification such as is always felt on the attainment of an end striven for."[9] To the degree that the object known is adapted to our faculties, their activity will be unhampered and so will produce gratification. With respect to the single datum of experience, where the datum is considered simply in relation to the apprehending subject, the reflective judgment is the aesthetic judgment and the gratification is aesthetic pleasure. But with respect to cognition, it is the relations among concepts and their objects, taken as part of our knowledge of the world, with which the reflective judgment is concerned, and to the degree that these are adapted to our faculties the result will again be a feeling of gratification. "This feeling of gratification may therefore be regarded as a sanction to the principle of the reflective judgment, and, in the last resort, it is this feeling of gratification alone which can decide whether the principle has been applied successfully in any given case."[10]

Veblen's interpretation of Kant leads to the result that we inevitably impute teleology to the world in our attempts to give coherence to our experience; this imputation is based on a subjective requirement, not objective fact.

> The finality which is attributed to external reality, on the ground of the adaptation found by the reflective judgment, is simply and only an imputed finality, and the imputation of it to reality is based on the same ground of feeling as every other act of the reflective judgment. Our imputation of finality to the things of the world, and our teleological arguments for an intelligent cause of the world, proceed on subjective grounds entirely, and give no knowledge of objective fact, and furnish no proof that is available for establishing even a probability in favor of what is claimed.[11]

This article is a discussion of Kant's third critique, not of Veblen's own position, and to draw conclusions from it about Veblen's views involves some risk. Nevertheless, the ideas discussed here play so important a part in Veblen's later thought that it is impossible not to draw certain connections. Whether he derived it from Kant or not, Veblen certainly believed that experience is a joint product of an active mind and sense data, the first supplying the conceptual order, the latter the material or data. But like many of his contemporaries in the post-Darwinian world, Veblen did not accept the idea of one fixed set of categories that were true for all men at all times. He did follow Kant (and most of the nineteenth century) in holding that Newtonian mechanics was not only true but the model that all other physical sciences must emulate, and he also seems to have followed Kant on the question of teleology. He accepted teleology as a description of the behavior of individual organisms but rejected it as applied to nature as a whole. But Veblen's comments about the reflective judgment and induction make it clear that he believed that we do impute teleology to nature, both to nature as a whole and to particular objects of nature, organic and inorganic. This imputation is subjective, but it is also universal because it is required by the mind. Veblen seems to have rejected entirely Kant's arguments of the Transcendental Dialectic and the second critique; he did not believe in God, or a noumenal world, and there is no evidence that he believed in freedom or immortality. But he did derive from the third critique his position on induction, which has the consequence that for him the truth of induction rests upon a feeling of gratification signifying a compatibility between the object known and "our faculties." Deleting the reference to the faculty psychology, this becomes a compatibility between what is known and the "apperceptive mass" brought to bear on it—in other words, it becomes a coherence theory of truth.

The Kantian psychology was a faculty psychology, and like most of his contemporaries in America, Veblen rejected this model of the mind. In his early writings (before 1914), Veblen drew heavily upon the "new" psychology of James, Dewey, and their followers. Thus he held that man is an active and unified being; the whole man is involved in every act, and although various aspects can be analytically distinguished in the mental processes, there are no separate faculties. Veblen accepted James's theory of the selective operation of attention upon the stream of thought. He also accepted the use of the term "habit" to encompass both learned patterns of behavior and beliefs, and the general outline of the doubt-belief theory of inquiry. The role of intelligence is to solve problems created by the failure of existing habits to lead to satisfaction in specific settings, and to create new habits that will provide a more adequate basis for action. The emphasis in this psychology is upon man's ability to overcome obstacles and to solve problems—in short, his ability to adapt to the world. Little emphasis is laid upon the invariable features of human nature that might limit the scope of adaptability. Veblen does introduce at least one instinct in this early period—the instinct of workmanship—but he does not discuss instinct as a psychological phenomenon and there is no evidence in these early writings that he used the term in any sense different from William James.[12]

In 1908, William McDougall published *An Introduction to Social Psychology*. McDougall's psychology was an instinct psychology, and the function of the instincts was described as providing the "essential springs or motive powers of all thought and action."[13] If these instincts could be defined, and shown to be common to all men, McDougall believed they would "afford a much needed basis for speculation on the history of the development of human societies and human institutions."[14] McDougall divided these innate tendencies into two classes—the instincts proper, and general nonspecific tendencies arising from the constitution and processes of the mind. Of these two groups, the first is the more important. His most precise definition of instinct was as follows:

> We may, then, define an instinct as an inherited or innate psycho-physical disposition which determines its possessor to perceive, and to pay attention to, objects of a certain class, to experience an emotional excitement of a particular quality upon perceiving such an object, and to act in regard to it in a particular manner, or, at least, to experience an impulse to such an action.[15]

These three aspects of instinctive action were designated "the cognitive, the affective, and the conative aspects; that is to say, every instance of instinctive behavior involves knowing of some thing or object, a feeling in regard to it, and a striving towards or away from that object."[16] From this it is clear that instinctive action is teleological, usually having for its end the welfare of the group and/or the individual. Furthermore, instinct involves the action of consciousness and intelligence, and so is fundamentally distinct from a mere reflex or tropism. Of particular importance for Veblen is the cognitive aspect of the instinct, which McDougall describes as follows:

> Now, the psycho-physical process that issues in an instinctive action is initiated by a sense-impression which, usually, is but one of many sense impressions received at the same time; and the fact that this one impression plays an altogether dominant part in determining the animal's behavior shows that its effects are peculiarly favored, that the nervous system is peculiarly fitted to receive and to respond to just that kind of impression.

The impression must be supposed to excite, not merely detailed changes is the animal's field of sensation, but a sensation or complex of sensation that has significance or meaning for the animal; hence we must regard the instinctive process in its cognitive aspect as distinctly of the nature of perception, however rudimentary.[17]

There is a functional similarity evident here between the Kantian categories and McDougall's instincts. Both are conceived to be generic to the human species and to be the fundamental grounds of thought and action. Both involve an active mind acting upon sense data through a preset mental process—that is, an innate tendency of the mind to order its data according to these principles. In both cases mental action is teleological and its innate principles are assumed to be basically unchangeable.

We do not know when Veblen first read McDougall, but he had certainly read him by the time he introduced his own instinct theory in *The Instinct of Workmanship* in 1914. Although he cites McDougall as the source of his instinct theory, Veblen's instincts are not McDougall's.[18] He defined them as general tendencies that arise from a combination of more specific psychological elements but that for the purposes of the social sciences may be treated as irreducible. Like McDougall's instincts, Veblen's are teleological; they are "teleological categories" that are best defined by reference to the end that each serves. But the underlying psychological processes out of which the instincts arise are not teleological; they are "of a quasi-tropismatic or physiological nature" that, although functional for the organism, involve no conscious purpose.[19] Thus, the teleological character of behavior, which Kant imputed to men (among other organisms) as a subjective requirement of the reflective judgment, is here grounded on the nature of instinct, but it arises as an effect of "mechanical" processes in the organism. Instincts are not only purposive, they involve consciousness and intelligence, but the role of intelligence is limited to the finding of means to the attainment of instinctively given ends. Intelligence therefore functions within the framework provided by the instincts and cannot transcend it. Veblen's instincts, like McDougall's, serve as *a priori* syntheses of thought and action.[20]

The most basic of these instincts Veblen called the "parental bent." Such specific instincts as the instinct of reproduction and the so-called maternal instinct he regarded as components of the parental bent, but the latter is more general and is taken to include all feelings of solicitude for the welfare of others and particularly for the welfare of the community at large. By "welfare" here Veblen means material welfare—the satisfaction of the community's needs for food, shelter, heat, clothing. The term "community at large" refers not just to the specific group (family, village, town) to which the person belongs but to the wider set of people who are linked to the person by economic interdependencies. In the modern world, this means the earth's population.[21]

The second instinct is idle curiosity. That curiosity was an instinct was generally agreed; Veblen's labeling of it as "idle" was specifically intended to assert its nonteleological character. This means of course that idle curiosity does not really fit his definition of an instinct as a teleological category; nevertheless, he named it as one of the three basic instincts. Veblen actually introduced idle curiosity as an instinct in 1906—before McDougall published—but his description of it is so similar to McDougall's that he could have cited the latter's authority for almost everything he said about it. Veblen accounted for idle curiosity psychologically by arguing that the selective processes of the mind in thinking leave some data that are rejected, and that some account must be given of their effects. Such data, Veblen thought, set up their own subsidiary chain of reactions that results in a wholly aimless curiosity. It is just because idle curiosity is idle—that is, not teleological—that it can lead to the apprehension of facts in terms of efficient cause rather than final cause, and it is from idle curiosity that Veblen believed our matter-of-fact and scientific knowledge is derived.[22]

In many respects the most important of the instincts is the instinct of workmanship. Like idle curiosity, it does not precisely fit the definition of instinct, for it belongs to the category of means rather than to that of ends; yet like the parental bent it is teleological and does have its distinctive end—a desire for a job well done, for the efficient use of means, and hence for effective workmanship. The end of the instinct of workmanship is thus the efficient use of the means that are employed in attaining the ends specified by the other instincts—for example, the parental bent.[23] But this is not an adequate description of this somewhat ubiquitous instinct, for its influence seems to pervade the mind to a greater degree than that of the other instincts. The reason for this is its peculiar relation to intelligence. Both are in the category of means, both are teleological, and both are closely connected with the knowing process. It was primarily to the instinct of workmanship that Veblen attributed the rise of man from the brute to his present position. Moreover, it is from the instinct of workmanship that the phenomenon of contamination results—a factor of the greatest importance in Veblen's system. It is therefore necessary to consider somewhat more closely the nature and role of intelligence.

In Veblen's analysis of human nature, man was essentially an active and purposive creature who strove to satisfy certain instinctive desires. The ends of action were determined by instinctive proclivity; with the choice of ends, therefore, intelligence had nothing to do. But the instinct is differentiated from the tropism by the fact that it involves intelligence and consciousness, and the role assigned to intelligence is that of finding means whereby the instinctive ends may be attained. It follows, therefore, that the pattern of intelligence—its mode of operation—is teleological; it operates within the framework of the instincts or teleological categories. The knowledge produced by intelligence conforms to this pattern. The instincts act selectively in the field of cognition and order the data of sensation in a fashion analogous to that in which the Kantian categories operate. Human knowledge is thus systematized according to its general compatibility with these categories.

Since action and thought are teleological, the mind seeks to find the means that will attain its ends. But even here it is under the control of instinct, for it is the peculiar function of the instinct of workmanship to regulate the choice of those means. The end of this instinct is efficiency, and intelligence will therefore seek to find such means as will attain the ends with the maximum of efficiency. Once action patterns that serve as means have been found, they will be repeated, and the constant repetition of one mode of action or thought results in the production of a habit, or a resistance to changing the established mode of action. When the process of habituation is extended over a protracted period, resistance to change may acquire sufficient strength so that habits are perpetuated even when they have become grossly inefficient. Like the instincts, the habits, in proportion to their strength, become principles that affect the ordering of sense data in a selective fashion. The mental framework may thus be conceived as composed of two basic factors; instincts and habits, the former providing the ends, the latter means.[24]

Veblen held that "habits of thought are an outcome of habits of life."[25] This claim does not imply a strict determinism, nor a simple copy theory. Action relates to thought in several ways. First, ideas are plans of action,[26] and the outcome of executing those plans can force a revision of the ideas. There is thus an interaction between thought and action, each modifying and being modified by the other. Second, and more broadly, thinking occurs within a problem context defined by the failure of some habit of doing to work successfully, and so is conditioned by the action context in which the problem occurs. Man satisfies his instinctive values by doing, and thinking is called for only where action fails. Habits of life thus give rise to habits of thought because thought is essentially a tool for developing habits of action that will produce satisfactions of the instinctive ends.

It is from this composition of the mind—a combination of instincts and habits in interaction—that one form of the phenomenon of "contamination" arises, for it follows from the vague and general character of the instincts that there will be a certain degree of overlapping among them, and hence to some extent the same mental processes will be involved in each. From this it further follows that habits contracted in the service of one instinct will to an appreciable extent carry over into the service of another, thus producing contamination of one instinct by another.[27] Superficially, the general nature of this contamination is that of obstruction—the blocking of the free operation of the instinct by habit—but the true seriousness of this situation can be seen only through Veblen's use of the term "apperceptive mass":

> All facts of observation are necessarily seen in the light of the observer's habits of thought, and the most intimate and inveterate of his habits of thought is the experience of his own initiative and endeavors. It is to this "apperception mass" that objects of apperception are finally referred, and it is in terms of this experience that their measure is finally taken.[28]

The apperceptive mass comprises the whole of the instincts and habits, desired ends and formulated knowledge, which the mind contains and which it brings to bear upon sense data in the process of knowing. In Veblen's theory of knowledge, data is systematized in terms of this apperceptive mass with the result that sense experience is interpreted through principles some of which are already outmoded and false. It follows then that human knowledge is never abreast of the actual situation and that there is always a time lag between environmental and institutional change. To the dictum "whatever is is right" Veblen answered "whatever is is wrong," at least to some extent.[29]

But there are two further types of contamination that are important for Veblen's theory. One of these is emulation, which arises from a contamination of the instinct of workmanship. Emulation is a crusical factor in Veblen's theory, but its analysis must be postponed to a later point. The second, and most important, type of contamination is animism or anthropomorphism. Veblen spelled out the significance of this phenomenon as follows.

> But the most obstructive derangement that besets workmanship is what may be called the self-contamination of the sense of workmanship itself. . . . The difficulty has been spoken of as anthropomorphism, or animism—which is only a more archaic anthropomorphism. The essential trait of anthropomorphic conceptions, so far as bears on the present argument, is that conduct, more or less fully after the human fashion of conduct, is imputed to external objects.[30]

Animism means the imputation of teleology to what are actually matters of fact and hence a failure to understand the true relations among these factors. To this end the first type of contamination contributes. For in any act of knowing, the apperceptive mass, or complete body of knowledge, habits, and instincts in the mind, comes into play, and the new data are brought into harmony with it. Data thus become assimilated into our knowledge of reality just insofar as we are able to bring them into a relation of logical consistency with our other knowledge. Since the action of the mind under its instinctive proclivities (idle curiosity excepted) is teleological, data are systematized under the canons of teleological order with reference to the teleological ends in view. The instinct of workmanship, by focusing attention on the means used in the attempt to attain ends, leads to a consideration of the means apart from the ends—with respect to what they are in themselves as opposed to what can be done with them—and so comes to explain their character on teleological grounds on the assumption that the things have ends of their own.[31] This leads to an animistic habit of mind whereby general efficacy if referred to some further ground of "intention" or "purpose" on the part of natural objects.

Veblen's catalogue of instincts seems at first glance entirely arbitrary. Other instinct psychologists posited the existence of instincts similar to Veblen's, but they also posited the existence of a number of further instincts—pugnacity,[32] self-assertion,[33] emulation,[34] acquisitiveness.[35] What justification has Veblen to offer for making the selection he did? Veblen has two answers to this question. The first is that rather than posit a long list of instincts it is more parsimonious to posit a minimum set of instincts and then to show that the other phenomena that might occur on such a list can be derived from the minimum set. It is obvious that Veblen chose his minimum set so as to emphasize man's altruistic motives and minimize the selfish ones. The problem then becomes one of explaining why human beings, who are basically altruistic, are so patently selfish, and this requires a method of deriving the egotistic motives from the altruistic. One function of contamination is precisely to permit the derivation of such motives as emulation and self-assertion from the three basic instincts, as we shall see below. The second answer lies in his theory of cultural evolution—a theory that seems bizarre by today's standards but that was based on impressive authorities at the time he formulated it.

The basic scheme of social evolution Veblen took from Lewis Henry Morgan. In *Ancient Society*, Morgan advanced a linear progressionist evolutionary scheme that he asserted to hold universally.

> As it is undeniable that portions of the human family have existed in a state of savagery, other portions in a state of barbarism, and still other portions in

a state of civilization, it seems equally so that these three distinct conditions are connected with each other in a natural as well as a necessary sequence of progress. Moreover, that this sequence has been historically true of the entire human family, up to the status attained by each branch respectively, is rendered probable by the conditions under which all progress occurs, and by the known advancement of several branches of the family through two or more of these conditions.[36]

Morgan posited three major stages, two of which were trichotomized. Beginning with the most primitive, these were Lower Savagery, Middle Savagery, Upper Savagery, Lower Barbarism, Middle Barbarism, Upper Barbarism, and Civilization. Each was correlated with a particular cultural configuration, and the transition from one to another was marked by an invention or cultural innovation such as the introduction of pottery or the domestication of animals. Moreover, the times occupied by the stages Morgan believed to form a geometrical progression, with savagery having by far the longest period.[37]

Veblen borrowed this general scheme from Morgan but modified certain elements of it for his own purposes. He believed that habits of thought are an outcome of habits of action. Habits of action in turn are determined by the modes of production and distribution that prevail in the community, for the requirements of survival are the most imperative demands faced by people and determine most of their activity. But the modes of production and distribution themselves are determined by the state of the industrial arts—that is, by the knowledge underlying and embodied in technology. Hence Veblen saw the state of the industrial arts as the chief dynamic factor in social evolution. The industrial arts are of course knowledge—that is, habits of thought—so we have a closed process in which the industrial arts, having determined a given mode of production and distribution and thus certain habits of action, will in turn be modified by those habits of action. The process so defined is dynamic and will generate an endless sequence of changes; it is also cumulative in that at each moment the course of the process depends on the outcome of the process up to that time, and it is continuous in that change is always underway. For purposes of analysis and description, Veblen used the stages drawn from Morgan, but these are not steady states with leaps from one to another; they are rather segments of a process of continuous change.[38]

The earliest stage Veblen called savagery in accordance with Morgan's scheme. It was characterized by group struggle for subsistence, in the form of agriculture and herding, minimal technology, peace, poverty, group cooperation, considerable animism, and a matriarchial family structure.[39] When the progress of technological knowledge reached the point at which indirect production became important—at which the means of production became important apart from the product—and at which a surplus could be produced, the transition to barbarism occurred.[40] This stage was marked by the appearance of war, since there was now a surplus worth seizing, patriarchy, ownership of booty leading to the development of private property, increasing inequality of wealth and emphasis upon status, slavery, tyranny, emulation, animism, monotheism, and pecuniary control.[41] Barbarism developed in two forms that often overlapped—the predatory phase, in which ownership rested upon seizure by prowess, with war as the principal means, and the commercial phase, in which war gave way to commerce based on ownership by prescriptive right.[42] Barbarism in turn gave way to civilization, of which Veblen distinguished two phases—the earlier handicraft phase and the later machine era. The handicraft phase began in the late feudal age and extended to the eighteenth century, a period of five or six hundred years, and was initiated by the growth of handicraft production, itinerant merchandising, and industrial towns. Central to this era was the "masterless man" or independent craftsman, who was at once the maker and marketer of his own goods, and so was involved in both industrial and pecuniary concerns. Technological progress was rapid in this era, but it was for the sake of pecuniary gain—goods were rated in terms of price and pecuniary acquisition was the objective. The emergence of the price system, however, had the consequence that new methods of accounting were introduced, which in turn led to the development of statistics and so furthered the development of science. Indeed, science made rapid strides in the handicraft era, with the concept of efficient cause—itself based on the model of the craftsman producing his product—as its fundamental postulate.[43]

With the industrial revolution of the late eighteenth century, civilization moved into the machine era, its present state. The machine era began with the development of mechanical means of production too extensive to be owned and operated by the independent craftsman. As mechanization grew, ownership of the means of production became divorced from operation; the owners specialized increasingly in the pecuniary manipulation of production and distribution while the actual operation of the machines became the domain of wage labor. The result was a separation into classes of owners and workers, the former becoming increasingly removed from actual contact with productive processes while the latter came to be almost entirely occupied with them. The institutional effects of the machine process are as yet unclear, owing to its recent appearance, but Veblen particularly emphasized its impact upon scientific thought and upon thinking about causality generally. Instead of the handicraft notion of an efficient cause producing its effect as a craftsman produces his product, Veblen believed the machine had introduced a new concept of efficient causality as a cumulative sequence of change free from any anthropomorphic residue. It is this essentially mechanistic view of causality that Veblen believes the discipline of the machine is instilling into those who tend it and which will become the premise of the industrial arts of the machine age.[44]

The process of social evolution just described is an evolution of "institutions," by which Veblen meant habits of thought that have become established in the community. But with respect to human nature itself, Veblen believed the process of evolution to be quite different. Here he confronted conflicting theories: on the one hand was Darwin's theory of fortuitious variation, on the other Mendel's theory of stable types. Veblen opted for the latter, as amended by DeVries's theory of mutations. Extreme environmental pressure, Veblen believed, caused similar mutations simultaneously in a number of members of the group. Stable types thus originated as mutations from preexisting types and remained constant until some further occurrence of extraordinary environmental conditions produced a further mutation or until hybridization—that is, interbreeding with other types—altered the genetic endowment. In the former case, the result was an alteration in the basic physical and/or psychological structure, the psychological structure for Veblen being the instinctive endowment, while in the latter case greater variability was added to the population and greater adaptability.[45]

Veblen applied this theory to the origins of "races" of men, using the term "race" with the latitude customary in the early years of the twentieth century. His most detailed treatment of the subject concerned the origin of the "dolichocephalic blond race" of northern Europe.[46] The earliest traces of this race, he believed, went back to the late glacial period and postdated the early traces of the Alpine and Mediterranean races in Europe. Veblen argued that the Mediterranean race had entered Europe from Africa and that shortly thereafter the Mediterranean bridge had sunk, cutting off their retreat. The advance of the last glacier would have sufficiently altered the climatic conditions in the Mediterranean basin to have caused mutations among the members of the Mediterranean race. The result was a wide variety of mutants of which he believed the dolichocephalic blond to have been one. Under the environmental conditions caused by the glacial invasion, the vast majority of these mutants would have been eliminated, but the blond was one of the survivors, apparently the only major one. As the glacier retreated, the blond followed it north in order to remain in the climatic conditions favorable to its survival and finally settled in the Baltic area where such conditions were relatively stable. The blond thus appears as a mutant of the Mediterranean stock. Furthermore, he is a hybrid, for having been produced in the midst of another stock, there has been constant crossing and recrossing of the parent and mutant lines. Veblen thought this conclusion confirmed by the contemporary evidence that indicated that there was no pure blond community in existence and in fact none where the proportion of blonds exceeded 50 percent. The result of this hybrid character was a greater adaptability than a purebred race would have had.[47]

The point to be noted here is that the survival of the dolichocephalic blond was not a matter of adaptation. The range of adaptability, even of a hybrid stock, was relatively narrow. The blond survived because by native endowment he happened to be fitted to survive under the conditions then and since prevailing—not because he could change his genetic make-up to meet the situation. The environment selects by eliminating those whose native endowment does not permit an adequate adjustment; ability to adapt has a relatively limited role for Veblen, unlike some of his contemporaries.

What is true of the action of the natural environment is also true, Veblen held, of the action of the social environment. The genetic endowment of a race must permit its members to meet the requirements of the culture under which it lives or the selective process will operate to eliminate that race. The selective action of the social environment, however, requires a long time to operate decisively. Veblen followed Morgan in believing that the period of savagery was much longer than the subsequent periods, and so concluded that only savagery had lasted long enough to have selected those races of man whose instinctive endowment best fit its requirements. And clearly those instincts that best fit men for savagery were the parental bent and the instinct of workmanship.[48] Thus Veblen's argument for the universality of these instincts rests on his evolutionary theses that psychobiological types are relatively stable, that savagery selected the present races of man because they were well fitted to survive its rigors, that none of the other periods of his social evolutionary scheme had lasted long enough to play this selective role, and that no changes in environmental conditions since the ice age had been severe enough to produce large-scale mutations in the instinctive endowment then selected.

There is a further consequence of this doctrine. If the present races of man were selected by their fitness to the savage culture, and if human nature is as inflexible as Veblen believed, it follows that as the cultures under which men live depart progressively from the savage original, the fit between culture and human nature must become ever worse. Cultural evolution may therefore create a social environment to which man is so maladapted that his only alternatives are extinction or mutation. Veblen did not say that this was the present situation, but this consequence of his position helps to explain his pessimism about the future.[49]

Veblen repeatedly attacked classical economics for being what he termed "a taxonomic science" and called for an economics that would be "an evolutionary science." What was it that Veblen wanted? Clearly he wanted a science that focused on the process of change and that analyzed it in terms of causality conceived as invariable sequence. This meant not only banishing final causes but interpreting efficient cause as sequences of change in which each part of the process is the result of all that has gone before. Applied to human culture, Veblen said

> The growth of culture is a cumulative sequence of habituation, and the ways and means of it are the habitual response of human nature to exigencies that vary incontinently, cumulatively, but with something of a consistent sequence in the cumulative variations that so go forward—incontinently, because each new move creates a new situation which induces a further new variation in the habitual manner of response; cumulatively, because each new situation is a variation of what has gone before and embodies as causal factors all that has been affected by what went before; consistently, because the underlying traits of human nature (propensities, aptitudes and what not) by force of which the response takes place, and on the ground of which the habituation takes effect, remain substantially unchanged.[50]

Understanding of the growth of human culture is not to be found in tools or weapons or machines but in men.

> The changes that take place in the mechanical contrivances are an expression of changes in the human factor. Changes in the material facts breed further change only through the human factor. It is in the human material that the continuity of development is to be looked for; and it is here, therefore, that the motor forces of the process of economic development must be studied.[51]

Man provides both the continuity in the process and the change. It is the instinctive nature of man that is the constant, at least over the period of recorded history; that instinctive endowment has not changed since the glacial age. Change therefore is to be found in habits, particularly in habits of thought. Veblen uses the term "habit" in a very broad sense to include learned ways of acting, such as driving a car, and learned ways of thinking, which include not only methods of thought but also beliefs. As Veblen argued in the passage quoted above, men respond to exigencies of their environment, which constantly changes. Thus old habits of beliefs are challenged by new data resulting from the changed situation in which men act, and men must constantly readjust their beliefs to conform to the dynamic reality they confront.[52]

A habit of course characterizes an individual at a particular time. But when habits are widely shared and become established within a group, Veblen calls them "institutions." Thus for Veblen institutions are not organizations or objects but habits or complexes of habits. For example, when Veblen said that private property was an institution, it was not the objects owned to which he referred but the set of established beliefs constituting prescriptive rights and duties by virtue of which the objects are made to be property. Institutions, then, are shared established beliefs, and as beliefs change so institutions change.[53]

The aggregate of our beliefs constitutes our knowledge. The term "knowledge" is usually restricted to those beliefs that are true, but if it is extended to include all of our beliefs that we think are true, it will fairly match what Veblen regarded as the totality of our habits of thought. This body of habits of course changes over time; it is cumulative, having been created by our predecessors over many generations, and constitutes the starting point for each new inquiry; it is conservative, since we seek to make our knowledge consistent and new beliefs that contradict established beliefs are likely to be rejected; and it defines the world for action, since we plan and execute action in terms of the environment as we believe it to be. As institutions are beliefs that are shared and established in the group, the history of institutions is really the history of knowledge.

Veblen was no idealist. In fact, it is not unlikely that he was a materialist. Certainly he seems to have regarded human beings as biochemical entities, and he rejected religion outright. The primacy that he gave to ideas and beliefs as factors in cultural history had nothing to do with any theory of mindstuff or world spirit. Veblen was interested in causal processes, and in his view causal processes in the history of culture centered on human instincts and habits. A change in the natural or the social environment could produce effects only through changing the behavior of men, and that meant either changing instincts or changing habits. Instincts are the basic motivational factors, but instincts change only by being contaminated, and the contamination involves habits. It is therefore to habits, and primarily to habits of thought, that one must look to understand cultural change.

It is in terms of this theory of human nature and cultural evolution that one must interpret Veblen's economics. Although a full treatment of his economics is impossible here, the point can be established by considering one of the most basic themes of his economic writings, the conflict between industry and business. By "industry," Veblen meant the production and distribution of materially serviceable objects—that is, of material objects that serve the instinctive ends of man. As the aim of the parental bent is the material welfare of the community at large, serviceable objects will be those providing nutrition, shelter, heat, clothing, comfort, and similar basic needs. When Veblen talks about production and distribution in the industrial sense, he refers only to the physical processes involved in producing and distributing such goods. The production of corn means the biochemical process of growing corn in a field; the production of a table means the physical process of turning wood into a table. Similarly, distribution means the physical processes of moving goods from the point of production to the consumer. Industrial processes do not involve money or ownership; they are the purely physical (or biochemical) processes of creating serviceable object from raw material and transporting it to the person who will consume it. As Veblen says repeatedly, the processes of industry are those of efficient causality only.[54]

Such a definition of industry seems bizarre because we at once ask what values would impel men to produce and distribute goods if no monetary gain were involved. Veblen's answer is the values defined by the generic instincts. If men really value the material welfare of the community at large and efficiency, then they will carry out the processes Veblen calls industrial without there being any need for pecuniary values to be involved. Assuming that men really do have instincts of the sort Veblen claims they have, the value problem is solved without the introduction of pecuniary values, and the whole pecuniary structure is irrelevant to the production and distribution of materially serviceable goods.

What then is business? In Veblen's view, business is concerned not with the production and distribution of serviceable goods but with the exchange of goods. What happens in a business exchange is an exchange of the ownership of goods; exchange value is the value something has as an object of ownership.[55] And the ends served by ownership, in Veblen's sense of ownership as prescriptive right, are emulative ends—that is, ends that arise from the contamination of the instincts rather than from the pure instincts.[56] Production in the business sense means the production of pecuniary values rather than serviceable goods, and distribution means the distribution of income. Business is not of course independent of industry, for business exchange requires goods to be exchanged and the making of goods is an industrial activity, but the production of pecuniary values bears a highly variable relation to industrial production. Thus although there are situations in which pecuniary gain will be maximized by increasing industrial production, there are also cases in which the opposite is true. In the classic "overproduction" case, pecuniary gain is maximized by reducing the output of goods. But of course "overproduction" here refers to business production only; people may be dying for want of the goods in question, yet if the price of the goods is deemed too low from the standpoint of the businessmen who control the process, the situation is described as "overproduction." Business then involves the manipulation of the industrial process for the purpose of maximizing the pecuniary gains of those who own the means of production and distribution. And the values underlying this desire to maximize pecuniary gains are emulative values, and so derive from the contamination of the instincts.[57]

If the history of culture is the history of knowledge, then both the development and the conflict of business and industry should be explicable in these terms. That this is true for industry is quite clear. Economists take the factors of production to be land, labor, and capital. Veblen rejected this triad as the factors of production in industry, but he substituted a triad of his own that is roughly comparable. What corresponds to land in his scheme is the material environment—indeed, Veblen defined industrial production as the turning of the material environment to account for man's use. But the material environment, Veblen held, has been roughly constant throughout man's recorded history; it cannot therefore be a dynamic feature.[58] Corresponding to capital for Veblen is the state of the industrial arts—that is, the knowledge of science and technology held by the community at a given time. It is not tools or equipment, which may be thought of as capital goods, but the knowledge upon which they are based and which informs their use that is industrial capital. Thus in savagery, the loss of all the tools used in production would be unimportant, because they were so simple they could be easily replaced; but the loss of the technological knowledge underlying the tools would be fatal. The industrial arts, which are habits of thought, are the dynamic factor in industrial production, for as that knowledge grows so does man's command of his material environment.[59] What corresponds to labor in this scheme is the community at large. The application of the industrial arts to the material environment is done by the community as a whole. Further, it is the community that is the carrier of the industrial arts, since the amount of knowledge involved is always far too great for any one individual.[60] Industrial development therefore depends upon the community, the material environment, and the industrial arts, with the industrial arts, or scientific and technological knowledge, as the key dynamic factor.

Business also depends upon habits of thought, but in a more complex sense because contamination is here involved. In his early writings, Veblen made emulation the key value of the pecuniary culture, and in *The Theory of the Leisure Class* he described its origin as follows:

> As a matter of selective necessity, man is an agent. He is, in his own apprehension, a center of unfolding impulsive activity—"teleological" activity. He is an agent seeking in every act the accomplishment of some concrete, objective, impersonal end. By force of his being such an agent he is possessed of a taste for effective work and a distaste for futile effort. He has a sense of the merit of serviceability or efficiency and of the demerit of futility, waste, or incapacity. This aptitude or propensity may be called the instinct of workmanship. Wherever the circumstances or traditions of life lead to an habitual comparison of one person with another in point of efficiency, the instinct of workmanship works out in an emulative or invideous comparison of persons. . . . The result is that the instinct of workmanship works out in an emulative demonstration of force.[61]

But after the publication *The Theory of the Leisure Class* the importance attached to emulation rapidly decreases and Veblen increasingly stresses animism as the basis of the pecuniary culture. The reason is not that emulation ceases to be important but that Veblen came to see it as a product of animism and therefore took animism as the basic factor. The animistic origin of emulation is evident in the above passage, for emulation arises from the invidious comparison of individuals with respect to efficiency or force. This of course involves the imputation to the individual of causal efficacy; the individual sees himself as the cause of his actions and achievements. But Veblen denies this status to the individual. In his analysis, the individual's actions are the result of his instincts and habits. But as the instincts are part of the race inheritance carried by the community at large, so too the habits, or knowledge, that make the individual effective as an agent are part of the cultural heritage of knowledge that is created and transmitted by the community at large. With respect to neither instinct nor knowledge (ends or means) therefore can the individual be regarded as independent or autonomous. He is an agent in the sense that the hammer is an agent in the driving of the nail, not in the sense of a prime mover who initiates his own course of action. The invidious comparison that underlies emulation is thus based upon an erroneous imputation of causal efficacy in which the individual's subjective sense of himself as an agent is taken for true, thereby misconstruing the actual nature of the process.[62]

Very much the same analysis applies to ownership. Veblen holds that ownership originates in barbarism, in which booty serves as a sign of individual prowess, and is continued in the commercial phase of the pecuniary culture, in which wealth similarly serves as a sign of individual force. As in the case of emulation, there is a mistaken imputation of causal efficacy to the individual. Furthermore, the motive underlying ownership is emulation—the desire to excel in invidious comparisons of individual efficacy—so that the institution of ownership is animistic with respect to both its foundation and its use.[63]

It is at this point that one can see how radically Veblen differs from writers such as James and Dewey. In Veblen's view it is the group—the community—that is important in understanding sociocultural change, not the individual. It is the group that carries the gene pool that determines the instincts or motives of its members, and it is the group that creates and transmits the habits that provide the means for their fulfillment. Individuals are just particular combinations of instincts and habits, and their behavior is explained by their twin heritage; there is no significant role for human freedom, if indeed there is any such thing. A causal explanation of social evolution is for Veblen an explanation in terms of the instincts and habits of the group. All self-regarding motives arise from a failure to grasp this basic truth, for all of them arrogate to the individual the causal efficacy that in fact the individual derives from the group. By their animistic imputation of causal efficacy to the individual, a ground is provided for invidious comparison either among individuals or between individuals and the group and so for self-enhancement at the expense of others. All egotism, all doctrines of economic competition and natural rights, are for Veblen products of the animistic contamination of the instinct of workmanship. Veblen thus derives all the selfish motives of human nature from the altruistic ones through contamination—that is, through the false imputation of causal autonomy to objects that are in reality parts of a mechanical process.

These considerations should make it clear why Veblen believed that the machine discipline had the capacity to subvert the pecuniary culture. The machine process he held to be a strictly mechanical process based on causality as invariable sequence. Those who work with the machine process must come to understand it and so become accustomed to thinking in terms of such mechanical processes. But if this mode of analysis is turned upon the pecuniary culture, it will reveal the animistic character of the whole activity. From Veblen's point of view, the entire pecuniary culture is a system of reasoned make-believe, and once recognized as such he believed those institutions on which it depended, such as ownership, would lose their credibility.[64]

But Veblen's theory is not one that leads to happy endings. Even if industry triumphed and the pecuniary culture was swept away, there was no guarantee that this outcome would be beneficial for mankind. For in Veblen's view, man's instinctive endowment dated from the late glacial era and man was best adapted to savagery—a culture in which animism was prevalent. The evolution of culture meant an ever-widening disparity between man's latest culture and that to which he was originally adapted. Veblen saw signs in the America of his day of a reaction against the machine process and the notion of impersonal causal sequence, and he thought it entirely possible that industrial culture would not be congenial enough to man's instinctual nature to permit a satisfactory adjustment. Moreover, there was no reason to believe that the state of the industrial arts had reached perfection, and its further development might well make the industrial order obsolete and replace it with some other economic order, the discipline of which would work to undermine the plausibility of just such causal analyses as that written by Veblen.[65] As Veblen rejected a teleological reading of evolution and with it the notion of progress, there was no guarantee that the races of man would prosper. As he put it on the eve of World War I,

> History records more frequent and more spectacular instances of the triumph of imbecile institutions over life and culture than of peoples who have by force of instinctive insight saved themselves alive out of a desperately precarious institutional situation, such, for instance, as now faces the peoples of Christendom.[66]

Notes

1. Morton White, *Social Thought in America* (New York: Viking, 1949).

2. Joseph Dorfman, *The Economic Mind in American Civilization* (New York: Viking, 1949), Vol. 3, p. 438.

3. Joseph Dorfman, *Thorstein Veblen and His America* (New York: Viking, 1947), Chaps. 3-5.

4. Thorstein Veblen, "Kant's Critique of Judgment," in Thorstein Veblen, *Essays in Our Changing Order*, ed. Leon Ardzrooni (New York: Viking, 1945), pp. 175-193. This volume of essays will be referred to hereafter as *ECO*.

5. *Ibid.*, p. 175.

6. *Ibid.*, pp. 179-180.

7. *Ibid.*, pp. 180-181.

8. J. D. McFarland, *Kant's Concept of Teleology* (Edinburgh: University of Edinburgh Press, 1970).

9. Veblen, "Kant's Critique," p. 181.

10. *Ibid.*, p. 192.

11. *Ibid.*, P. 186. See also Stanley Matthew Daugert, *The Philosophy of Thorstein Veblen* (New York: King's Crown Press, 1950), Chap. 1.

12. Thorstein Veblen, "Why Is Economics Not an Evolutionary Science?" in Veblen, *The Place of Science in Modern Civilization* (New York: Huebsch, 1919), p. 74. This volume of essays will be referred to hereafter as *PSMC*. Veblen, "The Instinct of Workmanship and the Irksomeness of Labor," in *ECO*, pp. 79–96; Veblen, "The Place of Science in Modern Civilization," in *PSMC*, p. 5; Veblen, "The Preconceptions of Economic Science III," in *PSMC*, pp. 155–157.

13. William McDougall, *An Introduction to Social Psychology* (London: Methuen and Co., 1908), p. 19.

14. *Ibid.*

15. *Ibid.*, p. 29.

16. *Ibid.*, p. 26.

17. *Ibid.*, pp. 27–28.

18. Thorstein Veblen, *The Instinct of Workmanship* (New York: Viking, 1946), pp. 12–37.

19. *Ibid.*, p. 3.

20. *Ibid.*, Chap. 1.

21. *Ibid.*, pp. 25–37.

22. *Ibid.*, pp. 86–88; Thorstein Veblen, "The Evolution of the Scientific Point of View," in *PSMC*, pp. 40–45.

23. Veblen, *The Instinct of Workmanship*, pp. 26–37.

24. *Ibid.*, Chap. 4. Veblen, "The Instinct of Workmanship," in *ECO*, p. 88.

25. Veblen, "The Evolution of the Scientific Point of View," in *PSMC*, p. 38.

26. Veblen, "The Place of Science," in *PSMC*, p. 5.

27. Veblen, *The Instinct of Workmanship*, pp. 40–41.

28. *Ibid.*, p. 53.

29. Thorstein Veblen, *The Theory of the Leisure Class* (New York: Random House, 1934), p. 207.

30. Veblen, *The Instinct of Workmanship*, p. 52.

31. *Ibid.*, pp. 54–62.

32. McDougall, *An Introduction to Social Psychology*, p. 62.

33. *Ibid.*, p. 65.

34. William James, *The Principles of Psychology* (New York: Henry Holt, 1910), Vol. 2, p. 409.

35. *Ibid.*, Vol. 2, p. 422.

36. Lewis Henry Morgan, *Ancient Society* (New York: World Publishing Co., 1967), p. 3. First published in 1877.

37. *Ibid.*, Chaps. 1 and 2.

38. Thorstein Veblen, "On The Nature of Capital," in *PSMC*, pp. 324–327.

39. Veblen, *The Instinct of Workmanship*, Chap. 3.

40. *Ibid.*, p. 150.

41. *Ibid.*, Chap. 4.

42. *Ibid.*, pp. 171–172, 202.

43. *Ibid.*, Chap. 6.

44. *Ibid.*, Chap. 7.

45. *Ibid.*, Chap. 1. On De Vries, see G. Allen "Hugo De Vries and the Reception of the 'Mutation Theory,' " *Journal of the History of Biology* II (1969): 55–87.

46. See Joseph Deniker, *The Races of Man* (Freeport, N.Y.: Books for Libraries Press, 1971), especially Chap. 9. First published 1900.

47. Thorstein Veblen, "The Mutation Theory and The Blond Race," in *PSMC*, pp. 457–476; Veblen, "The Blond Race and The Aryan Culture," in *PSMC*, pp. 477–496.

48. Veblen, *The Instinct of Workmanship*, p. 36.

49. *Ibid.*, Chap. 7.

50. Thorstein Veblen, "The Limitations of Marginal Utility," in *PSMC*, pp. 241–242.

51. Veblen, "Why Is Economics Not an Evolutionary Science?" in *PSMC*, pp. 71–72.

52. Veblen, *The Instinct of Workmanship*, Chap. 2.

53. Thorstein Veblen, "The Beginnings of Ownership," in *ECO*, pp. 32–49; "The Limitations of Marginal Utility," in *PSMC*, pp. 241; *The Instinct of Workmanship*, pp. 151–153; "Why Is Economics Not an Evolutionary Science?" is *PSMC*, pp. 74–79; "The Evolution of the Scientific Point of View," in *PSMC*, pp. 38–39.

54. Thorstein Veblen, *The Vested Interests and the Common Man* (New York: Huebsch, 1920), p. 55; "On the Nature of Capital," in *PSMC*, pp. 324–351; Veblen, *Absentee Ownership* (New York: Viking, 1945), p. 126; Veblen, *The Theory of Business Enterprise* (New York: Charles Scribner's Sons, 1935), Chap. 2.

55. Thorstein Veblen, "The Preconceptions of Economic Science II," in *PSMC*, p. 142; Veblen, "Industrial and Pecuniary Employments," in *PSMC*, pp. 296–298, 311; Veblen, "On the Nature of Capital II," in *PSMC*, p. 352; Veblen, *The Theory of Business Enterprise*, Chaps. 3 and 4.

56. Veblen, "Industrial and Pecuniary Employments," in *PSMC*, p. 299.

57. *Ibid,*; Veblen, *The Instinct of Workmanship*, Chap. 5; Veblen, *The Theory of Business Enterprise*, pp. 214–222.

58. Veblen, *Absentee Ownership*, pp. 125–126; Veblen, "Why Is Economics Not an Evolutionary Science?" in *PSMC*, p. 71.

59. Veblen, "On the Nature of Capital," in *PSMC*, pp. 324–386; Veblen, "Professor Clark's Economics," in *PSMC*, p. 185.

60. Veblen, *The Instinct of Workmanship*, p. 141; Veblen, "On the Nature of Capital," in *PSMC*, pp. 325–326.

61. Veblen, *The Theory of the Leisure Class*, pp. 15–16.

62. Veblen, *The Instinct of Workmanship*, pp. 103, 138–186; Veblen, "The Beginnings of Ownership," in *ECO*, pp. 33–49.

63. Veblen, *The Theory of the Leisure Class*, Chaps. 2 and 3; Veblen, "The Beginnings of Ownership," in *ECO*, pp. 32–49.

64. Veblen, *The Instinct of Workmanship*, pp. 318, 333; Veblen, "Industrial and Pecuniary Employments," in *PSMC*, pp. 314–323.

65. Veblen, *The Instinct of Workmanship*, Chap. 7.

66. *Ibid.*, p. 25.

8 | The "Two Cultures" and the Modern Imagination

Leon Edel

> Tell me where is Fancy bred
> Or in the heart or in the head?
> How begot, how nourished?
> William Shakespeare,
> *The Merchant of Venice*

Where lies the begetting in the human imagination?

In proposing to discuss this subject I return to C. P. Snow's 1959 Rede Lecture at Cambridge University, "The Two Cultures and the Scientific Revolution." In this lecture Snow refers constantly to intellectuals—"literary intellectuals"—at one pole, and at the other, "the physical scientists." The literary intellectuals, he says, are as ignorant of science as if they functioned in the time of the Plantagenets. On the other hand, literature is an open book to the scientists. This seemed to me in 1959, as it does now, a false comparison, a specious compartmentalization. It is inevitable that the creative spirit in the arts should take a different form from the creative spirit in science—but not in the underlying "imagination," which begets both. It is equally true (as Snow quite properly argued) that the

146

greatest ignorance resides in politics and government where decisions have to be made involving the uses of our scientific revolution and where only scientists are competent to explain what legislators too lightheartedly vote—such matters as the atom, the supreme terror and terrorist of our time—or such fantasies as "star wars." What I find strange in Snow's lengthy lecture, which fills fifty-two printed pages, is his avoidance of the word "imagination." Snow, at one moment, lets drop the phrase "imaginatively or intellectually," but he never again returns to the word. His key appellation is "intellectual." He looks constantly at our higher thinking power rather than at the sensations. He lets the rational mind suffice in describing the work of the mind's creative or constructive power. To illustrate his thesis, Lord Snow compares the thrill he derived from pondering the second law of themodynamics with the thrill he experiences reading Shakespeare. He is astonished to find that literary critics and other nonscientists are usually unaware of the second law. "Yet," he says, "I was asking something which is about the scientific equivalent of: *Have you read a work of Shakespeare?*"[1]

This statement, coming from a man who had begun as a scientist and then shifted to the writing of autobiographical fiction, lacks the exactitude we might expect of one scientifically trained. His phrase "about the scientific equivalent" is an equivocation. There is very little equivalence—save that both are works of the imagination. A scientific law is a work of the rational mind: it sets out to solve a specific problem. A play by a poet of Shakespeare's *envergure*—the spread of his wings of imagination and emotion, its use of language rather than formulae or mathematical logic—deals with human dilemmas usually depicted for us but never resolved save in hubris and death. Snow was wrong to speak of "cultures" when he meant simply difficulties in communication between two differently trained imaginations. Artists, being ignorant of mathematics and physics and the language of the laboratory, are likely to experience less emotion when confronted by a physical law, however much the beauty of its logic and thought; but the universal language of Shakespeare—a few archaisms aside—is emotionally intelligible to all who know the English language.

The true point of connection between Snow's "two cultures" resides in the ability of humans to have intellectual-emotional fusion. This we call the imagination. Although there exists a great difference in expression between scientist and artist, there is little difference in the deeper creative process, what we might call the imagination of discovery, which ends in finding and making on such a high level that we invoke the word "genius." In that high realm scientist and artist are creatively alike.

I speak empirically, having devoted many years to writing the lives of men and women of imagination. This has meant exploring their origins, their heredity, their inner natures, their personalities, their "conditioning," their psychological being—all the visible and invisible forces that may have led them into the expression in various ways of their uncommon being, their genius. Yet I have discovered, in my quest, that genius can give very little account and explanation of its particular self. The biographical surveyor and map maker faces mysteries and emotional obstacles and is often left in darkness with descriptions of secrets rather than answers to them. The wellsprings of creation remain in general invisible and must be explored as Freud and his successors explored the unconscious, through dreams, fancies, forms of utterance and of being. The explorer is reduced to inference and surmise.

We make too much of a difference between scientist and artist. We invent obstacles and conflicts simply because they work with different means to different ends. Yet in this work their imaginations belong to the common human order and function. Science, to be sure, is insistent on concretions the artist cannot produce save as finished work. In an early novel, Snow explained this with great lucidity:

> Science was true in its own field; it was perfect within its own restrictions . . . one goes to science for an answer . . . a scientific fact now does not enlighten us on the nature of all facts . . . [scientists] no doubt get their moments of ecstasy, as I did once in my youth, when I saw a scientific truth disclose itself to my mind. . . . Human intricacies I might enjoy for their own sense.[2]

Apparently between 1934 and 1959, Snow had become less flexible and forgotten that the "human intricacies" of which he spoke, are revealed in Shakespeare but not solved in the second law of thermodynamics or other laws of science. No play of Shakespeare is concerned with any one thing, any one answer. The plays contain mounting human inquiry and energy, profound and often unanswerable, save in the highly wrought emotion of the language—however inexact that language may be. Shakespeare himself described this:

> And as imagination bodies forth
> The forms of things unknown; the Poet's pen
> Turnes them to shapes and gives to airy nothing
> A local habitation and a name.
> *A Midsummer Night's Dream* (V:1:14)

It is from the imagination that the creator proceeds to concretions. Poets are not concerned with the genesis or even the process. They are willing to allow for associational magic and illumination. Ever since Freud's exploration of the unconscious through dreams we have come to recognize that both the hidden stuff of the unconscious and the hidden modes of the imagination elude our grasp. The imagination is a complex of hidden things, invisible and reinforced by preconscious memory, a gathering-in also of components of "experience." Trying to see them, William James wrote, was like turning on the light in order to examine the darkness. And when he sought to describe "consciousness" he fell back on the metaphor of a stream. Perhaps because of these difficulties, Snow preferred to stick to the concrete things brought up by the intellect and a world of scientific laws.

We tend often to overlook the simplest kind of fact (or so it seems)—the fact of our imaginative ability to match like with like, to see similarities hidden within dissimilarities, to recognize that the imagination contains ambivalence and strikes out into the fantastic and the incredible as well as into the "real." How many torments and disasters we can conjure up in an hour or a day! Henry Jame's phrase for this was "the imagination of disaster," which critics solemnly quoted without seeing that he was attempting to describe human anxiety.[3] The individual who doesn't experience anxiety is usually never a genius and is more likely to be a psychopath. Anxiety is an important element in the imaginative process and we persevere in order to overcome it in both science and the arts.

Imagination functions best when it performs the act of conquering anxiety; it then enters into creative action and by this means circumvents depression and a sense of futility. In moments of serenity it is capable of being decisive: it is then that it best leaps into the unknown, or makes combinations of disparate sensory and material experiences to arrive at a novel synthesis or fusion. If you tell me I speak in gross subjectivities, my answer can only be, yes, indeed—and these are the essences of artistic and scientific inquiries and creativities.

Creation is the imagination in action. We can discuss such action in reasonably concrete and even scientific terms. But when we attempt to touch the stuff of the imagination we deal in strange, often indescribable, forces. The magic of association is attended by unearthy divinities; at times we have a sense of dealing with the occult. What else does the word "inspiration" suggest? This may be why the Greeks invented extrahuman creatures to preside, under Apollo himself, as our Muses of inspiration and artistic performance. Imagination at its height is a moment of thought and connection, a mingling of disparate emotions and energies accompanied by an enormous sense of excitement and release. We partake of flashes of lightning not unlike those of the human sexual act, that cherished pleasure so intense and so driving that it seems to propel us—as Freud insisted—through our greatest acts of life.

Because I believe in a human order of life, and the processes of living, I have a feeling that all we can say about the imagination and creation is in reality a paradigm for the act of love, the supreme act—that coupling of male and female that assures the continuity of the race. The fusion of sperm and ovum makes a new life, equipped normally with human physicality and human sensory feeling in its state of evolution and growth; it is completed not only at adulthood but in all the subsequent stages leading to fulfillment of existence and death. If we accept the paradigm, it is possible to speak constructively of creation in the arts and sciences, and to recognize that they operate under a human law, a kind of supremacy of cause and effect. That is creativity.

The imagination belongs to another sphere, the sphere that precedes creation. The imagination is the act of believing and loving, of wooing, of coupling, a coupling of many forms. The strategies of courtship belong to the animal kingdom as well: one has only to observe animals in pursuit of mating to see that they too proceed with an intensity and fever that resembles the intensities of the human order. But they obey instincts: humans often creatively disobey. Sometimes the act of the imagination fails; there is rejection, there is mismating, there are accidents. We see a process of trial and error. And even such seemingly mechanical procedures as artificial insemination, on whatever level, are preceded by imaginative scientific and physical phases.

II

Let me not labor this parallel. I think, as I speak, of a rare moment of creation and emotion in the life of Jean Jacques Rousseau that he described in a letter to Chrétian Malesherbes, one of his admirers.[4] In it he told of his greatest moment of illumination, when he conceived his celebrated hypothesis that all men are born free and equal, that it is society that robs them of freedom and equality. A daring and magnificent hypothesis, and we still feel its effects. Anarchism was founded upon it. It inspired revolutions. Yet it remains a rather poorly tested hypothesis, given DNA and other scientific advances in our time. Unequal genes, unequal brains; but equality at the ballot box—when such are provided—and before the law, when there is justice. In his letter, Rousseau tells how he set out one day to walk to Vincennes, where his friend Diderot was imprisoned.

As he walked, Rousseau read a newspaper and in his casual strolling way, with his mind wandering freely, he suddenly saw a paragraph announcing an essay contest arranged by one of France's academies. The subject was corollary to our subject today—whether the arts and sciences had enlarged or corrupted civilization. Rousseau, from the moment he saw this paragraph, found his mind suddenly grappling with a tumult of ideas: the few words acted as a trigger to a kind of inner explosion. We must go by his account, there is no other; he was suddenly overcome by a powerful sensation that he was touching eternal truth. I can liken what happened only to the moment of orgasm. He wrote: "Suddenly I felt my mind dazzled by a thousand flashes of enlightenment; swarms of vivid ideas presented themselves to me with a force and confusion which threw me into a state of indescribable turmoil! I felt overcome by a giddiness resembling intoxication."[5]

What Rousseau is describing is an unusual moment of imaginative fusion. It doesn't matter, and serves us little to ask, whether he is making it up or not, whether he really had this idea in this way, or only had it when he was describing it in his letter. The point is that it originated within him, within his mind and his emotions. If it was a fiction it was a very beautiful fiction and certainly a very imaginative one, for he went on the describe the effects quite as if a sexual act had taken place. There was a series of moments of amnesia, and when he recovered his rational mind he found himself lying beside the road, under a tree. Tears were streaming down his face; his shirt was soaked with a salt-water bath it had received.

All this is to be found in Rousseau's astounding letter to Malesherbes. It was written thirteen years after the stroll to Vincennes. "Oh! Sir," wrote Rousseau, "had I been able to write down the quarter of what I saw and felt under that tree, how clearly would I have shown up all the contradictions of the social system; how forcibly I would have exposed all the abuses of our institutions; with what simplicity I would have demonstrated that man is good naturally and that it is by their institutions alone that men become wicked."[6]

Historians have wondered about the accuracy of Rousseau's memory and to what extent his account to Malesherbes may have been a dreamlike fantasy. To a critic imbued, as I am, with the nature of dream this has less importance than the emotional content.[7] Individuals undergoing psychoanalysis have on occasion boasted to me how they fooled their analysts by inventing a few dreams during long hours of anxiety-provoking silence. They little realized that an invented dream is an act of their imagination and quite as useful to the analyst as any other part of their verbal evocations. Rousseau's account is a description of his emotion and his imagination: there was a meeting of disparate items in the orgasmic moment he celebrated. He says to himself, look at society, it is bad, filled with evil and deceit and tyranny; look at the newborn babe, chaste and virginal, about to be bombarded by this antagonistic and coercive society. We can see in Rousseau's flight into liberty and equality how the idea of the noble savage arose in the minds of the Europeans—the idea that savages in their wild state were uncontaminated by the high civilization of the Enlightenment and the residuals of feudalism. Perhaps they did not have the example of the Hawaiian Islands, where the *alii*—the nobles—controlled the society; Rousseau would have rebelled against them quite as much as he did against the societies of the civilized. We may be sure that Rousseau's epochal bath of tears was not evoked by the simple title of the essay contest—the call for an essay on the corruption of the arts and sciences by civilization. What Rousseau's mind and emotions heard was the corruption of the human entity by social contracts and social evils. We predicate that what was occurring within Rousseau was a flood of memories of his own struggle with human institutions as against his simplistic romanticism; his instincts had been unduly subjugated and he cried to be free, to have the liberty of the American Indian roaming the unfurnished continent. And so he spoke for the innate goodness of men and women, his own sense of his own innate goodness and the quarrel of his own purities with the treacheries of the world.

III

These moments of inspiration, of insight, of imagination, of clairvoyance—of sharp and clear seeing—have deep emotional strength. They are intimately known to those who have embarked on scientific experiments or have suddenly, on the literary side, seen them arise in fusions of poetry and narrative, in documents and texts, when disconnected ideas and feelings acquire the subtlest kinds of connections, connections that take place mysteriously in our inner selves to form a new wholeness. James Joyce described, or tried to describe, this in his *A Portrait of the Artist as a Young Man*, using Shelley's formulation of the moment when the mind is like a glowing coal.[8] *Integritas, consonantia, claritas*—he was deep into the doctrines of St. Thomas Aquinas. Sometimes these moments of *claritas* may seem, when described, like small potatoes, but I have always vibrated and tingled in my own memories of this kind of moment. I experienced such a moment when I was eighteen. It remains unforgettable. I was in late adolescence, discovering the richness and wonder of reading. I had the freedom of the stacks in the college library and experienced a profound excitement, as if all the secrets of life were opening up for me. My imagination had been fired by my reading the stream-of-consciousness passages in Joyce's *Ulysses*, in a copy smuggled by someone from France, for it was then a banned book. One of my professors had suggested that I might look at the works of Henry James as one of Joyce's significant predecessors. I found an entire tier in the stacks devoted to James, then just ten years dead; and as I dipped into these volumes, mystified by so rich a use of language, I found myself fascinated by mention that between 1890 and 1895 James had stopped writing novels and tried to write plays—but had been a wretched failure. Then he resumed writing novels and brought into being the most complex fictions ever written.

The critics[9] who told me this also lamented Jame's wasting five years on bad plays when he could have gone on writing good novels. I did not have Rousseau's orgasmic moment, but my mind began to tingle; a lot of little bells rang along my spine. What if James had applied his play writing experiences, the experiences of his failure, to the writing of *The Ambassadors* or *The Spoils of Poynton* or *The Golden Bowl*? I shuddered with delight at this thought of cause and effect. I spent several days reading all available books to discover whether anyone else had had this idea. No one had. Everyone dismissed the play writing. James himself had been very secretive about it: he felt it was a sordid adventure for a man of letters to have to put up with mercenary managers and exhibitionistic actors and actresses. The hypothesis continued to thrill me. James had been, I said to myself, a novelist turned playwright. Could it be that in the end he was a playwright—even though a bad one—turned novelist again? carrying into the pages of his fiction the secrets he had learned?

As you see, to a scientist this might be small potatoes. But they had a delicious taste to my unformed self. When it came time to choose a doctoral subject at the Sorbonne, I chose Jame's "dramatic years." The Sorbonne, long before American universities, had a chair devoted to American studies. After a lot of research and talks with the actors and dramatists who had known James—Bernard Shaw and Harley Granville Barker among others—and months in the newspaper reading room of the British Museum at Colindale trying to unearth the precise details of each failed play, I defended my dissertation in the Salle Louis Liard before an august jury of French specialists in English and American literature.[10] The jury knew little about James, and couldn't be as enthusiastic as I was, but they grudgingly agreed that I had fulfilled the requirements for the degree.

I can hear the scientific members of this audience saying that my hypothesis remains a hypothesis, even though I had shown the dramatic structure of the later novels. All novels contain elements of drama. All novels use dialogue. I had convinced myself, and my published dissertation would convince a few others. But like thousands of dissertations, and my accompanying tingles of the spine, my discovery remained a conjecture. I went on to other work and other studies. At some point, about five years after taking my degree, the James family gave me access to Henry James's papers, then still in their possession. They would later give them to Harvard. I was allowed to rummage among vast quantities of letters and to look in trunks that appeared to have never been opened after Henry James's death. At the bottom of a sea-chest, amid typescripts of the failed plays, I found a batch of old scribblers containing notes—some of them dated—in which, as James said, he was taking blank sheets of paper into his confidence. I found outlines of stories and plays in his big scrawl, invocations to his guardian angel and the mysteries of his imagination, passages such as

> All life is—at my age, with all one's artistic soul the record of it—in one's pocket, as it were. . . . Try everything, do everything, render everything—be an artist, be distinguished, to the last. . . . I have only to live and to work, to look and to feel, to *gather*, to note. My *cadres* are all there, continue, ah, continue, to fill them.[11]

These goadings of the self into confidence and purpose illuminate his often dry pages of mechanical working out of plots. And then I came on the passages describing his defeat in the theatre, and suddenly on the following:

> Has a part of all this wasted passion and squandered time (of the last five years) been simply the precious lesson taught me in that roundabout and devious, that cruelly expensive way *of the singular value for a narrative plan too* of the (I don't know what adequately to call it) divine principle of the scenario . . . a key that working in the same *general* way fits the complicated chambers *of both* the dramatic and the narrative lock?[12]

I was eighteen again: the bells were ringing once more along my spine, and Henry James was saying, very elegantly and symbolically, what I had discerned in my immature youth. His posthumous words had validated my old hypothesis and in language that reminds me of the sperm and the ovum: the key that fits "in the same general way" the complicated chambers of drama and narrative. I am ready to be accused of being very Freudian, but even without Freud, the key and the lock, in our time, and after our sexual revolution, eloquently speak of the creative act as well as the perpetuation of the race.

IV

I hope I have demonstrated some small part of the way in which our imagination works, of how constructive we can be. The imagination of literature or the arts, the imaginations of love and of disaster, the anxieties and triumphs of our bringing together moments of insight and perception, resemble the moments in science when chemicals mix and explode or physical laws are juggled in impressive formulae involving mass, weight, velocity, the speed of light—I offer you the typical jumble of a nonscientific person. We know too that once the imagination takes its leap, whether to small potatoes or earth-shaking (and earth-destroying) discovery, there follows a great deal of donkey work—my apologies to the helpful donkey! Who can say how many years of inner struggle and ferment and drudgery lit up Rousseau's lightning stroke on the road to Vincennes? I think at this moment of the donkey work Pierre and Marie Curie carried out for seemingly endless days melting down tons of pitchblend in order to extract a tiny bit of dangerous radium. The donkey work is a part of the adventure. My researches at Colindale were quite like melting down pitchblend: my quest was for evidence that might explain my illumination. James had written in his notebook after his remarks about the key and the lock, "I almost hold my breath with suspense as I try to formulate it"—and the "it" was, he said, "a portentous little discovery." So it had been for me. And James also wondered whether he was exaggerating the importance of this "little discovery," its magicality. I have heard scientists describe the same kind of magicality, and I often think, in this respect, of Fleming's coming on penicillin when he found the molds destroying bacteria.

In writing the lives of men and women I have found that the new psychology—that is, the psychoanalytical psychology of Freud and his successors—has greatly enlarged our understanding of the universality of the imagination, its mischievous ambiguities and its action in the creative process. We all imagine things. The negative imagination tries and succeeds in frightening us with the imagination of disaster. The positive imagination sets us daydreaming about palaces, privileges, divans and dancing girls, miracles and wonders. It is a great source of fiction in the form of wishful thinking; among scientists too hypotheses often express fiction before they become fact. That is why science has so rigidly pursued evidence and proof. Psychological evidence, whether in a physical gesture or in our use of words, in our dreams or our behavior, often can reveal secrets, but we tend to be inattentive to this kind of evidence.[13]

What did Freud do to further our understanding of the imagination? His greatest contribution was to make us aware of the unconscious and to demonstrate the truths that lie within the fantastic in our dreams—truths we refuse to tell ourselves during our waking hours. He showed how a slip of the tongue or of the pen is often a truth we were concealing from ourselves. Harry Stack Sullivan, adapting Freud, and William James spoke of "selective inattention" —our tendency in anxiety not to see or hear what is disagreeable to us.[14] The 1984 American presidential election showed how a great part of this television-fixated nation prefers role playing and fiction to the hard facts of government. We are by nature self-deceivers. Our imagination, which tries constantly to lead us astray, also provides us with a wide-ranging ability to grasp at all that we mythologize and beneficently understands the human capacity for metamorphosis. Psychoanalytical psychology distinguishes between the imagined unreal and the real, and helps keep us on guard against self-delusion and paranoia. Advertising long ago tuned in to human self-deception. The language of advertising is spread thick across our lives: it is a kind of euphemism that has been changing our language in significant ways to tell half-truths. Undertakers become morticians; elderly persons become senior citizens; street cleaners and garbage men become sanitation squads. We can all testify to this obfuscating process. We have all seen television commercials that associate in our minds the frenetic behavior of drunkenness with bubbling soft drinks. The euphemisms are designed to make us "feel good." Advertising knows the nation's oral and anal needs. It is quite as effective as propaganda in totalitarian states. Who has not sung a commercial in the shower? The instruments we create can be horrendous as well as benign. The language of the unconscious is extremely important for the understanding of any form of creativity.

We have metaphors of disease and illness as well, and the language of the unconscious creates them. There is a relation between illness and creativity: it has been the subject of some of the most striking works of the imagination of our time, as those who have read Thomas Mann's *The Magic Mountain* know. The biographer reads the language of pathology or disease in the writings of genius. We have studied literature as if it were an intellectual process untouched by emotion. The reverse is true. It is an emotional process that is constantly being rationalized. I have demonstrated in my book *Stuff of Sleep and Dreams*[15] and other writings how depression colors every creative life and its phases are reflected in the life-pattern and the life-work. The romantics used to call it melancholy; Benjamin Rush, the inspired physician who was a signer of the Declaration of Independence, called it *tristimania*. We know that none of us escape it—and usually the most euphoric individuals are often compensating for their chronic blues. Different stages in life have their depressions; the depressions of aging, or youth, are marked among all of us and notably among writers, for they give voice to it. We need no test-tube science to observe this and to see it written out in poetry, in Keats or Whitman, and in music, in the long sad and depth-shaking slow movements of Mozart or Beethoven and in many passages of even so stolid-seeming a citizen as Johann Sebastian Bach, the least mercurial of geniuses. Creation siphons off stored aggressive feelings that have found no outlet, grievances that have had no escape, the hidden hatreds of the heart. Even before Freud, William James and Bergson demonstrated how we are great repositories of undischarged feelings. The civilization Jean Jacques Rousseau blamed for our troubles does indeed put barriers in front of our primitive instincts and our imagination of disaster; it does breed our anxieties. The writer, the composer, the painter, discharge such stresses in a kind of creative self-therapy that brings release. Small wonder that Kafka spoke of writing as being a form of prayer—both supplication and fulfillment. But like the sexual drive, or the hunger drive, we move from release to stress, from fulfillment to further need. As vessels of wrath empty themselves, they are inevitably filled up again. If the frustrations and stresses are extreme, we use desperate measures. Two notable examples in our time are those of T. S. Eliot, who reduced his abulia by writing "The Waste Land," and Virginia Woolf, who after many years of manic depression—and some forty-five books—finally achieved her suicide.

V

Some scientists or their researchers shrug off the unconscious as something we can't taste, or smell, or touch, or perceive. They insist upon the palpable and the material. It is true: the unconscious is perceived only through the shadows it casts, the data it projects; we study it by inference. But its data is abundant. I usually reply to such scientists, "And your atom? I have never tasted, knowingly touched, smelled or seen an atom, or a quasar or a quark" (and the quark exists as a joke in the pages of James Joyce, probably one of his derivations from the snark). Is it not a matter for wonder that the great discoveries of our time belong to the invisible?[16]—testimony indeed to the remarkable creative energy lodged in the human imagination, its ability to pick up signs and wonders and discover hidden patterns, and deduce the unknown from the known. The imagination proceeds from fiction to truth, or from truth to fiction—and we must be on constant guard against its wonderful fantasies and learn how to use them—from hypothesis to demystification. I am certain that the greatest discoveries of science, those that have diminished disease and may decrease poverty and suffering, which are supposed to banish rage and war, will go on creating their Frankensteins as well. Life is a constant mixture of good and evil—fertilizers that provide more food poison us, sprays are health-giving and destructive of animal life, radiation heals and destroys.

Empirical evidence and scientific evidence, deduction and induction, walk hand-in-hand: our proof may not be absolute but we often have clouds of witnesses. Artists differ from scientists in the forms they use that are distinctive and invariably related to their different senses—the plasticity of the painter, the verbal memory of the writer, the ear of the musician. In science it is above all the eye and reason, the presence of the deductive and formulating mind, with the senses as auxiliaries. Each medium has its message. But the model for both is human sexuality.

"If I have seen farther, it is by standing on the shoulders of giants," Newton said.[17] He was implying another of his laws, an unwritten law—that giants beget giants, that genius helps to create genius. So too creation becomes procreation, procreation engenders creation: I offer this, if no one else has named it, as Edel's axiom.

Those of us who have lesser imaginations—and there are all kinds—can't climb to the shoulders of giants. So we sit on their knees. That may be called talent. And those who cannot climb to their knees have imagination of a more mundane form. Yet each individual is king or queen of a particular personal creative domain. The question is not one of democracy; it is one of degree and scope. To be sure, there are persons who can imagine nothing. We may condescend and call them flat-footed: but their literalness is also helpful. They are the ones who on occasion tell us distinctly whether the emperor has his clothes.

Notes

1. Charles Percy Snow, *The Two Cultures and the Scientific Revolution* (Cambridge: Cambridge University Press, 1959), p. 14.

2. C. P. Snow, *The Search* (New York: Charles Scribner's Sons, 1959), pp. 278–282.

3. Henry James, *Letters to A. C. Benson and August Monod*, ed. E. F. Benson (New York: Charles Scribner's Sons, 1930), p. 35.

4. F. C. Green *Jean-Jacques Rousseau* (Cambridge: Cambridge University Press, 1955), pp. 95–99.

5. *Ibid.*, p. 100.

6. *Ibid.*, p. 99.

7. Leon Edel, *Stuff of Sleep and Dreams, Experiments in Literary Psychology* (New York: Harper & Row, 1982), pp. 22–43.

8. James Joyce, *A Portrait of the Artist as a Young Man* (London: Jonathan Cape Ltd., 1924), pp. 241–245.

9. In particular see Oliver Elton, *Modern Studies* (London: Edward Arnold, 1907); Ford Madox Hueffer (Ford), *Henry James, A Critical Study* (New York: Dodd, Mead, and Co., 1916); Dixon Scott, *Men of Letters* (London: Hodder and Stoughton, 1916); Helen Thomas Follett and Wilson Follett, *Some Modern Novelists* (New York: H. Holt & Co., 1918); Joseph Warren Beach, *The Method of Henry James* (New Haven: Yale University Press, 1918); Percy Lubbock, *The Craft of Fiction* (London: Jonathan Cape, 1921); Van Wyck Brooks, *The Pilgrimage of Henry James* (New York: E. P. Dutton & Co., 1925).

10. Leon Edel, *Henry James: Les années dramatiques* (Paris: Jouve et Cie., 1931); See also Edel (ed.), *The Complete Plays of Henry James* (Philadelphia and New York: J. B. Lippincott Company, 1949).

11. Edel and Powers (eds.), *The Complete Notebooks of Henry James* (New York: Oxford University Press, 1986), pp. 57–58.

12. Ibid, p. 115.

13. See Edel, *Stuff of Sleep and Dreams*, "The Nature of Psychological Evidence."

14. Helen Swick Perry, *Psychiatrist of America, The Life of Harry Stack Sullivan* (Cambridge, Mass. Harvard University Press, 1982), pp. 166, 236.

15. Edel, *Stuff of Sleep and Dreams*, especially the chapters on T. S. Eliot, Virginia Woolf, and Willa Cather.

16. I have been told it is now possible to photograph an atom: however this advance into visibility does not seem to me to alter our past ventures into the invisible without the aid of an exploring camera.

17. Robert K. Merton, *On the Shoulders of Giants* (New York: Harcourt Brace Jovanovich, 1985), p. 1 *et seq.*

9 | Truths of Fiction: Value as Metaphor in Modern Literature

Chaim Potok

Writing is a mystery to most writers. It is the task of current philosophy to help dispel mysteries. This is a report about one writer's recent reading in philosophy on a matter pertinent to language and writing.

Ernest Hemingway wrote: "All good books are alike in that they are truer than if they had really happened"; and Picasso once said: "Art is a lie which makes us realize the truth." One of the tools in this artistic reach for truth is the metaphor. Reading at some length about the nature of metaphor, I discovered this: philosophers discuss metaphors and do not like to use them; writers use metaphors and do not like to discuss them. I am a writer-*cum*-philosopher, at times precariously balanced between those two worlds.

I read *Philosophical Perspectives on Metaphor*, edited by Mark Johnson; *Metaphors We Live By*, by George Lakoff and Mark Johnson; *Illness as Metaphor*, by Susan Sontag; and a number of other works that I will refer to in due course. I began my reading with a novelist's sense of wonder at the mysterious process whereby a certain kind of truth is created by the imagination, and at the predisposition that humankind appears to have for uniting disparate entities and producing as a result "two ideas for one," as Samuel Johnson once expressed it. We possess a passion for figuration, Jean Jacques Rousseau informs us, for the process of meaning transfer that expands human language. The Akkadian (Sumerian? Assyrian? Babylonian?) author of the *Epic of Gilgamesh* writes: "Huwawa—his roaring is the flood-storm, His mouth is fire." The Egyptian author of the *Story of Sinuhe* writes: "An attack of thirst overtook me, I was parched and my throat was dusty." The Israelite author of the *Song of Songs* writes: "I am a rose of Sharon, A lily of the valleys." The Greek author of *Agamemnon* writes: "I medicine my soul with melody."

A writer would probably be rendered inarticulate were he or she to be asked: In what sense(s) is (are) the mouth of Huwawa fire; the throat of Sinuhe dusty (literally, with the dust of travel? figuratively, with the dryness of thirst? both, at the same time?); and a young woman a rose of Sharon? What does it mean to medicine a soul with melody? What kind(s) of truth(s) do those metaphors contain?

Following the outline in Mark Johnson's introduction to his *Philosophical Perspectives*, I read Plato, Aristotle, some Roman rhetoricians, a few medievalists, Thomas Hobbes, John Locke, Bishop Berkeley, John Stuart Mill. I read papers by the better-known among the modern and contemporary masters and disciples. Plato's negative view of poetry—and, one assumes, of metaphor as well—has always seemed to me a bit odd, coming as it does from one of the most poetic and metaphor-prone of philosophers. Aristotle, we know, focused on words rather than sentences; distinguished between literal and figurative usage; pointed out that metaphors should be drawn "from things that are related to the original things, and yet not obviously so related"; stated that metaphors "must fairly correspond to the thing signified: failing this, their inappropriateness will be conspicuous"—and established the agenda for all discussions on metaphor for more than two thousand years.

The ambivalence of medieval thinkers on the subject of metaphor is intriguing. On one hand, they appear to regard it as an example of pagan grandiloquence and warn the pious Christian writer to avoid it; on the other hand, they cannot get around the fact that metaphors abound in Scripture. Some sort of consensus seems to have developed: scriptural metaphor is superior to that found elsewhere; scriptural metaphor is revelatory of truth, all others are obfuscatory. Mark Johnson puts it well when he points out that, for the most part, the medievalists regarded metaphor as "a *deviant* use of a *word* to point up *similarities*."[1]

As we enter the world of ideas that appears to be more hospitable to the modern temperament, we find Hobbes equating metaphors with senseless, ambiguous words and absurdities (we shall return to that notion of ambiguity);

Locke warning us that figurative applications of words bring about wrong ideas, "mislead the judgment," and are "wholly to be avoided"; Bishop Berkeley urging philosophers to abstain from metaphors; Hegel regarding metaphor as nothing more than ornamentation for a work of art; John Stuart Mill doubting that a metaphor can be considered an argument; and Kant's apparent hesitation about attributing cognitive significance to metaphors. Virtually alone in this indifferent or hostile landscape is Neitzsche, who regarded metaphor as pervasive and fundamental to all speech and thought; not as a linguistic arabesque but as the essential way that we encounter reality. Truth, Neitzsche claimed, is "a sum of human relations which become poetically and rhetorically intensified." We experience and think the world through metaphors. Nietzsche's view was largely ignored by philosophers.

In the early decades of this century, the positivist notion of metaphor as a rhetorical and emotive trope—as the opposite of the literal utterances that form the basis of verifiable or falsifiable cognitive statements—left metaphor in the shadows of philosophical discourse. Even the claim of I. A. Richards, in *The Philosophy of Rhetoric*, that metaphors are not so much located between words, as Aristotle believed, but are in fact a "borrowing between and intercourse of *thoughts*"; that "*thought* is metaphoric, and proceeds by comparison, and the metaphors of language derive therefrom"; that metaphors have significant cognitive content; that they cannot be replaced by literalist reductions; that they function in a complex epistemological network of projections and superimpositions: "Our world is a projected world, shot through with characters lent to it from our own life"—even this went unnoticed.[2] *The Philosophy of Rhetoric* was published in 1936, and most philosophers then, as Mark Johnson astutely points out, were in no mood to take thought metaphorically and metaphor seriously.

And there the matter of metaphor rested until fairly recently.

Current philosophy, still characterized by an acute and at times polemical preoccupation with language, appears now to be newly and startlingly involved with this strange and fuzzy linguistic entity called metaphor. Among the papers and books that I read were those by certain contemporary philosophers whose thoughts on metaphor and truth were of special significance to me as a writer.

In "Metaphor" (*Philosophical Perspectives*), Max Black concludes his refutation of a certain view of metaphor with the following remarks:

We need the metaphors in just the cases where there can be no question as yet of the precision of scientific statement. Metaphorical statement is not a substitute for a formal comparison or any other kind of literal statement, but has its own *distinctive* capacities and achievements. . . . It would be more illuminating . . . to say that the metaphor *creates* the similarity than to say that it formulates some similarity antecedently existing.[3]

Mark Johnson, in his introduction, comments: "If metaphors actually *create* similarities, any ontological description of the way things stand forth or reveal themselves to us as meaningful will itself be inextricably linked to metaphor."[4]

Black makes an additional point. In his account of I. A. Richards's view of metaphor as interaction (Richards talks about the "cooperation" and "interillumination" of two thoughts that are "active together"), Black writes that he has "no quarrel with the use of metaphors (if they are good ones) in talking about metaphor." And, as if in keeping with that dictum, he goes on to describe metaphor as a filter. A metaphor like "man is a wolf" utilizes, in Black's words, a "system of associated commonplaces" and involves the "acceptance of a set of standard beliefs about wolves that are the possession of the members of some speech community. . . . The wolf-metaphor suppresses some details, emphasizes others—in short, *organizes* our view of man."[5]

Black argues that with regard to both the substitution theory of metaphor (something is being *indirectly* said about another thing) and the comparison theory (the epigram *presents* some comparison between two things), the original statements are easily replaceable by literal translations: "Richard is a lion" = "Richard is brave" (substitution); "Richard is *like* a lion (in being brave)" (comparison); the difference between the two being, of course, that the comparison notion offers a more elaborate paraphrase of the original metaphor, "inasmuch as the original statement is interpreted as being about lions as well as about Richard." But metaphors appear also to function in still another way: they interact. That is to say, in the statement, "man is a wolf," two sets of subjects interact in such a way that all of our general commonplace knowledge about wolves is superimposed upon, acts as a filter for, and organizes our knowledge of man. At the same time, our notion of "wolf" is also subtly altered, for it says something about "wolf" to have it linked with "man": it renders the animal more human. The two subjects (man and wolf) are "active together and . . . produce a meaning that is the resultant of that interaction." Black sees this as a unique act of cognition, "a distinctive intellectual operation . . . demanding simultaneous awareness of both subjects but not reducible to any comparison between the two."[6]

That metaphors have the capacity to create similarities rather than constantly echoing old ones; that they interact with their subjects and serve as filters that superimpose our commonplace knowledge of one subject upon another; and that in making metaphors we are involved in an irreducible act of cognition—all this is of singular import to me as a writer.

In *Languages of Art*, Nelson Goodman writes:

Metaphor, it seems, is a matter of teaching an old word new tricks. . . . Briefly, a metaphor is an affair between a predicate with a past and an object that yields while protesting. In routine projection [see his *Fact, Fiction, and Forecast*, III.5, IV] habit applies a label to a case not already decided. . . . But metaphorical application of a label to an object defies an explicit or tacit prior denial of that label to that object. Where there is metaphor there is conflict: the picture is sad rather than gay even though it is insentient and hence neither sad nor gay. Application of a term is metaphorical only if to some extent contra-indicated.

But he quickly adds: "Metaphor requires attraction as well as resistance—indeed, an attraction that overcomes resistance." And, further: "A metaphor might be seen as a calculated category-mistake—or rather as a happy and revitalizing, even if bigamous, second marriage."[7]

This tropical flowering of metaphors to describe the workings of metaphor is somewhat mind-wheeling. Goodman is aware of this; he tells us in "Metaphor and Moonlighting" (*Philosophical Perspectives*): "Metaphor permeates nearly all discourse; thoroughly literal paragraphs without fresh or frozen metaphors are hard to find in even the least literary texts." In Goodman's terminology, a metaphor "involves withdrawing a term or rather a schema of terms from an initial literal interpretation and applying it in a new way to effect a new sorting of the same or of a different realm."[8] As for the truth content of metaphors: "The question why predicates apply as they do metaphorically is much the same as the question why they apply as they do literally. And if we have no good answer in either case, perhaps that is because there is no real question."[9]

Neither kind of statement is without difficulties as regards truth. The thick classic positivist wall between the literal and the figurative has turned paper thin, if indeed it still stands at all.

In *Metaphors We Live By*, George Lakoff and Mark Johnson argue that "human *thought processes* are largely metaphorical" and that "the human conceptual system is metaphorically structured and defined." I found helpful their elucidation of the notion of metaphor as metaphorical concept (for example, the metaphorical concept "time is money" finds expression in: You're *wasting* my time; This gadget will *save* you hours; How do you *spend* your time these days; You're *running out* of time; He's living on *borrowed* time). Especially helpful were the chapters on *structural metaphors* (language about language seems to be structured as a conduit metaphor: It's hard to *get* that idea *across* to him; Your reasons *came through* to us; Your words seem *hollow*); on *orientational* and *spatialization metaphors* (for example, "Conscious is up, unconscious is down": Get *up*; Wake *up*; He *fell* asleep; He's *under* hypnosis; and another such metaphor, "Good is up, bad is down": He has a *lofty* position; He's at the *bottom* of the social hierarchy; and so on); *ontological metaphors*, that is, our ways of viewing events, activities, emotions, and ideas as substances and entities (for example, the words we use to express the notion that for us inflation is an entity: *Inflation is backing us* into a corner; and, as another example of entity-making, "The mind is a machine": I'm *a little rusty* today")—and so on throughout the volume.[10]

Of high importance to me was the chapter called "Truth," a search into the truth value of metaphor. The authors write:

> We do not believe that there is such a thing as *objective* (absolute and unconditional) *truth*, though it has been a long-standing theme in Western culture that there is. We do believe that there are *truths* but think that the idea of truth need not be tied to the objectivist view. We believe that . . . truth is always relative to a conceptual system that is defined in large part by metaphor.[11]

Many truths emerge from our direct experience of the world around us and are cast in terms of categories like object, substance, purpose, cause. Other truths are the result of the way we "sometimes project these categories onto aspects of the physical world that we have less experience of. For example, we project a front-back orientation in context onto objects that have no intrinsic fronts or backs. . . . Similarly, our on-off orientation emerges from our direct experience with the ground." They continue this point with the assertion that

> we perceive various things in the natural world as entities, often projecting boundaries and surfaces on them where no clear-cut boundaries or surfaces

exist naturally. Thus we can conceive of a fogbank as an entity that can be *over* the bay (which we conceive as an entity) and *in front of* the mountains (conceived as an entity with a FRONT-BACK orientation). By virtue of these projections, a sentence like "The fog is in front of the mountain" may be *true*. As is typically the case in our daily lives, truth is relative to understanding, and the truth of such a sentence is relative to the normal way we understand the world by projecting orientation and entity structure onto it.[12]

An analysis of how it is that we come to understand a simple nonmetaphoric sentence ("John fired the gun at Harry") as being true in a given situation reveals that what is required is "an understanding of the sentence and having an understanding of the situation." We understand a statement as true if our understanding of the statement fits closely enough to our understanding of the situation. And understanding a situation that could fit our understanding of a statement about it often requires entity and orientation projections, experiential gestalts ("shooting someone"), and acquiring an understanding of the statement in terms of its categories (gun, firing, and so on). This is a far more complex process than I make it out to be here; for my purposes, the important point has to do with the truth content of conventional and new metaphors. In the case of conventional metaphors ("Inflation has gone up"), Lakoff and Johnson state that

> and understanding of truth in terms of metaphorical projection is not essentially different from an understanding of truth in terms of nonmetaphorical projection. The only difference is that metaphorical projection involves understanding one kind of thing in terms of another kind of thing ["inflation" = an ontological metaphor; "up" = an orientational metaphor] . . . while nonmetaphorical projection ["The fog is in front of the mountain"] involves only one kind.[13]

A new metaphor—say, "Life's . . . a tale told by an idiot, full of sound and fury, signifying nothing"—is analyzed in terms of a conventional metaphor, "Life is a story":

> What makes it possible for many of us to see this metaphor as true is that we usually comprehend our life experiences in terms of the LIFE IS A STORY metaphor. We are constantly looking for meaning in our lives by seeking out coherences that will fit some sort of coherent life story.

The authors point out that

issues of truth are among the least relevant and interesting issues that arise
in the study of metaphor. The real significance of the metaphor LIFE'S . . . A
TALE TOLD BY AN IDIOT is that, in getting us to try to understand how it
could be true, it makes possible a new understanding of our lives. . . . What
the LIFE'S . . . A TALE TOLD BY AN IDIOT metaphor does is to evoke
the LIFE IS A STORY metaphor, which involves living with the constant
expectation of . . . a sane life story. The effect of the metaphor is to evoke
this expectation and to point out that, in reality, it may be constantly
frustrated.[14]

Johnson echoes this last point in his introduction to *Philosophical Perspectives*
when he claims that "we encounter our world, not passively, but by means of
projective acts influenced by our interests, purposes, values, beliefs, and language.
*Because our world is an imaginative, value-laden construction, metaphors that
alter our conceptual structures (themselves carried by older metaphors) will also
alter the way we experience things*" (emphasis mine).[15]

The notion of our world as a value-laden construction that affects, and is
affected by, metaphor is illustrated by Susan Sontag in her work *Illness as
Metaphor*, a study of the web of lurid metaphoric langauge that has grown up
around the diseases of tuberculosis and cancer in western civilization. Sontag
writes: "A disease of the lungs is, metaphorically, a disease of the soul. Cancer,
as a disease that can strike anywhere, is a disease of the body."[16]

She makes the point that

epidemic diseases were a common figure for social disorder. . . . Feelings
about evil are projected onto a disease. And the disease (so enriched with
meaning) is projected onto the world. . . . And it is diseases thought to be
multi-determined (that is, mysterious) that have the widest possibilities as
metaphors for what is felt to be socially or morally wrong.[17]

Regarding the metaphors surrounding tuberculosis and cancer, she writes:

TB is described in images that sum up the negative behavior of
nineteenth-century *homo economicus*: consumption; wasting; squandering
of vitality. . . . Cancer is described in images that sum up the negative
behavior of twentieth-century *homo economicus*: abnormal growth; repres-

sion of energy, that is, refusal to consume or spend. . . . The controlling metaphors in descriptions of cancer are, in fact, drawn not from economics but from the language of warfare.[18]

Cancer cells are "invasive." Cancer cells "colonize" from the original tumor. We talk of the body's "defenses." The goal of treatment is to "kill" the cancer cells.

The cancer metaphor is often used by those in positions of power: "To describe a phenomenon as a cancer is an incitement to violence. The use of cancer in political discourse encourages fatalism and justifies "severe" measures."[19]

Sontag concludes her analysis with the claim that

our views about cancer, and the metaphors we have imposed on it, are so much a vehicle for the large insufficiencies of this culture, for our shallow attitude toward death, for our anxieties about feeling . . . for our inability to construct an advanced industrial society which properly regulates consumption, and for our justified fears of the increasingly violent course of history.[20]

We have come a long way, I think, from Aristotle's idea of metaphor as "things that are related to the original things and yet not obviously so related," and from Hegel's view that metaphor is nothing more than ornamentation for a work of art.

A writer creates metaphors out of an intuitive sense of their appropriateness, their expansiveness, their resonance, their coherence, their loveliness, and out of a sheer delight in the power of language to unite discrete elements of human experience. He (let "he" be generic for "he/she" here) does not (ought not, lest it render the creative act self-conscious and thereby throttle it) consciously ask himself: What is the truth value of my metaphor? Where do I draw it from? What value system does it mirror? What is its epistemology? How does it work? He might ask himself: Is it a conventional or new metaphor? Is it appropriate; that is, does it fit what I want to convey? But the answers will come not from a carefully reasoned set of rational responses but from a blur of images, words, ideas, memories, and from a *feeling*, and *intuition* about the rightness and wrongness of the thing.

Sometimes, however, a writer will work methodically to create a certain kind of metaphor: a value-charged metaphor upon which an entire novel, say, might depend. I have always found it difficult to believe the account by Edgar Allen Poe of his writing of *The Raven*. But his attempt points up the postpartum self-awareness that sometimes comes upon a writer after the fit of creativity dissipates and some measure of normalcy returns: the writer hopes to restore a semblance of order to the jumping chaos of a creative process in which he is unable to keep careful track of his thoughts, fears, and feelings. Hemingway's and Picasso's utterances about the truths of art are indicators of that self-awareness, that need to give configuration to the process of *creating* truths. And my recent reading about metaphor has brought a measure of that self-awareness to me.

Very early in the planning of *The Chosen* I made a list that consisted of the following requirements: I need a frame that will reflect the combat between the two groups; I need a uniquely American setting, because this story cannot take place anywhere but in America; I need a frame that will echo the war in Europe; I need a frame that will lead from the world of the sons to the world of the Hasidic father.

I made a second list. I needed a counterframe, one that would be the reverse of the first, that would mirror the world of the Hasidic father and lead from that world to the world of the sons.

The first frame had to take in the outer world and its involvement in, and reaction to, the noise of nearby and distant events. The second frame had to mirror an inner world and its reaction to those same events. Both frames were going to be brought into conflict as *opposing ways* of seeing the world, experiencing and communicating values, and dealing with the frightful possibility of ontological meaninglessness.

I wrote the first list down on paper; the second I kept in my head. I would say, on reflection, that the first was worked out cognitively; the second was *intuited, felt*.

The first frame became the metaphor of the baseball game; the second, the metaphor of the silence. Baseball and silence were *value metaphors* drawn from *categories of experience*. They served to *organize* the world I was going to write about.

Where did those metaphors come from? One morning, after many days of contemplating that written list, I remembered having once seen a group of Hasidic boys playing at a game of running bases in a Brooklyn park. That was a clear image that surfaced from my past: the boys playing, holding on to their skullcaps as they ran, fringes flying, from base to base. But running bases was clearly too frail and inappropriate a metaphor for my needs. The metaphor quickly evolved into the baseball game—which *fit* the criteria on my list.

That metaphor was drawn from memory and from the normal language of one kind of domestic "warfare": baseball. But I have no recollection of the process that led me to the silence metaphor; one day it was suddenly there.

The Chosen is also about a clash of ideas from the cores of two cultures: the baseball-game metaphor comes from, and adds to, the values of the general culture; the silence metaphor comes from, and adds to, the culture of Reb Saunders.

A value metaphor is a certain mapping of the world through a celluloid of large questions: What am I really doing here? Does what I do with my life truly matter in an intrinsic way? What am I ready to go to the barricades for? Who are the really important people, and what are the really important things, in my life? and so on. The writer probes and explores personal terrain, then makes a map of it that he superimposes upon similar terrain (or upon new terrain) experienced by the world outside him. It is this mapping that he gives to the world. At times the mapping is too familiar, and the world yawns. At times it is sharply new; it *creates* similarities that are startling surprises. Sometimes the world ignores the new map; it lies beyond commonplace understanding. Sometimes it adopts it and carries it whenever venturing out upon that terrain. Since the publication of *The Chosen*, the silence metaphor has become a map superimposed upon the old landscape of Hasidism, as well as upon father-son relationships; and the baseball-game metaphor has been used a number of times in connection with Hasidim, something few would have thought to do with that apparently pacific and anti-sports minded sect from the world of Eastern Europe. In time new metaphors become old truths.

How new value metaphors are created and used might be a worthwhile field of exploration for philosophy.

An additional point about *The Chosen* came to mind during my reading about metaphors. Hobbes equated metaphors with senseless and ambiguous words. The avoidance of ambiguity is admirable in a world that regards fixity as a possibility and objective truth as a reality. But that world is gone for most writers who deal seriously with humankind in these last decades of the twentieth-century. We are the children of Kafka; ambiguity encircles us, webs us about. We plow its fields and harvest its ambivalences. Max Black wrote that we need metaphors where exact scientific statements are not yet possible. Well, they are not nearly possible in most instances having to do with the human condition, and least of all when we confront our century's evil. The silence metaphor fit precisely because of its prismatic ambiguity: Is silence good or bad? How does a compassionate man raise a son in silence? Yet the resulting pain yielded the desired effect. Is it a value metaphor drawn from Reb Saunders's world or is it a metaphor for God's silence in the twentieth century? Do you respond to ontological silence (God and the Holocaust) with existential silence (Reb Saunders and the Holocaust)?

Nelson Goodman observes, in "Metaphor and Moonlighting," that "metaphor and ambiguity are closely akin."[21] They are especially akin to writers who, struggling with the crucial dilemmas of our time, often invent metaphorical concepts: a trial; a castle; a man transformed into a monstrous vermin; a wasteland; a wanderer; a deserting soldier; a tuberculosis sanitarium; a cancer patient; a plague. The reader is then presented with these ambivalences and participates in the writer's attempt to half-reveal and half-conceal his meaning as a way of giving expression to his sense of ambiguity about a world that is a puzzle with many missing pieces and with others that seem not to fit.

I would not have undertaken this task at self-analysis had it not been for my reading on metaphor. This writer is grateful to philosophy for some measure of clarification of the mystery of writing and the nature of the truths of fiction. It is in such ways that philosophy helps the writer and the writer, it is hoped, helps philosophy.

Notes

1. Mark Johnson, ed., *Philosophical Perspectives on Metaphor* (Minneapolis: University of Minnesota Press, 1981), p. 11.

2. *Ibid.*, p. 60.

3. *Ibid.*, p. 72.

4. *Ibid.*, p. 43.

5. *Ibid.*, pp. 73–75.

6. *Ibid.*, p. 79.

7. Nelson Goodman, *Languages of Art* (Indianapolis: Hackett Publishing Co., 1976), p. 69ff.

8. Mark Johnson, *Philosophical Perspectives on Metaphor*, p. 224.

9. *Ibid.*, p. 129.

10. George Lakoff and Mark Johnson, *Metaphors We Live By* (Chicago and London: The University of Chicago Press, 1980), Chaps. 1–7.

11. *Ibid.*, p. 159.

12. *Ibid.*, pp. 161–162.

13. *Ibid.*, p. 171.

14. *Ibid.*, pp. 172–173.

15. Mark Johnson, *Philosophical Perspectives on Metaphor*, p. 41.

16. Susan Sontag, *Illness As Metaphor* (New York: Farrar, Straus and Giroux, 1978), p. 18.

17. *Ibid.*, p. 58.

18. *Ibid.*, pp. 63–64.

19. *Ibid.*, p. 84.

20. *Ibid.*, pp. 87–88.

21. Mark Johnson, *Philosophical Perspectives on Metaphor*, p. 222.

IO | Rationality, Ritual, and Relativism

Lawrence Foster

"I have nightmares every night," the woman said. "Now I've got it in my head to find out who those unknown people are whom one meets in one's dreams."

She plugged in the fan. "Last week a woman appeared at the head of my bed," she said. "I managed to ask her who she was and she replied, 'I am the woman who died in this room twelve years ago.'"

"But the house was built barely two years ago," the colonel said.

"That's right," the woman said. "That means that even the dead make mistakes."

Gabriel García Marquez, "No One Writes to the Colonel"

I

For a good part of the twentieth century, anthropologists have questioned the status of alien world views and practices in traditional societies. Recently, nonanthropologists have entered the debate and with good reason. For, ultimately, claims about the existence of "primitive minds," the rationality or irrationality of traditional thought, the similarities and differences between scientific and ritual practice, and related issues concerning relativism raise questions broad in scope and philosophical in nature.[1]

This paper attempts to contribute to the ongoing discussion by taking as its starting point the justly celebrated and widely discussed writings of John Beattie[2] and Robin Horton[3] concerning the correct analysis of magico-religious beliefs, myths, and rituals. How are we to interpret traditional beliefs and practices that are *prima facie* irrational, that appear bizarre and senseless to us? Horton claims that traditional thought can be correctly viewed as analogous to scientific thought, that it is a product of a theoretical model-building process. Beattie, on the other hand, argues that ritual, unlike science, can be more correctly and fruitfully viewed as essentially expressive and symbolic; ritual—be it myth, magic or religion—is more like the arts than like science in that its function is to dramatize experience rather than to analyze it.[4]

These contrasting claims raise important issues for the philosopher as well as for the anthropologist—issues that have not yet been fully explored in the literature. Both views rest on a particular conception of science, a conception, I will argue, that is wanting. Beattie's arguments, in addition, presuppose a theory of the function of art and of the differences between art and science that also needs rethinking. An evaluation of the views of Horton and Beattie, therefore, cannot be divorced from a wider investigation of some of their more philosophical claims and assumptions concerning the nature of science and art. It is to these more philosophical issues and their consequence for the study of other cultures that I address myself in this paper.

Horton's views represents a philosophical advance over the pioneering work of Evans-Pritchard who, in turn, rightly criticized Levy-Bruhl's attribution of a primitive, prelogical mentality to traditional people.[5] Yet, Evans-Pritchard believed that the social content of "savage" thought differed from the social content of western, scientific thought in that the former relied on suprasensible (and hence, mystical) entities while the latter did not. Horton correctly rejects this distinction.

According to Horton, both the traditional thinker and the scientist postulate theoretical entities for the purpose of explanation and prediction. An understanding of traditional thought, therefore, is not in essence different from an understanding of science. The twin goals, explanation and prediction, are present in each, as are the processes for obtaining these goals. The attempt by some anthropologists to contrast scientific and traditional thought on the grounds that one is empirical and the other nonempirical will not be successful. Resort to so-called nonempirical, or better, nonobservable, entities is as much involved in science as it is in traditional thought.

To support this view, Horton cites examples from his fieldwork among the Kalabari people of the Niger Delta, showing how their postulation of theoretical entities, albeit unusual ones, is used for the purpose of explanation and prediction.[6] Further support for Horton's thesis easily could be gathered by citing countless other cases from traditional African thought or by looking at traditional thought in such areas as Mexico where explanations incorporating terms for theoretical entities (for example, ancestral spirits) are used to account for observable phenomena and also to elucidate the purpose of certain rituals, for example, curing ceremonies performed by a shaman.[7] When traditional thought is viewed in this way, questions concerning its rationality are on a par with questions concerning the rationality of scientific thought.

What then marks the difference between traditional and scientific thought? As Horton initially saw it, the primary difference was that "traditional cultures are 'closed' and scientifically oriented cultures 'open.' "[8] In traditional cultures there is an absence of awareness of alternative theories. As a result traditional beliefs are held to be sacred, and any threat to them evokes great anxiety. Scientific thought is different. It is "characterized by awareness of alternatives, diminished sacredness of beliefs, and diminished anxiety about threats to them."[9] In making this distinction, Horton apparently accepts a form of Evans-Pritchard's realism that assumes scientific notions are those that accord with objective reality, while magical-mystical notions do not. I will say more on this later.

Several problems with Horton's views have been pointed out in the literature and subsequently responded to by Horton. On one hand, as Beattie has noted, even the most traditionally minded Africans today are aware of alternatives, yet traditional African beliefs continue to thrive.[10] On the other hand, as Beattie failed to note, but as Thomas Kuhn had clearly shown several years prior to the publication of Horton's article, scientific thought itself is characterized by sacredness of beliefs and anxiety about threats to them.[11] Indeed, Horton's characterization of the reaction to predictive failure in traditional cultures is just the reaction described by Kuhn as characteristic of scientific thought. Reading Horton's description of traditional thought, one would think one was reading Kuhn's account of scientific thought. Kuhn writes, "What scientists never do when confronted by even severe and prolonged anomalies . . . [is] renounce the paradigm that has led them into crisis. They do not, that is, treat anomalies as counterinstances."[12] Kuhn goes on to assert that "by themselves they [anomalies] cannot and will not falsify that philosophical theory, for its defenders will do what we have already seen scientists doing when confronted by anomaly. They will devise numerous articulations and *ad hoc* modifications of their theory in order to eliminate any apparent conflict."[13] And Horton asserts,

In the theoretical thought of the traditional cultures, there is a notable reluctance to register repeated failures of prediction and to act by attacking the beliefs involved. Instead, other current beliefs are utilized in such a way as to "excuse" failure as it occurs, and hence to protect the major theoretical assumptions on which prediction is based. The use of *ad hoc* excuses is a phenomenon which social anthropologists have christened "secondary elaboration."[14]

Because resort to *ad hoc* hypotheses is common in both scientific and traditional thought, it cannot be a key feature distinguishing them. Whereas Horton viewed scientific thought, but not traditional thought, as open and critical, Kuhn correctly, I believe, argued that "in a sense . . . it is precisely the abandonment of critical discourse that marks the transition to a science."[15] Although Horton was well aware of Kuhn's work and even referred to it, he seemingly missed its force and continued to urge that the "scientist's essential scepticism toward established beliefs . . . above all . . . distinguishes him from the traditional thinker."[16]

In a recent article, Horton acknowledges some of these objections.[17] He recognizes the untenability of both the open versus closed dichotomy and the distinction between traditional and scientific thought based on the presence or absence of anxiety about threats to beliefs. Horton notes that traditional African thought has responded to recalcitrant experience not simply by taboo reaction but also by theoretical innovation.[18] Not all responses to anomalous experiences in traditional thought take the form of denying or suppressing the data. Again, traditional thought in Mexico provides additional examples in support of Horton's revised views. Surely, one of the most striking cases involves the Aztec modification of the Quetzalcoatl myth to explain what certainly ranks as one of the most startling anomalous experiences in history—the appearance of white Spaniards, led by Cortés, clothed in iron armor astride monstrous, supernatural, snorting animals (horses).[19]

Drawing on the work of Lakatos and Feyerabend, Horton now argues that the presence or absence of intertheoretic competition marks an important distinction between traditional and scientific thought. Whether this anti-Kuhnian view is correct is too complex and controversial a matter to be explored here. But any exploration along these lines for distinguishing between the two types of thought should also consider Kuhn's proposed criteria for counting a field as a mature science. I suspect that a good part of traditional thought may fail Kuhn's third and fourth conditions; namely, that the theory suggests means for the improvement of predictions in both precision and scope, and that "the improvement of predictive techniques must be a challenging task, demanding on occasions the very highest measure of talent and devotion."[20] The painstaking working out of the details of a paradigm, Kuhn's so-called mopping up operations, does not, I believe, characterize much of traditional thought. This, no doubt, is at least partly attributable to the absence of the high degree of literacy in many traditional societies that is required for scientific maturity.

As mentioned above, willingness to abandon a theory in light of recalcitrant experience fails to distinguish scientific from traditional thought, despite Horton's early belief that it did. Horton argued this position because he mistakenly believed that only scientific thinkers were aware of alternative systems of belief. But his mistake was deeper and more complex, for Horton's arguments are based on the popular view of an emotive free science that will continue to plague the science-ritual controversy unless examined more closely.

Scientific thought provides numerous cases of predictive failure, awareness of alternative theories, yet reluctance to abandon the existing theory. What appears to be required for a theory to be abandoned is not simply the awareness of an alternative but the perception of crisis in the existing theory.[21] In the absence of perception of crisis, neither the existence of predictive failure nor the awareness of an alternative theory is sufficient alone or in combination to give rise to the abandonment of existing theory. Since this conservatism holds for scientific thought, it should not be surprising that it characterizes traditional thought as well.

The perplexing question concerning the causes of the perception or lack of perception of crisis is not one that I can explore deeply here. Horton, however, proposes an answer, at least, for traditional thought. He suggests that in traditional but not scientific thought emotional and aesthetic factors weigh heavily. He writes,

There is little doubt that because the theoretical entities of traditional thought happen to be people, they give particular scope for the working of emotional and aesthetic motives. Here, perhaps, we do have something about the personal idiom in theory that does militate indirectly against the taking of the scientific attitude; for where there are powerful emotional and aesthetic loadings on a particular theoretical scheme, these must add to the difficulties of abandoning this scheme when cognitive goals press towards doing so. Once again, I should like to stress that the mere fact of switching from a personal to an impersonal idiom does not make anyone a scientist, and that one can be unscientific or scientific in either idiom. In this respect,

nevertheless, the personal idiom does seem to present certain difficulties for
the scientific attitude which the impersonal idiom does not.[22]

There are problems with this suggestion, however. In scientific as well as in
traditional thought, aesthetic factors (such as simplicity or elegance; for example,
in Ptolemaic astronomy, the complexity and ugliness of epicycle upon epicycle),
religious or metaphysical factors (for example, the identification of circular
motion with perfect, heavenly motion), and personal and practical factors (for
example, who perceives the anomaly, or proposes the alternative theory) can play
an important role in the perception of crisis. And these factors may play a role
not significantly different from the "nonrational" aspects of traditional thought.
They may hinder or promote the perception of crisis in existing theory. Horton's
suggestion that emotional and aesthetic considerations enter into traditional
thought because the theoretical entities happen to be people (or, perhaps, more
accurately, because they are anthropomorphic) is no doubt correct. He goes wrong,
however, in suggesting that the scientific attitude precludes such considerations.

Despite identifying what he believes to be the differences between scientific and
traditional thought, Horton rejects the idea that a superior rationality operates in
western scientific thinking. Instead, he posits a universal rationality that functions
in particular technological, economic, and social settings, and that supposedly
accounts both for the cognitive success of the sciences and the rationality of
traditional thought. Without working out this universal theory of rationality,
Horton does reject a relativistic view.[23] Although he alludes to certain views
on translation as the ostensible reason for this rejection, I suspect that another
important source can be traced to his acceptance of the popular notions of a single
objective reality and the independence of words and the world.

Let us first consider the latter view and its consequences for a nonrelativist or
universal notion of rationality. Horton perceives a difference between traditional
and scientific thinkers in their attitude toward the power of words. The traditional
thinker believes that words and reality form a dependent relationship; the scientist
views words and reality as independent.[24] Horton writes,

> If ideas and words are inextricably bound up with reality, and if indeed
> they shape it and control it, then, a multiplicity of idea-systems means a
> multiplicity of realities, and a change of ideas, means a change of things.
> But whereas there is nothing particularly absurd or inconsistent about this
> view, it is clearly intolerable in the extreme. For it means that the world
> is in the last analysis dependent on human whim, that the search for order

is a folly, and that human beings can expect to find no sort of anchor in reality.[25]

At first glance this distinction holds promise. Indeed, as Horton notes, from the time of ancient Egypt, traditional thinkers have understood words as having the power to create and affect reality.

> A central characteristic of nearly all the traditional world-views we know of is an assumption about the power of words, uttered under appropriate circumstances, to bring into being the events or states they stand for. The most striking examples of this assumption are to be found in creation mythologies where the supreme being is said to have formed the world out of chaos by uttering the names of all things in it. . . . In traditional African cultures, to know the name of a being is to have some degree of control over it. In the invocation of spirits, it is essential to call their names correctly; and the control which such correct calling gives is one reason why the true or "deep" names of gods are withheld from strangers. Yet again, it is widely believed that harm can be done to a man by various operations performed on his name-for instance, by writing his name on a piece of paper and burning it.[26]

Horton believes that scientists surely refuse to attribute such world-making power to words. But do they? The answer may depend on which modern "scientist" one consults. Beginning with Kant and continuing through such twentieth-century pragmatic thinkers as C. I. Lewis, philosophers have held that the mind, at least through its concepts, plays a major role in the construction of reality. And Nelson Goodman has argued persuasively that language plays a major role in our determination of which hypotheses constitute scientific laws, which kinds in nature constitute real rather than artificial kinds, and which theories or hypotheses possess the greatest simplicity.[27] In recent writings, Goodman continues this theme, arguing that through language and other symbols we make worlds. "Now as we thus make constellations by picking out and putting together certain stars rather than others, so we make stars by drawing certain boundaries rather than others. Nothing dictates whether the skies shall be marked into constellations or other objects. We have to make what we find, be it the Great Dipper, Sirius, food, fuel, or a stereo system."[28] Although we don't bring stars into existence simply by uttering the word "stars," nevertheless there are no stars without words or other symbols. And we do bring kinds and projectible categories into existence, in part, by habitually projecting certain predicates and not others. Admittedly, Goodman's position differs in important respects from the traditional view cited by Horton. Goodman is no shaman—as far as I know.

Further support for this position can be gathered from numerous thinkers who have discussed the role that language and other symbols play in our perceptual judgments and our construction of reality.[29] And, at one time, Kuhn went so far as to suggest that "when paradigms change, the world itself changes with them."[30] The belief in the "magical" power of words, then, does not easily distinguish traditional from scientific thought.

I cannot at this point resist noting one additional western "scientific" view on the "magical" power of words, for it was formulated by one of the more distinguished twentieth-century philosophers from the British Empire, the birthplace of many of the anthropologists writing about traditional African thought. I am referring to J. L. Austin and his theory of performative utterances. According to Austin, in uttering certain expressions under the appropriate circumstances we are doing something or bringing something into existence rather than merely describing it. For example, "I now pronounce you man and wife" uttered by the appropriate person under the appropriate circumstances *makes* the couple man and wife. Here again we see that words and reality, even in western scientific societies, are not always perceived as independent variables.[31]

Sorting out the differences between the scientific and traditional views of the power of words would be a challenging project, but it is not one that I am prepared to carry out here. Nevertheless, the dichotomy drawn between scientific and traditional thought on the basis of the alleged independence of words and the world still awaits argument. Further, Horton is surely wrong in suggesting that if words and reality are not viewed as independent variables, then any change of ideas amounts to a change of things, and the search for order is a folly. On one hand, not all ideas are correct and hence not all world-making successful; on the other hand, the order in the universe that we "discover" is certainly as much a creation of language and other symbols as it is a discovery. Among other reasons, Goodman's grue-paradox has clearly shown this to be so.[32]

What can now be said about Horton's nonrelativistic views on rationality? Frequently, discussions in the anthropological-philosophical literature about rationality and relativism assume either that there is an intimate connection between the rationality of a belief and the belief's correspondence with a single independent reality or that rational beliefs follow rules or "procedures that can be trusted to lead us to truths."[33] The previous comments on the "magical" power of words serve to undermine the first assumption and suggest that other arguments in support of a universalist theory of rationality are needed. The second alternative, establishing that certain inductive procedures "can be trusted to lead us to truths," apparently would constitute just such an argument. Unfortunately, despite numerous attempts to do this, none, I believe, have overcome Hume's fundamental objections. And so another ground for universalism is removed.[34]

In fact, the Humean-Goodmanean account that construes inductive justification in terms of the conformity of inductive rules with accepted inductive practice provides us with a more promising response to the quest for justification. But once we divorce inductive justification from any connection with producing truths, and relate it instead to inductive practice, we find that legitimate differences can arise at the level of what are accepted inferences and accepted rules. Therefore, there can be equally legitimate and justifiable yet conflicting sets of inductive rules. Since any theory of the rationality of beliefs will have to appeal in part, at least, to rules of induction or confirmation, some kind of relativistic position on rationality would appear to be forthcoming. This relativity would seem to be all the more plausible when we are considering traditional systems of thought with beliefs and patterns of accepted inferences and practices quite different from our own. And the relativity of rationality at the level of beliefs would be supported further by the recognition that the rationality of a belief is dependent in part upon the available evidence, which clearly can vary both spatially and temporally.

The case for a universal theory of rationality fades with the rejection of the correspondence theory of truth and the failure to answer Hume's challenge to induction. But with these supports gone, and with many realities replacing the one ready-made objective reality, relativism gains plausibility. Indeed, Goodman has gone so far as to propose that ultimate acceptability is a sufficient condition for truth. He argues further that "since acceptability involves inductive validity, which involves right categorization, which involves entrenchment, habit must be recognized as an integral ingredient of truth."[35] Obviously, this view of truth could lead to a notion of conflicting truths and multiple realities, a conclusion that Goodman readily accepts and argues for on other grounds.[36] But where truths conflict, and worlds are many, can rationality be far behind? Or, rather, the relativity of rationality?

II

Horton's perceptive analysis, although widely discussed, has not been widely received. Legitimate questions arise concerning whether the scientific analogy adequately captures traditional thought and practice; whether Horton's analysis, like those of his predecessors in the intellectualist tradition, does not in fact ultimately lead to disturbing conclusions about the irrationality of traditional thinkers; and whether the persistence of bizarre traditional beliefs and practices in light of abundant contrary evidence does not call out for a different mode of interpretation.

In several of his writings, John Beattie rejects Horton's scientific model and argues for a symbolic interpretation of traditional thought instead. He writes, "The 'bizarre and senseless features' of such beliefs do not become immediately comprehensible to me at any rate, when they are seen as the product of a model-building process comparable with that of modern science. If they were this, their presence and persistence would indeed be inexplicable."[37] "Ritual," Beattie claims, "is essentially expressive and symbolic. . . . In this respect it is allied with art rather than with science, and it is susceptible to similar kinds of understanding."[38] Myth functions differently from science. "While science analyses experience, myth, magic, and religion dramatize it. The mythmakers . . . are on the side of the poets, not of the scientists; both find 'order underlying apparent disorder,' but they find very different kinds of order, and they seek them by very different means." Beattie holds that the key difference between traditional and scientific thought must be found "in the nature and grounds of the beliefs themselves." And here we find that what distinguishes traditional from scientific thought is "ritual's essential quality, namely its expressive character." Thus, the traditional and scientific approaches represent "fundamentally different and mutually irreducible ways of looking at the world."[39]

Earlier I noted that nonevidential factors enter into the scientific acceptance and rejection of theories. Although Beattie does not acknowledge this aspect of science, his account of the expressive quality of traditional thought shows how these factors enter there as well, and he provides an intriguing explanation of why apparently irrational and senseless beliefs and practices continue to be adhered to despite strong evidence to the contrary. But Beattie's account, I believe, rather than replacing or contradicting Horton's may be more fruitfully viewed as supplementing it, just as accounts of the nonevidential aesthetic and emotional factors that enter into scientific practice augment and illuminate theories of confirmation, explanation, and theory choice in science. And Beattie's view of art and science as diametrically opposed ways of understanding the world warrants closer examination.

The promising analogy that Beattie draws between traditional thought, practice, and art has important implications for understanding traditional thought, implications not fully foreseen by Beattie. Beattie implies that art and science differ in that the former but not the latter is primarily expressive. Hence, to understand art, (and given the analogy, ritual also) one must primarily understand what is expressed. But this view oversimplifies the multifunctional nature of both art and ritual. Consider painting. Indeed, some paintings may be primarily expressive, but some are essentially representational, and others, as Goodman has pointed out, like a late Mondrian, may express little or nothing but exemplify much.[40] Similar remarks apply to rituals as well as to other art forms. Some rituals, such as bloodletting among the ancient Maya, were powerfully expressive.[41] But the bloodletting ritual also served a major nonexpressive function; it was utilized to bring forth a vision of an ancestor or god and the blood itself was believed to nourish the gods. In other rituals, such as certain house ceremonies among contemporary Zinacantecos in Mexico, the expressive power may be minor or absent. But in such cases the ritual, like a nonexpressive work of art, may nevertheless have other functions. As Scheffler has pointed out, the notion of reenactment which is virtually absent in the arts, plays a major role in ritual, a role, we may add, that is played even in the absence of a ritual's expressive effect. It "gives some body to the notion of tradition" and serves "to form a conception of community."[42] To understand ritual, therefore, just as to understand art, one needs to explore more than what is expressed.

I am suggesting that we cannot understand the reluctance to give up apparently irrational beliefs and practices unless we understand the multifunctional aspects of ritual, that the expressive force of ritual no more than the evidential data of science can alone account for the presence and persistence of questionable beliefs and practices.[43] The argument that ritual like art is primarily expressive can lull us into neglecting important aspects of both, aspects that link art and ritual with science and others that differentiate them. This point is brought home by Goodman in relation to art when he writes,

> Even among works of art and aesthetic experiences of evident excellence, the emotive component varies widely—from, say, a late Rembrandt to a late Mondrian, or from a Brahms to a Webern quartet. The Mondrian and the Webern are not obviously more emotive than Newton's or Einstein's laws; and a line between emotive and cognitive is less likely to mark off the aesthetic from the scientific than to mark off some aesthetic objects and experiences from others.[44]

Other dangers attach to a primarily expressive interpretation of ritual. This can be seen as a result of an important observation made by Evans-Pritchard in *Witchcraft, Oracles and Magic Among the Azande*. He wrote,

> When a man chooses a suitable tree and fells it and hollows its wood into a gong his actions are empirical, but when he abstains from sexual intercourse during his labour we speak of his abstinence as ritual, since it has no objective relation to the making of gongs and since it involves ideas of taboo. We thus classify Zande behavior into empirical and ritual, and Zande notions into common sense and mystical, according to our knowledge of natural processes and not according to theirs. For we raise quite a different question when we ask whether the Zande himself distinguishes between those techniques we call empirical and those techniques we call magical.[45]

Although Beattie is well aware that ritual actions, like scientific ones, are performed to bring about certain results, his stress on the essentially expressive aspects of ritual, when combined with Evans-Pritchard's point, yields certain unwelcome consequences. Anthropologists, in distinguishing between empirical and ritual behavior on the basis of their own (perhaps naive) view of natural processes may too easily force the expressive element on to the bizarre and unusual behaviour and too easily ignore other important aspects. But the behavior may, in fact, be primarily aimed at getting results, perhaps unsuccessfully, or as we are quickly learning, the strange beliefs may turn out to be true; the "bizarre and senseless" behaviors may in fact be causally efficacious and no expressive interpretation may be required to explain their persistence.[46] It would be a remarkable coincidence indeed if the division between essentially expressive and nonexpressive behavior did, in fact, correspond to the distinction between the causally nonefficacious and efficacious. After all, we judge what is efficacious, like the anthropologists, based on our present yet ever-changing commonsense beliefs that are sometimes scientifically informed, yet ever fallible.

I alluded above to other aspects of ritual and art of no less importance than expression. If Beattie is correct in his analogy between art and ritual, then the multifunctional nature of each should be apparent. Representation, of course, is prevalent. In certain Zinacanteco curing ceremonies, for example, fifty-two grains of maize of each of four colors are used to represent the four world directions and thirteen parts of the soul. Wooden crosses placed at the foot and top of certain mountains in Zinacantan represent the doorways to houses of the ancestral gods. And pine tree tops fastened to the crosses represent a forest and symbolize the "pines which surround the supernatural corrals located in the mountain homes of the gods where the wild animal companions of the Zinacantecos are kept."[47] Similarly, in art it is frequently important that we understand the referents, whether we are viewing Picasso's *Guernica* or Daumier's *The Audience Pleased*.

And where we have cases of fictive representation, whether in art or ritual, understanding what puports to be represented is of no less importance. Viewers would miss much if they dismissed and ignored Michelangelo's *Creation of Adam* in the Sistine Chapel on the grounds that it lacked an actual referent.

Granted, in ritual, as in art, what is expressed and exemplified is of no less importance for understanding. And as Beattie recognizes, but downplays, there are significant causal or instrumental aspects of ritual. Rites of baptism in Zinacanteco society are believed to fix the soul of the child more securely in the body. Ritual drinking of cane liquor is believed to be efficacious in curing illness and repairing social relations. The placing of pine needles on the ground is believed to insulate the practitioner from the Earth Lord.[48] But in these practices and others, the instrumental aspects are but one set of features of the practice, and the relative importance of instrumentality, representation, expression, exemplification, reenactment, and other features of ritual may vary from ritual to ritual. Anthropologists, like art critics, who focus on one aspect to the exclusion of the others, will miss out on important aspects of ritual practices. Ritualistic practices, like art forms, perform various functions. In sorting them out and understanding them, we learn to perceive the world in new and interesting ways—and, as a side benefit, we may, in fact, learn about "bizarre" but actually plausible ways to explain or bring about certain events.

In summing up the differences between his approach and that of Horton, Beattie says,

> The principal difference between us now seems to be that while I find it useful to regard the scientific and the "traditional" as two approaches representing fundamentally different and mutually irreducible ways of looking at the world, Horton thinks that they can be understood in terms of the differences between "closed" and "open" societies.[49]

As we saw earlier, Horton now has abandoned the open versus closed distinction. But if we ask why Beattie believes that the scientific and the traditional represent fundamentally different and mutually irreducible ways of looking at the world, we seem led back to the analogy between traditional thought and art.[50] But this analogy will not support Beattie's claims, although the irreducibility thesis appears sound. A Cézanne painting of Mont Sainte-Victoire cannot be reduced to a scientific description. But nothing startling follows. Presently, we cannot reduce biology to physics. These fields probably represent irreducible ways of looking at the world. Does it follow that they represent fundamentally different ways of looking, or that their cognitive status differs, or that criteria of rightness and rationality are not equally applicable to them?

If challenged, Beattie may rest his fundamental-difference thesis on the grounds that science is primarily cognitive whereas ritual is primarily emotive or expressive. For this reason traditional thought is more aligned with the poets, painters, and musicians than with Horton's scientists. But even this thesis stalls. We saw earlier that emotional factors enter into science, and they may be absent in certain aspects of art. Further, the cognitive-emotive dichtomy, like the analyzing-dramatizing distinction, is suspect as a basis for distinguishing between science and art. As Feyerabend has argued,

> The existing separation between the sciences and the arts is artificial. . . . A poem or play can be intelligent as well as informative . . . and a scientific theory pleasant to behold. . . . The choice between theories which are sufficiently general to yield a comprehensive world view and which are empirically disconnected may become a matter of taste. . . . Matters of taste are not completely beyond the reach of argument. Poems, for example, can be compared in grammar, sound structure, imagery, rhythm, and can be evaluated on such a basis. . . . Even the most elusive mood can be analyzed and should be analyzed if the purpose is to present it in a manner that either can be enjoyed or increases the emotional, cognitive, perceptual, etc. inventory of the reader. Every poet who is worth his salt compares, improves, argues, until he finds the correct formulation of what he wants to say.[51]

On a related theme, Goodman claims,

> In science, unlike art, we are indeed usually less concerned with what is exemplified or expressed than with what is asserted. But to say that truth is asked of science, but not of art is far too simpleminded a way of drawing the distinction between them. Much else besides—and sometimes even rather than—truth is asked of science. Moreover, when we examine our tests for truth in science we find them far from alien to tests for quality in art.[52]

Artists have not neglected to reflect on the cognitive and analytic nature of their work. Constable insisted that "painting is a science and should be pursued as an inquiry into the laws of nature. Why then, may not landscape painting be considered a branch of natural philosophy, of which pictures are but experiments?"[53] And talking about Cézanne, the painter Albert Silvestre reported that "he never ceased declaring that he was not making pictures, but that he was searching for a new technique. Of that technique, each picture contained a portion successfully applied, like a correct phrase of a new language to be created."[54] Beattie's analyzing-versus-dramatizing thesis breaks down; it marks no radical distinction between science and art, or between scientific and traditional thought. Traditional thought and art, just like science, can forge new associations, effect novel emphases, and restructure and reorganize our world. In short, there is no real opposition between the dramatic and the analytic. And what is emotive can, nevertheless, be cognitive.

The analogy drawn between traditional thought and art appears to illuminate traditional thought in ways not entirely foreseen by Beattie, and it brings ritual and science closer together than Beattie envisioned. This point is strengthened when we consider Beattie's claim that "we need to distinguish between the 'truths' of practical experience (whether 'science' or 'common sense') and those also 'true' but in a different way, of religion, myth, and poetry."[55] Some art forms (for example, painting) because nonverbal, lack truth value. But others, as Beattie notes, can be true or false. A sonnet, for example, although literally false, may be metaphorically true. And, as Goodman has argued, in contrast with Beattie who holds to a correspondence theory of truth, at least for science,[56] the tests for metaphorical truth are not significantly different from the tests for literal truth. Further, even nonverbal aesthetic symbols are tested for their rightness in ways not significantly different from scientific hypotheses. Goodman purposes that

> Truth of a hypothesis after all is matter of fit—fit with a body of theory, and fit of hypothesis and theory to the data at hand and the facts to be encountered. . . . But such fitness, such aptness in conforming to and reforming our knowledge and our world, is equally relevant for the aesthetic symbol. Truth and its aesthetic counterpart amount to appropriateness under different names. If we speak of hypotheses but not works of art as true, that is because we reserve the terms "true" and "false" for symbols in sentential form. . . . [This difference] marks no schism between the scientific and aesthetic.[57]

If we acknowledge the existence of different kinds of truths and can accept the connection between truth and appropriateness we may better understand the status of traditional beliefs and some of the charges of irrationality. Consider Evans-Pritchard's famous example of the Nuer belief that twins are birds.[58] Taken literally, the belief is obviously false. Since the Nuer do not also believe that twins have feathers and beaks, the Nuer belief would also appear irrational. But as Evans-Pritchard suggests, this belief is not taken literally by the Nuer themselves and should not be so construed by the anthropologist. For it was the literal interpretation that led anthropologists to postulate mistaken theories about the prelogical mentality of traditional peoples. Examined in context, the Nuer belief can be seen to involve an association of twins and birds with multiple births, Spirit, and the sky. Understood metaphorically, the belief takes on new meanings and fashions novel associations, and the charges of inconsistency, irrationality and prelogical mentality lose much of their force.

A statement that is literally false may nevertheless be true, for example, on metaphorical grounds. Indeed, this may be Beattie's point when he claims that "a Nuer's assertion about twins is not to be regarded as a scientific proposition."[59] Presumably what Beattie means here is that such a belief is not to be taken literally; to take it literally amounts to a failure to understand the complexity of the Nuer belief system and the Nuer language. And here Beattie's remark about not subjecting a sonnet to the same kind of testing as a scientific hypothesis is both illuminating and somewhat misleading.[60] It is misleading in the suggestion that empirical evidence is not relevant for testing statements that are metaphorical. It is illuminating in that for the most part statements in science are to be taken literally. But always to construe poetry or other literary works literally is to miss the point. On the test of literal truth, such works frequently will be bizarre, senseless, and false. But literal truth is not the only truth, and a statement in poetry or myth that is literally and metaphorically false may nevertheless express certain properties and exemplify others. Hence, to view ritual (myth) as art, in this case along the lines of the literary arts, may not only be doing justice to certain traditional views but may also enable us to see the world in unexpected and interesting ways.

To view some traditional thought in this vein is not necessarily to be guilty of the charge brought by Gellner of being excessively charitable and blinding us to "the possibility of . . . absurd, ambiguous or inconsistent doctrines."[61] For, on one hand, the doctrine or myth under study may be literally absurd, inconsistent, or false even though metaphorically true. On the other hand, it may not even be metaphorically true and may express or exemplify little or nothing. Not all metaphors are apt; not all metaphors stand the test of experience. But if a myth (or associated practice) is both literally and metaphorically false, yet expresses or exemplifies much—or serves other important functions—it possesses significance. Further, the prospects for irrational, inconsistent, or false beliefs do not fade when rationality is understood to link up with inductive practice, when words and worlds are viewed as connected, and even when truth is tied to fitness. A detailed study of traditional beliefs, for example, like a similar study of nontraditional ones, would no doubt show some to be in accordance with inductive practice and others not; some rational, others not; some literally or metaphorically true, others not. Neither the distinction between rational and irrational beliefs nor that between true and false beliefs vanishes under the approach proposed here.

Which traditional beliefs turn out to be rational and which true still must await a detailed study of particular traditional systems of beliefs as well as the development of a satisfactory theory of rationality. In the meantime, questions about the irrationality of traditional thought and practices or the existence of "primitive minds" must be dealt with less directly, as they have been here, by examining their presuppositions, whether they concern the nature of science, the nonrelativity of rationality, the independence of reality, the oneness of truth, or the fundamental difference between science and art and scientific and traditional thought.

To argue for viewing traditional thought not only on the model of scientific theory but also on the model of the arts, to investigate ritualistic practice not only instrumentally along the lines of scientific practice but also in terms of symbolic functions characteristic of the arts is, I believe, to do justice to the many and varied aspects of traditional thought and practice, just as it would be the only adequate way to view our own culture. Yet to look at ritual as one does art is not to downgrade ritual or to sharply disassociate it from science. As Goodman has remarked, "The arts must be taken no less seriously than the sciences as models of discovery, creation, and enlargement of knowledge in the broad sense of advancement of understanding."[62] And as Peter Winch has noted, "What we may learn by studying other cultures are not merely possibilities of different ways of doing things, other techniques. More importantly, we may learn different possibilities of making sense of human life, different ideas about the possible importance that the carrying out of certain activities may take on for a man, trying to contemplate the sense of his life as a whole."[63]

Notes

Acknowledgment: I am indebted to Lynn V. Foster for very helpful criticisms of several drafts of this paper.

1. For a sample of the literature, see B. R. Wilson (ed.), *Rationality* (New York: Harper and Row, 1970); R. Horton and R. Finnegan (eds.), *Modes of*

Thought: Essays on Thinking in Western and Non-Western Societies (London: Faber and Faber, 1973); and M. Hollis and S. Lukes (eds.), *Rationality and Relativism* (Cambridge, Mass.: MIT Press, 1982).

2. See John Beattie, "Ritual and Social Change," *Man: Journal of the Royal Anthropological Institute* I (1966): 60–74; Beattie, "On Understanding Ritual," in Wilson (ed.), *Rationality*; Beattie, *Other Cultures* (New York: The Free Press, 1964).

3. Robin Horton, "African Traditional Thought and Western Science," in Wilson (ed.), *Rationality*, pp. 131–171. A fuller version of this article appeared in *Africa* XXXVII (January and April, 1967): 50–71 and 155–187. When the latter article is referred to an asterisk will accompany the page reference. A number of writers have correctly pointed out that much traditional thinking and practice is quite straightforward and involves no mystical-magical elements, whereas the Western scientific world encompasses ritualistic elements as well as scientific ones. So, the differences we are examining here concern more what is distinctive about each world than what is peculiar to each.

4. Beattie, "On Understanding Ritual," p. 261; Beattie, "Ritual and Social Change," p. 65. There is some confusion in the literature that results from looking at science at the level of theory and ritual at the level of practice. Comparing them consistently with regard to theory or practice would eliminate some of the confusion. Although I have not done that here, I hope to do so in another article.

5. See E. E. Evans-Pritchard, *Witchcraft, Oracles and Magic Among the Azande* (Oxford: The Clarendon Press, 1937), pp. 11–12; Evans-Pritchard, "Levy-Bruhl's Theory of Primitive Mentality," *Bulletin of the Faculty of Arts*, Egyptian University, Cairo, 1934; Evans-Pritchard, "Science and Sentiment," *Bulletin of the Faculty of Arts*, Egyptian University, Cairo, 1935.

6. Horton, "African Traditional Thought," p. 142.

7. See, for example, Evon Z. Vogt, *The Zinacantecos of Mexico* (New York: Holt, Rinehart, and Winston, 1970); and Vogt, *Tortillas for the Gods* (Cambridge, Mass.: Harvard University Press, 1976).

8. Horton, "African Traditional Thought," p. 153.

9. *Ibid.*, p. 155.

10. Beattie, "On Understanding Ritual," pp. 264–265.

11. Thomas S. Kuhn, *The Structure of Scientific Revolutions*, 2nd ed. (Chicago: University of Chicago Press, 1970). See also W. V. Quine, "Two Dogmas of Empiricism," in Quine, *From a Logical Point of View*, 2nd ed. (Cambridge, Mass.: Harvard University Press, 1961).

12. Kuhn, *Structure of Scientific Revolutions*, p. 77. See also Nelson Goodman, "Science and Simplicity," in Goodman, *Problems and Projects* (Indianapolis:

Bobbs-Merrill, 1972); and P. Duhem, *The Aims and Structure of Physical Theory*, trans. P. P. Wiener (Princeton: Princeton University Press, 1959), Part 2, Chap. 6, especially pp. 183–190.

13. Kuhn, *The Structure of Scientific Revolutions*, p. 78.

14. Horton, "African Traditional Thought," p. 162. Horton remarks in a footnote that this "idea of secondary elaboration as a key feature of prescientific thought-systems was put forward . . . by Evans-Pritchard in his *Witchcraft, Oracles and Magic Among the Azande*." See pp. 201–204 of Evans-Pritchard's book for his account of the twenty-two reasons why the Azande fail to "perceive the futility of their magic."

15. Thomas Kuhn, "Logic of Discovery or Psychology of Research?" in I. Lakatos and A. Musgrave (eds.), *Criticism and the Growth of Knowledge* (Cambridge, England: Cambridge University Press, 1970), p. 6.

16. Horton, "African Traditional Thought," p. 163. Horton claims that "this underlying readiness to scrap or demote established theories on the ground of poor predictive performance is perhaps the most important feature of the scientific attitude" (p. 164).

17. Robin Horton, "Tradition and Modernity Revisited," in Hollis and Lukes (eds.), *Rationality and Relativism*, pp. 201–260.

18. *Ibid.*, pp. 219–220.

19. See Esther Pasztory, *Aztec Art* (New York: Harry N. Abrams, Inc., 1983).

20. Thomas Kuhn, "Reflections on My Critics," in Lakatos and Musgrave (eds.), *Criticism and the Growth of Knowledge*, pp. 245–246.

21. For an illuminating example of the existence of such an alternative theory which nevertheless was not adopted until approximately two thousand years after it was first propounded, see Kuhn's remarks on Aristarchus' heliocentric theory in *The Structure of Scientific Revolutions*, pp. 75–76.

22. Horton, "African Traditional Thought," p. 161. For an intriguing different perspective on this personal idiom, see Mary Douglas, *Purity and Danger* (London: Routledge and Kegan Paul, 1966), Chap. 5.

23. Horton, "Tradition and Modernity Revisited," pp. 256–260.

24. Horton, "African Traditional Thought," p. 157. See ATT*, pp. 157–161.

25. *Ibid.*, p. 157.

26. *Ibid.*, pp. 155–156.

27. Nelson Goodman, *Fact, Fiction and Forecast*, 4th ed. (Cambridge, Mass.: Harvard University Press, 1983), Chaps. 3 and 4. See also Goodman, "Science and Simplicity," and Goodman, "The Test of Simplicity" both in Goodman, *Problems and Projects*. For Goodman's more recent statements about the role of language and other symbols in worldmaking see his *Ways of Worldmaking*

(Indianapolis: Hackett Publishing Co., 1978), Chaps. 1, 6, and 7; and *Of Mind and Other Matters* (Cambridge, Mass.: Harvard University Press, 1984), Part 2.

28. Goodman, "Notes on the Well-Made World," in Goodman, *Of Mind and Other Matters*, pp. 30–39.

29. See, for example, E. H. Gombrich, *Art and illusion* (New York: Pantheon Books, 1961). At one point Gombrich writes, "There is no reality without interpretation; just as there is no innocent eye, there is no innocent ear" (p. 363).

30. Kuhn, *The Structure of Scientific Revolutions*, p. 110.

31. J. L. Austin, "Performative Utterances," in Austin, *Philosophical Papers,* O. J. Urmson and G. J. Warnock (Oxford: The Clarendon Press, 1961).

32. Goodman, *Fact, Fiction and Forecast*, Chaps. 3 and 4. See also C. G. Hempel's example of the order creating concept of time in his *Fundamentals of Concept Formation in Empirical Science* (Chicago: University of Chicago Press, 1952) pp. 73–74.

33. Steven Lukes, "Some Problems about Rationality," in Wilson (ed.), *Rationality*, pp. 194–213. See especially pp. 208–213.

34. For a defense of this position, see "Inductive and Ethical Validity" *American Philosophical Quarterly* VIII (January 1971): 35–44.

35. Goodman, "Notes on the Well-Made World," p. 38.

36. *Ibid.*, pp. 30–38.

37. Beattie, "On Understanding Ritual," p. 263.

38. Beattie, "Ritual and Social Change," p. 65. Beattie notes "that causal efficacy is often attributed to ritual . . . [and] serves to distinguish the magico-religious field from that of art, but it does not . . . in any way invalidate this approach" (p. 72).

39. Beattie, "On Understanding Ritual," pp. 261, 265.

40. Much of what follows draws on Goodman's penetrating analysis of symbol systems in his *Language of Art* (Indianapolis: Bobbs-Merrill, 1968). See especially Chaps. 1, 2, and 6.

41. See Linda Schele and Mary Ellen Miller, *The Blood of Kings* (Fort Worth: Kimball Art Museum, 1986).

42. Israel Scheffler, "Ritual and Reference," *Synthese* XLVI (March 1981): 435.

43. This claim needs to be taken in conjunction with what was said in Part I of this paper concerning the reasons for the presence and persistence of apparently irrational beliefs and practices.

44. Goodman, *Languages of Art*, pp. 246–247.

45. Evans-Pritchard, *Witchcraft, Oracles and Magic*, p. 492.

46. See, for example, Horton on the social causes of illness, "African Traditional Thought," pp. 135–139. In similar vein, one is reminded of Galileo's
unfortunate attack on Kepler for suggesting that the moon had some influence on
the tides. Galileo wrote, "Among all the famous men who have philosophized
upon the admirable effect of Nature, I wonder more at Kepler than at any of the
rest, who, being of a free and penetrating intellect, has, for all that, given his
ear and assent to the Moon's predominance over the water and to occult properties and such-like trifles" (Galileo, *Dialogue on the Great World Systems*, trans.
Salusburg [Chicago: University of Chicago Press, 1953], p. 469).

47. Vogt, *Tortillas for the Gods*, p. 6.

48. *Ibid.*, pp. 18, 20, 25, 46.

49. Beattie, "On Understanding Ritual," p. 265.

50. We are also led back to Beattie's positivistic views on science. At one
point he argues that "ritual is not science and is nothing like it, it operates not
by trial and error, guided by observation, but by symbolism and drama" ("Ritual
and Social Change," p. 65). Feyerabend notes, "The Copernican view at the time
of Galileo was inconsistent with facts so plain and obvious that Galileo had to
call it 'surely false.' 'There is no limit to my astonishment,' he writes in a later
work, 'when I reflect that Aristarchus and Copernicus were able to make reason
so conquer sense that in defiance of the latter, the former became mistress of their
belief.' Newton's theory of gravitation was beset, from the very beginning, by a
considerable number of difficulties which were serious enough to provide material
for refutations. . . . Bohr's atomic model was introduced and retained in the face
of very precise and unshakable contrary evidence" (P. K. Feyerabend, "Against
Method: Outline of an Anarchistic Theory of Knowledge," in M. Radner and
S. Winokur [eds.], *Minnesota Studies in the Philosophy of Science* [Minneapolis:
University of Minnesota Press, 1970.], Vol. 4, p. 37. For additional examples see
pp. 37–48, 71–72, 83.

51. Feyerabend, "Against Method," p. 91.

52. Goodman, "Some Notes on *Languages of Art*" in Goodman, *Problems
and Projects*, p. 132.

53. Quoted by Gombrich, *Art and Illusion*, p. 175.

54. Quoted by Theodore Reff in "Painting and Theory in the Final Decade,"
in *Cezanne: The Late Work* (New York: The Museum of Modern Art, 1977),
p. 37.

55. Beattie, "On Understanding Ritual," pp. 257–258. Elsewhere Beattie
writes, "No sensible person subjects a sonnet or a sonata to the same kind of

examination and testing as he does a scientific hypothesis, even though each contains its own kind of 'truth'. Likewise, the sensible student of myth, magic and religion will . . . be well advised to recognize that their tenets are not scientific propositions, based on experience and on a belief in the uniformity of nature, and they cannot be adequately understood as if they were" ("Ritual and Social Change," p. 72). Note here Beattie's fairly simple view of science, which is, I believe, a source of some of the provocative but mistaken dichotomies he draws. For another source, see the following footnote for Beattie's acceptance of the correspondence theory of truth.

56. Beattie writes, "For the magician, as for the artist, the basic question is not whether his ritual is 'true', in the sense of corresponding exactly with some ascertainable reality" ("Ritual and Social Change," p. 68).

57. Goodman, *Languages of Art*, p. 264.

58. E. E. Evans-Pritchard, *Nuer Religion* (New York: Oxford University Press, 1974), pp.. 129–132.

59. Beattie, *Other Cultures*, p. 68.

60. See note 55.

61. Ernest Gellner, "Concepts and Society," in Wilson (ed.), *Rationality*, p. 43.

62. Goodman, *Ways of Worldmaking*, p. 102.

63. Peter Winch, "Understanding a Primitive Society," in Wilson (ed.), *Rationality*, p. 106.

II | A Limited Defense of the National Interest

Robert L. Simon

In both the theory and practice of international relations, the court of last resort frequently is appeal to the national interest. Pursuit of the national interest is cited not only as an explanation for the actual behavior of nations but also as a justification of it.

However, although the explanatory power of appeal to the national interest may be of theoretical interest, the appeal to the national interest as a normative justification of the behavior of states has come under increasing moral criticism. Nations that single-mindedly pursue their national interest have been compared to egoistic individuals who trample on the rights of others. Charles Beitz maintains that from a Rawlsian global original position, national boundaries would lack fundamental moral significance. Other theorists reject the very idea of the national interest as intellectually incoherent. Thus, Noam Chomsky tells us that the concept of " 'national interest' is a mystification that serves to conceal the ways in which state policy is formed and executed."[1]

Considerations of national interest surely have been used far too often as mere rationalizations for the aggrandizement of national power or private gain. However, it is possible for the critical pendulum to go too far. Although we surely should not follow Machiavelli in pursuing the national interest "against faith, against charity, against humanity and against religion," it is far from clear that appeal to the national interest always lacks justificatory force in international affairs.

On the contrary, it is possible that illegitimate appeals to the national interest have rhetorical impact precisely because they are parasitic on legitimate uses that do have justificatory force. The misuse of appeal to the national interest is, in this view, simply part of "the tribute that vice plays to virtue." Indeed, a parallel point can be made about normative appeals to the public interest in domestic political discourse. Although claims about the public interest sometimes may function as ideological rationalizations for the pursuit of private or group interests, such claims have impact only because the public interest is generally conceived of as a value worth pursuing.[2] Perhaps, then, appeal to the national interest can sometimes play a coherent if limited justificatory role in international affairs, just as appeal to the public interest sometimes plays a coherent justificatory role in domestic political discourse.

Although such a thesis is at most suggested rather than established in this paper, perhaps enough can be said to show that the national interest is a more interesting notion than many philosophers have acknowledged and is well worth further philosophic scrutiny.

I. Conceptual Considerations

It is important to distinguish the *concept* of the national interest from different *conceptions* of what constitutes that interest.[3] Similarly, the concept of the public interest can be distinguished from various conceptions of the public interest. Thus, the public interest has been identified with the aggregate of individual interests, the common interests of all members of the public, the interests of individuals *qua* members of the public, and the interest in preserving public institutions and ways of life. But for each of these conceptions to be conceptions of the public interest, they must contrast with our diverse interests as individuals in pursuing our own private satisfactions.[4]

Similarly, the national interest must be distinguishable conceptually from the private interests of individuals or groups within the nation. Thus, the national interest may require sacrifices from citizens that are not in their interests *qua* individuals. In extreme cases, dissolution of the state may be in the individual interests of the citizens although it could hardly be in the national interest as well.

Once the national interest is distinguished from individual interests, certain kinds of criticisms of the national interest can be defused. Thus, Peter G. Brown writes that "by referring to any sort of well-being of the citizens of a nation, the national interest can serve to sound the alarm for the slightest actual or potential incursion on . . . privilege. . . . It can be thought to justify nearly any policy which might enhance the well-being of Americans."[5] But once the national interest is distinguished from private or group interests, it no longer follows that any policy that enhances the well-being of Americans as individuals also is in the national interest. Thus, Brown's remarks are better construed as warnings against misuse of appeal to the national interest rather than as undermining all use of that appeal altogether. Brown is quite right to claim that if the national interest is confused with individual interests, the national interest can be construed in a dangerously broad way, but better understanding of the distinction between national and individual interest can help us avoid this confusion.

Should the national interest simply be identified with the public interest? After all, both are employed to demarcate an area of broad public concern from purely private interests. Thus, it is tempting to conclude that the only difference is one of usage. The "national interest" is employed when discussing international relations and the "public interest" is employed when discussing domestic politics. But in this view, the interests being appealed to are in each case the same.

Although the thesis that the public and the national interests are identical is plausible, there are good reasons for considering alternative views. It is even arguable that in some contexts, the national and public interests can actually conflict, which would be impossible on the supposition that they were identical. For example, open discussion of intelligence-gathering institutions might be in the public interest, because it would stimulate public understanding of the proper role of intelligence gathering in a democracy, but may damage the national interest by revealing our hitherto unsuspected capacity to obtain secret information. In this view, we sometimes have to choose between a degree of enhancement of public life and a degree of damage to national security, a key element of national interest.

Although consideration of such examples is not likely to be conclusive, it suggests that there may be important differences between the national and public interests. For one thing, "national" seems narrower in scope than "public." By picking out the state as its target of concern, those practices, rules, and institutions that have to do with the nation's existence and status as a political entity are made central. The public interest, however, can encompass cultural and social as well as political factors; for example, public support for research in the humanities.

More important, the national interest seems to function in a comparative context in a way that the public interest does not.[6] Thus, the public interest can be pursued within an entirely self-sufficient nation that has no contact with lands beyond its borders. However, determination of the national interest requires comparative analysis in a way that determination of the public interest does not. This may be because national security is (necessarily) an element of national interest and can itself be assessed only relative to overt or covert threats from across national boundaries.

A full consideration of the concept of national interest requires more extended treatment than has been provided here. For our purposes, it is enough to note that the concept of national interest is no more suspect conceptually than the parallel notion of public interest, that in both cases the interests in question are viewed from a broader perspective than that of individuals or interest groups within the state, and that it is at least arguable that the national and public interest, while overlapping, are distinct.

II. Conceptions of the National Interest

The concept of national interest has to do with the interests of the national community and not with the private interests of its constituents. However, there can be and are different conceptions of what constitutes that interest. In particular, conceptions can differ over what constitutes the nation, over the nature of the nation's interest, and over what particular policies are best suited to secure that interest as so defined.

For example, is the nation to be identified with a particular territorial configuration, with the preservation of a particular set of political institutions and rules, or with the continued sovereignty of a particular group? Thus, should the nation of Saudi Arabia be identified with the continued rule of the royal family or with the stability of Saudi territory or with the dominance of a set of religious and cultural values? Clearly, one's conception of the national interest of Saudi Arabia may vary depending upon one's conception of what constitutes the Saudi nation.

Dispute is possible not only over what constitutes the nation but also over the nature of its interests. Perhaps the most useful distinction here is between "realist" conceptions of interest, which define interest soley in terms of power and security, and normative conceptions that appeal to national ideals and values as constituents of the national interest.[7] Felix Oppenheim has recommended that "interest" be construed in the former sense because such a construal not only makes empirical analysis of the national interest possible but also allows for the clear separation of ethical and empirical questions.[8] Thus, in such a view, we could determine empirically whether a given policy enhanced the U.S. national interest, that is, increased the power of the United States, and consider independently whether such a policy was or was not immoral.

On the other hand, ideal conceptions of the national interest appeal not only to such factors as security or power but also to values that are held to be fundamental to national existence. For example, an ideal conception of the U.S. national interest might include, over and above a concern for national security, an emphasis on the preservation of constitutional and democratic values.

Of course, the more one packs into the national interest, the greater the chance of conflict among the discrete elements. What previously was a conflict between the national interest, narrowly construed, and some other value will simply reappear as a conflict between two different constituents of the national interest broadly construed; for example, between national security and preservation of democratic values.[9]

Should we therefore accept the recommendation that the national interest be explicated only in such "realist" terms as power and security? Such a recommendation at least seems to be supported by the gains in clarity it promotes. I suggest nevertheless that the issue is more complex than supporters of the "empirical" realist approach maintain.

For one thing, terms like "power" and "security" raise difficult conceptual problems themselves. Is security to be measured only in terms of military might, or does it also encompass such less tangible and perhaps value-laden notions as the loyalty of the citizenry and commitment to important national values? Is the nation less secure, for example, the less people understand and respect the principles underlying the Bill of Rights? If power is to be understood as the ability to get others to carry out one's desires, does that omit the power to shape the desires of others to begin with, so that their wishes do not differ from one's own? How broadly or narrowly is "power" to be understood? It is far from self-evident, then, that the realist conception of national interest is either conceptually simple or value-free.

Perhaps more important, it is difficult to understand why a nation's interests must be exclusively concerned with power and military security any more than an individual's interests should exclusively involve domination of others and protection from force. Just as it may be in an individual's interest to be a decent person, not because the image of decency promotes covert power over others but because that is the way the individual wants to be, so it may be in a nation's interest to be a decent state, just because that is the way the nation most deeply conceives of itself. Although such a view surely involves problems, it hardly seems unintelligible or incoherent. Moreover, as we have seen, the narrow realist conception of national interest is not without its problems as well.

Perhaps the best thing to conclude is that it is important to avoid two conceptual pitfalls. The first involves packing so many disparate values into the national interest that appeal to the national interest becomes empty of all but rhetorical force, performing no other role than that of expressing general moral approval. The second is that of excessive narrowness, where all conceptions of national interest except that of the realist are dismissed without a hearing. Rather, different conceptions of the national interest, each value-laden to different degrees and containing different normative packages, need to be evaluated on their own merits.

Accordingly, rhetorical appeal to the national interest should not be allowed to obscure the point that often the very nature of the national interest itself should be at the center of political debate. As Charles Frankel has told us,

> A national interest is not a chart pinned to the wall from which one takes one's sense of direction. The heart of the decision making process . . . is not the finding of the best means to serve a national interest already perfectly known and understood. It is the determining of that interest itself: the reassessment of the nation's resources, needs, commitments, traditions and political and cultural horizons—in short, its calendar of values.[10]

III. Realism and Morality in International Affairs

We can now turn to what is perhaps the major problem concerning the national interest; namely, an exploration of the role the national interest should play in the formation of national policy. When, if ever, does appeal to the national interest justify the behavior of states that act in its name?

Normative political realism is the view that moral considerations should not influence the conduct of nations. In the view of the realists, national policy is best formulated on a basis of national interest, narrowly conceived. However, the conceptual considerations advanced so far undermine one of the major arguments offered in support of such alleged realism.

According to this argument, if states pursue their own moral ideals in the international arena, their behavior will be unstable, unconstrained, and unpredictable. As Hans Morganthau warned us, "What is good for the crusading country is by definition good for all mankind and if the rest of mankind refuses to accept such claims to universal recognition, it must be converted with fire and sword."[11] On the other hand, the realists argue, if each state realistically calculates its own interests and restricts itself to their pursuit, its behavior becomes stable, predictable, and above all constrained. The kind of compromise that often is impossible on matters of deep moral principle becomes a predominant means of securing national interest. Accordingly, peace, security, and tolerance of national differences is best assured if every state avoids pursuit of abstract moral ideals and pursues its own national interest instead.

Such an argument does serve as an important warning against an overzealous crusading moralism in foreign affairs. However, it does not establish that pursuit of the national interest always should take precedence over conflicting moral values. Although a number of important criticisms might be raised against it, the objection that the account of national interest presupposed by the argument is defective is of special interest here.

That is, the realist's argument assumes that the national interest will be discovered and understood the same way by all observers regardless of their own normative commitments or ideological frameworks. However, as we have seen, different conceptions of the national interest may have significantly different implications for policy. Disaster in international affairs can arise not only from crusading moralism but also from one state basing its foreign policy upon mistaken assumptions about what conception of the national interest is dominant in a rival nation. Ideologues may be all too eager to assume that other nations have similar notions of national interest when they do not. Some conceptions of the national interest, such as those that identify it with national hegemony, can be inherently destabilizing. Finally, the conception of the national interest dominant in a nation at one time may no longer be dominant at another. Thus, the assumption of the realist that the national interest provides a clear, easily ascertainable basis for predicting the behavior of nations and for ensuring stability of policy is open to serious objection. The very account of national interest on which it rests is at best an extremely oversimplified one.

Moreover, it hardly is necessary to add that the role of morality in international affairs need not be restricted to a dogmatic and intolerant form of crusading moralism. The realist characterization of morality in international relations is as much a caricature as the equation of morality in domestic affairs to the simplistic mechanical application of rigid, exceptionless rules to complex situations. On the contrary, appreciation of special circumstances, willingness to compromise, tolerance of differences, and sensitivity to the consequences of action are just as much elements of a rational approach to the application of moral principles in international affairs as they are to the application of morality within a social framework.[12]

Thus, the realist notion of national interest and of morality are both unrealistic. We can conclude that the claim that universal pursuit of national interest will best promote peace has yet to be adequately defended.

IV. National Interest and Moral Justification

Even if the national interest is not literally an incoherent notion, it still may not have justificatory force in the formation and assessment of policy. According to the cosmopolitan moralist, the pursuit of national interest should be subordinated to moral principle in international affairs just as the pursuit of selfish personal interest should be subordinated to moral principle in domestic affairs.

The traditional response of the realists is that international affairs, unlike domestic society, is a Hobbesian state of nature. Since no nation can rely on any other to behave morally toward it, no state is morally required to sacrifice its interests for moral principle. Morality does not require (although it may permit) extreme self-sacrifice. But that is exactly what the pursuit of morality would entail in a context where morality is not generally followed. As Hans Morganthau has argued, "a foreign policy guided by universal moral principles . . . relegating the national interest to the background is under contemporary conditions . . . a policy of national suicide actual or potential."[13] Accordingly, pursuit of the national interest is at least morally permissible, because its abandonment is not morally required.

The claim that international affairs closely resembles a Hobbesian state of nature is controversial and has been attacked most recently, and in my view successfully, by Charles Beitz in his book *Political Theory and International Relations*.[14] What has not so often been noticed, however, is that even if international relations do closely resemble such a state of war of all against all, the extreme conclusions of the realists do not follow.

That is, the premises that (1) no nation can count on other nations to act morally toward it and that (2) no nation is morally required to take extreme risks to its national interest do not entail that (3) no moral requirements at all exist in international affairs. Rather, (1) and (2) establish at most that nations are not required to undergo severe risk, not that they are permitted to do anything that enhances their national interest to any degree. Similarly, an individual in a

Hobbesian state of nature may not be morally required to unilaterally disarm. It does not follow that he is morally permitted to attack the helpless, murder babies, rape women, or torture those who have done him no harm.

But if there are moral requirements that apply in international affairs, what are they? Just as the realists err in their overly simplistic construal both of morality and of national interest, there is a tendency of the moralist to err in a similar fashion. This can result not only in the kind of overzealous, crusading moralism that realists rightly fear but also in a tendency to oversimplify the moral factors that bear in actual international relations. Thus, appeals to ideal conceptions of morality, such as Rawl's conception of justice, may be thought to give direct guidance in actual international dilemmas. States may be held to the same standards of behavior that would apply to individuals functioning within a well-ordered domestic society. The range of considerations bearing upon a situation may be too narrowly construed in a too rigidly individualistic fashion.[15]

Thus, although I am in strong sympathy with the view that the pursuit of the national interest ought to be constrained by moral principle, and that the requirement of respect for individual persons surely is the most fundamental of such restraints, I suggest there is also a danger in construing moral restraints in an overly ideal manner. Although morality surely applies in international relations, the kind of morality that applies may not be strictly analogous either to ideal models of justice or to the moral relations that might hold among individuals conceived of in a socially isolated, atomistic manner.

Consider, for example, Beitz's claim when he recommends that we

> dispense with the idea of national interest . . . and appeal directly to the rights and interests of all parties affected by the choice. . . . It is the rights and interests of persons that are of fundamental importance from the moral point of view and it is to those considerations that the justification of principles for international relations should appeal.[16]

The claim that the ultimate justification for the principles of international relations lies in the rights and interests of individuals seems both plausible and correct. However, this claim should not be confused with the superficially similar assertion that securing the rights and interests of individuals *qua* isolated atomic individuals is the primary requirement of an ethic of international affairs. In addition to their rights and interests *qua* persons, individuals may also have rights and interests *qua* members of political communities.

Consider an example from a different context. Suppose that the administration of one's university proposes that courses in Greek and Latin be dropped because of lack of enrollment. As a member of the faculty committee charged with evaluating that proposal, you can respond from a number of perspectives. From the point of view of your own interests, effects on your salary might well be considered. However, as a member of the committee, you are committed to asking how the proposal is to be evaluated from the perspective of the university. Once you take this perspective, features such as the balance of the curriculum, the importance of a classical background for appreciation of other subjects, and the rights of affected faculty become paramount. These considerations involve the entitlements and interests of individuals; but the rights and interests in question arise because of individual relationships to the university and so are not independent of it.

Similarly, in appealing to the national or public interests, we thereby delineate the range of considerations that are held to be relevant to the issue at hand. For in addition to the purely individualistic human rights said to be possessed by all individuals, such as the right to liberty from coercion, individuals may also have interests in, as well as rights to, association in political communities of their choice and in promoting the welfare of such communities without unjustified outside interference.[17]

Once it is recognized that associational rights and interests should be taken account of in international affairs, the application of individualistic moral principles to the world as a whole becomes exceedingly complex. Consider, for example, the principle of rights over interests which, as articulated by Peter G. Brown, states that "In every case of conflict between the promotion of an interest to which no one has a right and the promotion of a right, the right takes priority over the mere interest.[18] As developed by Brown and applied to international affairs, this principle requires that respect for individual human rights take precedence over pursuit of national interest. Such a view is plausible precisely because in domestic affairs it is one function of rights to protect individuals against the unrestrained pursuit of either private or collective interests. However, although the principle of rights over interests faces difficulties even when applied internally, these difficulties are especially acute in the international arena.

For one thing, as Brown himself would acknowledge, the national interest itself might involve or affect significant rights, including the associational rights referred to earlier. In such a case, it would be better to speak of a conflict of rights rather than a conflict of rights with pure national interests. That is, we cannot just assume, to use Brown's language, that national interests always are interests "to which no one has a right."

However, even if we ignore this point, difficulties remain. Suppose, for example, that the inhabitants of developing nation A are especially needy and have human rights to aid from the more affluent nations. Does it automatically follow that nation B, which is threatened by A, has an obligation to provide the aid, regardless of national interest? Does Israel, for example, have equal obligations to provide aid to both Syria and Chad?

Again, suppose countries have at least a *prima facie* obligation to protect smaller helpless nations from external aggression. Does it follow that this obligation must be met regardless of cost to the rescuer's national interests?

Does the principle of rights over interests require that nations must not violate human rights abroad or does it also require that they must take positive action, regardless of its effects on national interest, to prevent violation of rights by others? Must a nation refrain from even a minimal risk of violating rights abroad, even if it thereby places its own national interest in severe jeopardy? Is *any* degree of risk to rights through the pursuit of interest prohibited, or is a state more justified in promoting its national interest the lower the probability of rights being adversely affected? Do more defensible conceptions of the national interest have greater moral weight than less defensible ones when balanced against risk to rights?

These questions suggest that the principle of rights over interests is far from self-evident, at least in international affairs. Stated as a simple formula, it is just too simple to apply easily to the kinds of questions raised above. A more complex version might well be defensible, but how is it to be formulated? Although I am not able to offer a version of the principle that is defensible, I would like to conclude by suggesting three errors that should be avoided when trying to balance concern for national interest against regard for human rights.

First, in formulating a human rights policy, we should avoid what Robert Nozick has called a simple utilitarianism of rights, which justifies the violation of some rights in order to secure greater respect for rights in the future. Such a view faces difficulties parallel to those facing classical utilitarianism, particularly those involving the need for a fair distribution of benefits and burdens. For example, such a utilitarianism of rights allows for imposition of sacrifices on those with the least ability to bear them in order to achieve future benefits. Thus, as Beitz has pointed out, development policies that impose heavy burdens on the poorest unproductive members of today's third world societies in order to promote future production raise disturbing distributive issues.[19] Although it is doubtful if consequentialist calculations of future effects on human rights can or should be entirely avoided, distributive as well as aggregative considerations need to be considered.

Second, the moral constraints set by rights on interests in international affairs are unlikely to parallel those that hold among individuals within a well-ordered society. For although the claim of the realists that international affairs is a Hobbesian state of nature seems overdrawn, the world as a whole is not yet a global society either. It is true that some writers, such as Beitz, argue that increasing economic interdependence among nations has transformed the international arena into the analogue of a world society.[20] Beitz uses such a conclusion as his basis for maintaining that whatever principles of justice should apply within states—in his view those of John Rawl's theory of justice as fairness—should thereby apply to the world as a whole.

However, and here is where the realists may have a point, even if economic interdependence is one precondition for the existence of social bonds, reciprocity seems to be another. Mutual acknowledgment of fundamental norms, a willingness to generally abide by them, and provisions for protection from and punishment of violators all seem to be crucial. Thus, Rawls characterizes a society as an "association of persons who in their relations to one another recognize certain rules of conduct as binding and for the most part act in accordance with them."[21] Such a view captures the idea of many that a society is far more than a marketplace.

If this suggestion has force, then the moral principles that apply in the international arena may differ significantly from those that apply to individuals within a reasonably well-ordered state. In particular, the ethic of international relations, as it applies to states, may resemble much more an ethic that would apply to individuals under conditions of unusual risk than an ethic that would apply to individuals under conditions of law and order. Of course, even under conditions of unusual risk, states, like individuals, would be presumptively obligated to avoid violating the rights of others and to aid those in danger, when provision of such aid is not especially risky. Moreover, even under conditions of risk, an individual normally is not entitled to use an innocent person as a shield against an attacker or expose the innocent to risk, at least not without an extraordinary moral justification.

On the other hand, the failure to meet less stringent obligations might be excused, even if in the absence of risk similar failure might be unjustifiable. For example, preventive attack against a perceived threat surely is easier to justify under conditions of partial compliance than in a well-ordered domestic society. Again, individuals at risk who are justified in doubting whether others will comply with moral restrictions may be excused for making alliances with unsavory characters whom they would have a duty to turn over to the police in a well-ordered state. Similarly, in extreme circumstances, democracies may make alliances with undemocratic states, at least when it is unclear there is a viable democratic altenative and the dangers of not entering into such an alliance are clear and present. In such cases, it is not that the state is "beyond" morality, as the realists might have it, but rather that the peculiar morality applied in international relations justifies or at least excuses conduct that under better circumstances would be unwarranted.[22]

Thirdly, when it comes to balancing pursuit of the national interest against concern for the rights of others, we should avoid hard-and-fast prohibitions and rely on sliding scales instead. For example, instead of saying that rights always have priority over interests, no matter what, we should say that the greater the risk of rights violation and the lower the risk of harm to the national interest, the less justification there is for pursuing the national interest at the expense of rights. A second sliding scale might stipulate that the more defensible the conception of the national interest at stake and the less central the kinds of rights being threatened, the greater the justification for promoting the national interest at some risk to rights. Policy-making would reflect complex judgments, not only about the points of balance on particular scales, such as one comparing risks to rights versus risks to interests, but also judgments that combine the readings on a variety of different scales as well. In my own view, there ought to be a strong presumption against violating rights that can be overridden only when the scales lean decisively toward the national interest in the context in question; but that is a long way from saying that talk about the national interest is unintelligible, let alone that it should have no weight in the policy-making process.

It might be objected that if policy makers are given leeway to make such rough-and-ready calculations about national interest, they are likely to misuse their discretion. As a result, indefensible conceptions of the national interest will be constantly misapplied. In order to avoid misuse, wouldn't it be better to adopt an absolutist and simple version of the principle of rights over interests, rather than allow officials the wiggle room provided by more complex versions? Although there may be particular cases where the kind of flexibility and weighing of moral costs and benefits would produce the best result, wouldn't we do better on the whole, morally speaking, to forbid such critical calculations and insist on strict adherence to the rights-over-interests principle?

Although it is tempting to accept such a conclusion, on the ground that although ideally the balancing of complex values is necessary, actual leaders in the actual world cannot be trusted to do it. In the actual world, so this argument goes, we are better off with an absolute limit on pursuit of the national interest, precisely because we are not ideal moral agents.

However, if the major arguments of this paper are sound, we are not likely to procure the best overall moral results simply by ignoring defensible appeals to the national interest. We need to stop viewing the conflict between concern for the national interest and concern for human rights as always a conflict between selfishness and morality. As we have seen, although concern for rights should perhaps be assigned priority, different conceptions of the national interest may have moral weight of their own. To reconcile conflicts of value by always ignoring one of the conflicting elements is simply to ignore one of the morally relevant factors; such a policy is hardly likely to yield morally defensible results over time.

V. Terrorism and the National Interest

Consideration of terrorism, and attempts to defend against it, may provide a concrete example of the sort of considerations discussed so far. Although a thorough examination of the topic cannot be conducted here, perhaps enough can be said to illustrate at least an intuitive case of how the national interest can have justificatory force in international affairs.

"Terrorism" can be explicated in a morally laden manner, such that one has to make a moral judgment before determining whether a case of violence can appropriately come under that heading. A crude example of such a value-laden account would equate terrorism with *unjustified* violence employed for some political purpose. Alternately, one might attempt to explicate terrorism in a less value-laden way, perhaps by equating it with violence directed against innocent, that is, nonthreatening, individuals for the purpose of terrorizing a population so as to achieve some political goal. If terrorism is described in such a relatively neutral way, we need only make factual judgments in order to agree on whether particular acts of violence are instances of terrorism. However, we would still need to make a further moral judgment in order to decide whether terrorism, as so defined, is justified or unjustified.

Because the linguistic question of how terrorism should be defined cannot be used to stipulate a solution to moral questions, for a moral judgment must be made whether or not we employ a value-laden definition if terrorism is to be condemned, we need not dwell on definitional questions here. I shall simply indicate that the kind of terrorism I am concerned with involves violence directed at innocent individuals with the intent of terrorizing a population so as to attain a political goal. I shall take it for granted, although it is not crucial to my argument, that terrorism as so understood therefore is *prima facie* wrong since it involves harm to innocents. It of course remains an open question, not to be settled by linguistic stipulation, who is to count as innocent, or whether terrorism, in some other sense, carries different moral implications with it.

Three important points, suggested by our earlier discussion, are these.

(1) Barring highly unlikely circumstances, states are not entitled to react to terrorism in any way their national interest dictates, regardless of moral restraint.

(2) Nations may react to terrorism in ways not permitted to individuals in well-ordered domestic societies.

(3) Within limits, the national interest can play a legitimate justificatory role in determining the response of states to terrorism.

Let us consider these points in turn.

In light of the earlier critique of realism, and of the Hobbesian argument, (1) should not need extensive defense. For example, outside the direst of circumstances one can imagine, nations attacked by terrorists would not be justified in rounding up babies of the same nationality as the terrorists and executing them, even if such a practice would have some deterrent effect in reducing attacks. On the other hand, nations clearly can take some steps that would not be open to threatened individuals in a well-ordered society. Thus, individuals in such a society would not be entitled to take the law in their own hands and conduct reprisals. However, it seems clear that nations may do so, at least where the innocent are not likely to be harmed by retaliatory action.

Turning to the role of national interest in these matters, note that although nations sometimes may be morally permitted to retaliate against terrorists, they do not seem morally required to do so. Surely, one factor that can justify policy makers in deciding not only whether to retaliate but also how to retaliate can be the national interest. How much force the national interest will have in a given case will depend upon the kind of factors discussed in the previous section, but it is at least theoretically possible, and arguably actually the case, that in some contexts the national interest will be decisive.

In some cases, surely in most actual cases, the national interest may have to be weighed against competing moral factors. For example, perhaps the form of response most in the national interest will carry with it some significant risk to innocent lives. That is surely a strong reason for not responding in the way suggested. But suppose the risk is relatively low, suppose there is good reason to believe not only that many more innocent lives will be lost if the response will not be made but also that damage to the national interest will be very great, and that there are strong moral reasons (although not necessarily atomistic individualistic ones) for supporting the national interest. Suppose, for example, that lack of a strong response will cause a failure of nerve among people in the democracies, which will in turn undermine the security of the democracies. It is at least arguable that in such circumstances, the national interest has some weight relative to the prohibition against risking harm to the innocent.[23]

Critics might reply that if this is so, it is because protection of the security of democratic states is tied to protection of individual rights and interests. Perhaps they would acknowledge that some risk to the innocent justifiably can be tolerated in order to combat terrorism. But if so, it is not because of the national interest but because of the need to protect the rights and interests of other individuals.

What such critics may fail to acknowledge, however, is that, in part, the rights and interests of individuals are constituted by their membership in political communities. Thus, citizens of relatively decent democratic states may have interests and rights arising from citizenship that are either built into the national interest (in an ideal definition) or provide a moral reason for protecting such interest (in a nonideal definition). For example, in addition to human rights, Jewish citizens of Israel may have a right, based in part on the historical and continuing failure of others to protect their basic human rights, to a state in which their way of life is given full recognition. Americans may have an interest, over and above whatever human rights they might possess in a state of nature, in determining their own fate as a political community, and a response to terrorism might protect the national interest by helping preserve that communal autonomy. Moreover, the national interest may sometimes weigh against retaliation. Thus, the United States seems perfectly justified in considering the response in the Arab world and its effect on the national interest before deciding whether to retaliate against Libya for the 1985 terrorist raids at the Rome and Vienna airports.

Specific claims, such as those made above, about the nature of individual rights and interests, and the bearing of national interest in particular contexts, of course are controversial. Clearly, they need much more defense than can be given here. However, whether they ultimately are or are not defensible, they at least illustrate the importance of not begging the issue by simply taking for granted a particular conception of what constitutes individual rights and interests.

To reiterate, the discussion here suggests that states, under appropriate conditions, are morally permitted to take steps, including military ones, to deter terrorism. The national interest can play a justificatory role as one factor bearing upon whether retaliation should take place and, if so, what form it should take. As such, the national interest functions—or can and should function—not as a factor "outside" morality but as one of the constituents that determines the requirements of morality in particular situations.

VI. Conclusion

Many Americans rightly have feared the extent to which pursuit of the national interest might be used to justify gross violations of human rights. Such concerns are legitimate and unfortunately are hardly unrealistic. What I have suggested, however, is that within proper limits, concern for the national interest also may be legitimate.

In particular, perhaps enough has been said to cast doubts on both the claims of the realists, to the effect that morality should play no role in international affairs, and the cosmopolitan dismissal of talk of the national interest as a disguised rationale for pursuit of individual interest. Although the cosmopolitans are correct in arguing that pursuit of national interest is constrained by moral principles, such side constraints may differ from those that would apply within a well-ordered society. Moreover, depending upon the way it is conceived, the national interest itself may have moral components, or may be supportable by moral arguments, which need not be egoistic in character. For example, the national interest of the United States might encompass such values as preservation of a democratic way of life. At the very least, promotion of the national interest may be a vital means of promoting democratic values. Moreover, although the national interest as so conceived may be ultimately reducible to individual rights, those rights may include associational entitlements that hold because of membership in the nation and that hence do not arise through common humanity alone.

Whatever justificatory force the national interest might have, we should reject the contention of the realists that morality has and should play no role in international affairs. On the other hand, the moral principles that apply in international affairs may differ in significant ways from those that apply to individuals within a well-ordered domestic society. In international relations, a more appropriate model might be the principles that apply to individuals under conditions of partial compliance and unusual risk. This suggests both that ideal conceptions of some sphere of morality, such as Rawls' theory of justice, have only limited application to international affairs and that the morality of individual relationships can be applied to international relationships only if modifications are made to allow both for associational rights and for the special conditions under which agents must function in the international arena.

Our discussion, then, has suggested that the national interest raises questions of greater interest and complexity than suggested either by the equation of national interest with power and security, on one hand, or the reduction to individual interest, on the other. Although the discussion here has raised questions rather than settled them, it at least suggests that policy decisions in international affairs frequently will involve more than a simple choice between enhancement of the national interest, grossly understood, on one hand and respect for justice, morality, and human rights on the other. Although we certainly need to beware of the dangers of excessive nationalism, which may lead us to trample the individual while misled by inflammatory rhetoric of national interest, we also need to be sensitive to the complex moral factors that sometimes can lie behind appeals to national interest. Although the former danger is perhaps the greater, in more complex cases, appeal to defensible conceptions of the national interest need not lack all justificatory force. If so, the national interest properly conceived remains one, although only one, of the values among which we must choose in the formation and evaluation of the behavior of states in world affairs.

Notes

Acknowledgment: Elizabeth Flower first called problems of ethics and international relations to my attention during a discussion of Hobbes in a seminar in, I believe, 1965. Although I fear she will disagree with much of what I say here, my rejection of realism and suspicion of the Hobbesian paradigm of international affairs go back to discussions with her of the need to explore ethical issues in international affairs.

1. Noam Chomsky, symposium on "Human Rights and American Foreign Policy," *Commentary* LXXII (1981): 30. Charles Beitz argues for the application of a Rawlsian model of justice to international affairs in his book *Political Theory and International Relations* (Princeton: Princeton University Press, 1979), p. 151.

2. Of course, the concept of public interest also has been attacked as hopelessly obscure but has tended to receive a better press from philosophers than the concept of national interest. Perhaps this is because the public interest is con-

ceived of as being connected to social concerns whereas national interest has been associated with pure power politics and the quest for dominance by one nation over others.

3. Here I follow John Rawls, who employs the distinction between the concept of justice and conceptions of justice in *A Theory of Justice* (Cambridge, Mass.: Harvard University Press, 1971), p. 5.

4. Which conception is most justified is of course a different question from that of which conceptions are conceptions of the public interest. However, even the latter question is not purely semantic or definitional since what is of primary philosophical interest is not likely to be how words are used but rather the substantive implications of making distinctions one way rather than another.

5. Peter G. Brown, ". . . in the National Interest," in Peter G. Brown and Douglas MacLean (eds.), *Human Rights and U. S. Foreign Policy* (Lexington, Mass.: D. C. Heath and Co., 1979), pp. 163–164.

6. I owe this suggestion to George Sher, although he might not agree with the use I make of it here.

7. For a discussion and partial defense of national interest conceived of in terms of power, see Hans Morganthau, *Politics Among Nations* (New York: Alfred A. Knopf, 1978), especially pp. 5–10.

8. Felix Oppenheim, "National Interest, Rationality, and Morality," *Political Theory* XV (1987): 369–389.

9. That is, the more distinct values one includes under the heading of national interest, the greater the chances of conflict among them. Thus, although one may attempt to sanitize the national interest by stretching it to include a variety of virtues, substantive moral disputes between elements of the national interest cannot be avoided by such conceptual engineering.

10. Charles Frankel, "Morality and U.S. Foreign Policy," *Headline Series* No. 224 (1975), p. 52.

11. Hans Morganthau, *In Defense of the National Interest* (New York: Alfred A. Knopf, 1951), pp. 33–39.

12. For a similar point, see Marshall Cohen, "Moral Skepticism and International Relations," *Philosophy and Public Affairs* XIII (1984), pp. 299–346.

13. Morganthau, *In Defense of the National Interest*, p. 35.

14. Beitz, *Political Theory and International Relations*, Part 1.

15. For discussion of Beitz's attempt to apply Rawls' theory of justice to international affairs, see Robert L. Simon, "Global Justice and the Authority of States," *The Monist*, LXVI (1983): 557–570.

16. Beitz, *Political Theory and International Relations*, p. 55.

17. See Michael Walzer, "The Moral Standing of States," *Philosophy and Public Affairs* IX (1980), particularly pp. 225–226 for a defense and discussion of such a position.

18. Brown, ". . . in the National Interest," p. 165.

19. See Charles Beitz, "Economic Rights and Distributive Justice in Developing Societies," *World Politics* XXXIII (1981): 321–346 for thoughtful discussion of such issues.

20. Beitz, *Political Theory and International Relations*, pp. 42–46, 143–154.

21. Rawls, *A Theory of Justice*, p. 4. For criticisms of Beitz along such lines, see Brian Barry, "Humanity and Justice in Global Perspective," in J. Roland Pennock and John W. Chapman (eds.), *Ethics, Economics and the Law* (New York: New York University Press, 1982), p. 233.

22. The provisos attached to this claim make it much more difficult to justify support for right-wing dictatorships than many U.S. foreign policy makers might acknowledge. However, if the line of argument sketched out in this article is correct, whether such support is morally defensible depends on a variety of factors that might differ from case to case. For discussion of the broader issue of whether there is a distinct morality that applies to international relations, or whether "ordinary" morality applies, but in an unusual way because of the special features of international relations, see Cohen, "Moral Skepticism and International Relations."

23. This does not mean that risking harm to the innocent is ever to be taken lightly. However, if risk of harm to the innocent, *however slight*, was taken as an absolute prohibition on action, nations would never be permitted to defend themselves, even against blatant aggression or the Nazi threat in World War II. That is why Israeli retaliatory raids against terrorists, whether or not they are morally justified, are of an entirely different moral order than terrorist raids directed against civilians. The former are designed to minimize the risk of harm to innocents, even at some risk to the attacking force, whereas the latter are aimed at harming innocent civilians.

I2 | Teaching "Ethics in Business": Leave It to Sisyphus

Ivar Berg

Introduction

We can conveniently date the increasingly widespread concern with the subject of values in the teaching of business ethics from the widely heralded appearances of separate reports by the Ford and Carnegie foundations urging business schools to address questions about the social correlates of corporate conduct, among other novel proposals, in the spring of 1959.[1] A colleague and I began teaching a course that fall on corporate conduct essentially along the lines suggested by the foundations, in accord with curriculum reforms mandated by the Columbia Business School's faculty on the eve of the publication of the foundations' reports. I accordingly join in a celebration of Elizabeth Flower's work as a professional philosopher and widely celebrated ethicist in this festschrift in her honor on the twenty-ninth anniversary of my own efforts to join and deal with several of the issues that fall under the rubric of "applied ethics." My remarks, interestingly enough, derive from a presentation originally prepared for the Luce Foundation

Distinguished Lecturers' Series, Department of Religion, Wake Forest University, in 1983. As we will see later, I believe that departments of religion and philosophy are better venues for the study of ethics than business schools.

The Market Paradigm

The history of the efforts urged by the foundations, and by workers in what became a thriving cottage industry in many prestigious business schools, has been nicely reviewed by Charles W. Powers and David Vogel in one of the volumes in the series published by the Hastings Center's Institute of Society, Ethics, and the Life Sciences entitled *The Teaching of Ethics in Higher Education.* Powers and Vogel not only review what has been done in hundreds of courses on "business and society," "business responsibility," and "business ethics" over a twenty-five year span but offer helpful ideas about what might be done better, given the shared experiences of a great many lecturers who teach what, at my former school, they call the Conceptual Foundations of Business. I may anticipate my conclusions by suggesting that I do not share Powers's and Vogel's optimistic conclusions about this area's continuing progress; perhaps I am the scarred victim of my own receding background.

I should quickly add that my scars are from self-inflicted wounds; indeed, many colleagues regularly indulged my well-intended preachings. And students have been more than tolerant of my courses' distractions of their attentions from accounting, finance, marketing, and other tools in the equipage of their would-be calling. Business students' postcollege interests in "reducing business uncertainties" are, after all, far better developed than their interests in addressing moral ambiguities in what are dramatically called decision-making situations.

Nor are my bruises linked to serious doubts that we would likely have a better world were our men and women of business attentive to ethicists' and their disciples' concerns. Whitehead's dictum that "great men of business think greatly of their functions" is more a consummation to be wished than a practice to be often observed.

The fact is that my efforts, insofar as I can gauge them, were no more productive than those attempted by Sisyphus; in my judgment those who were skeptical from the beginning of what became the business and society movement were correct in their assessments, and I hereby retire from any further efforts to induce either aspiring captains of industry or a more sizeable group of prospective corporals of industrial bureaucracies to be applied ethicists. The redeemable souls in those roles are no more numerous than active NHL hockey players who attend thoughtfully to lectures critical of violence.

My sense of failure derives from the difficulties one encounters in persuading student proponents and some teachers of economic science, the most widely accepted paradigm for analyzing the environment of business in other courses, that the discipline's main canon is far from being neutral toward value-laden issues. Economists allow, of course, that ethical issues attaching to economic transactions may well need to be joined. But the paradigm itself, as they view things, is a scientific one; it is, in and of itself, neutral on matters of what choices ought to be selected from among those options shown to afford different mixtures of measurable efficiencies in the allocation of resources (and thus the measurable tradeoffs among them).

I refer, of course, to the widely shared view that there is, in the words of Victor R. Fuchs, a distinction between "allocative efficiency" and "distributive justice."[2] "Economics," Fuchs writes, "has a great deal to say about the former, but the justice of any particular distribution of income cannot be established by economics . . . the economic perspective [that is, paradigm] can help clarify the effects [of public policies, for example, but] it cannot provide the final answers. These must come from our *values*."[3] Fuchs, however, thereupon admiringly cites Sir Edwin Chadwick's famous dictum that "when the sentimentalist and the moralist fails, he will have as a last resource to call in the aid of the economist."[4] A few pages later Fuchs certifies the bottom line of all bottom lines by calling upon Chicago's Gary Becker, who defines "the market paradigm" pithily, if not felicitously: "The combined assumptions of maximizing behavior, market equilibrium, and stable preferences, used relentlessly and unflinchingly, form the heart of the economic approach."[5]

In this perspective, for example, the justice of any particular distribution of income is not, in Fuchs's usage, "established"; what *is* established is an exceedingly constrained apparatus for (implicitly) defining allocative choices as if distributive choices were simply not involved therein; the allocative and distributive choices, according to what I may call ledgerdemain, are not only analytically but empirically quite distinguishable.

At its core—what Becker in a romantic lapse calls its heart—there is (Fuchs's, Chadwick's, and Becker's question-begging formulations notwithstanding) a moral imperative according to which the collective interests of a society's members are best served in a social system in which free men and women doggedly pursue their (legal) personal interests in accord with their individual preferences. What "moralists" and "sentimentalists" might reasonably regard as choices among admixtures of virtue-filled and vice-ridden wants (for churches and child-porn movies, for example) most economists, as such, regard simply as preferences and indifferences toward goods and services comparable only in terms of prices. These preferences and indifferences are translated by consumers into actions that maximize what are termed their utilities. Sizeable numbers of Americans, claiming themselves to be a moral majority, might very well view the social costs of such an equanimous position vis-à-vis churches and X-rated films with considerable misgivings.

The economist-*cum*-citizen will, of course, deplore some legal but distasteful or obnoxious demands described by one or another indifference curve. And Fuchs, a most thoughtful citizen, makes a number of such value-laden statements. As an *economist*, though, he is relentless and unflinching in his loyalty to the implications of his brethrens' understanding of the axiom that the pursuits by individuals of their self-interests sum to the best interests of us all.

When Adam Smith articulated that proposition, in *The Wealth of Nations*, he rejected his own earlier urgings in *The Theory of Moral Sentiments*, but he did so, we recall, while continuing to occupy the Chair in Moral Philosophy at the University of Glasgow. There are at present in the United States very few professionally trained moral philosophers among those whose courses and writings are so frankly organized around the so-called market paradigm; Herbert Simon and Phillip Drucker are among a few notable exceptions. The overwhelming majority of such courses and scribblings are afforded us by card-carrying economists or by specialists in business subjects based on the paradigm.

Economists would not (and do not) deny that there are unspecified supplements to private interests that help to convert essentially free individual actors into communities and societies; these add-ons presumably include, at a minimum, shared norms of behavior, shared prejudices, and shared sentiments. But even business professors who favor regulatory measures as safeguards of the public's interests assume an incredibly high order of trust to be automatically operative among the actors in an economy.

The bases of community standards and interpersonal trust across myriad persons and interest groups, I submit, are regarded as having been factored *out* of the economist's scientific paradigm; they are, by the profession's logics, the fit subjects of study by economists only when they step *back* from their scientific roles to play their citizens' roles. Many economists are very chary of consumer protection laws, for example, preferring the view that the market, as a for instance, will drive false advertisers' products off sellers' shelves; the hazards of a product are to be known preferably by the body counts, deformed babies, and cancerous lungs they generate.

For sociologists, the economist's leap from individual to collective interests is particularly arresting; sociologists, after all, are the social science fraternity's self-appointed demystifiers, thriving as they do on the study of the pieces of social technology, including rites and rituals that operate to foster "social solidarity." Antireductionists by trade, they study wholes and wonder only that economists can so readily reify their Cartesian and Newtonian metaphors in their moves from vacuous models to a real world in which personal greed is literally equated with collective well-being and in which markets are often, well, less than "perfect."

For ethicists, and for academics otherwise, who seek to explore "ethics in business," the leap from individual motives to the commonweal is viewed as a perfectly extraordinary one if only because the paradigm's devoted followers can eat their ethical cake and have it as well: their assertedly value-neutral model is urged upon the value-conscious community simply with assurances that value considerations have been extracted from the technical apparatus and, as we have noted, that these considerations can be taken up after the technical economic analysis has been completed.

It is not my purpose to suggest that economists should be maligned for their problematical posturings when they gainsay value questions by euphemizing about "tradeoffs," tradeoffs, for example, between equity and efficiency. Nor are my doubts about the value neutrality of economists' models unknown to most of the persons who chance to read these words.

Indeed, I would be in the front ranks of those who applaud the best of our professional economists for having correctly forecasted, as Paul Samuelson once jibed, "thirteen of the last eight recessions"; given the difficulties, for instance, of dealing with exogenous shocks—OPEC as a case in point—they do exceedingly well in their forecasts, indeed. And, yes, my own discipline, though hardly dominated by them, is well populated by investigators who deem their statistical and mathematical methods to be neutral—they are "after just the facts, ma'am"! In any event, it would be unseemly of me to disallow the value of econometric techniques, for example, that we have borrowed with considerable alacrity (and to many good effects) for applications to problems under examination in the other social sciences.

No, my purpose is to suggest that the economic model, with its "theodicy of paradox" and its construction of "a long, dark moral tunnel,"[6] derives from a widely shared and deeply rooted cultural-scientific tradition in accord with which we *start* our analysis of the social and physical world using Descartes's, Hobbes's, Newton's, Locke's, Mill's, or Galileo's reductionist metaphors. These metaphors differ, for present purposes, only in the degree to which they are "mechanistic" or "mathematical." In Descartes's writings the metaphor, as one distinguished natural scientist put it, "described the earth, and the whole visible world in general, as if it were a machine in the shape and movements of its parts."[7]

The fact is, however, that the metaphor, the "as if," *becomes* for many of us (and for long uncritical periods at a time) the reality. In biologist R. C. Lewontin's words, "What has happened, since 1637, is that in the minds of natural scientists and a large fraction of social scientists as well, the world has ceased to be *like* a machine, but instead is seen as if it *were* a machine," a particular reductionism that Lewontin describes as Cartesian.[8]

The specific version of reductionist thinking most often borrowed in the social sciences, especially in economics, is from Newtonian mechanics, especially the notion of equilibrium. Not many economists are aware that one of their most fundamental ideas was advanced by a former chemical engineer; Wilfredo Pareto's excursion into the social sciences was a second career. One is tempted to suggest that he came by what is in fact a "fallacy of misplaced concreteness" quite honestly; his borrowings from the intellectual capital he accumulated as a natural scientist are, however, rarely acknowledged by later economists for the metaphors they are.

As I see it, the "market paradigm"—Becker's trinity of "maximizing behavior," "stable preferences," and "equilibrium"—is problematic vis-à-vis ethical questions in business education simply because economic modeling, "financial analysis," modern double-entry bookkeeping, and the rest of business schools' intellectual armamentaria figure to such extraordinarily large degrees as *the* "basics" of all of business education. A sophisticated treatment of business ethics, *in a course or two*, in an undergraduate or graduate business program thus tends to pick up on the ethical issues only after endless treatments of economic, financial, and accounting facts in which ethical issues are treated as residual, "postscientific" ones; the bulk of business programs' curricula, replete with technical and "functional" courses, are not seen, *themselves*, as value-laden intellectual apparatuses. A one-course treatment, a philosophical collop, organized around the proposition that the behavior of competing economic agents does take particular forms, from culture to culture, that result from choices among competing *values* is simply overpowered by the rest of the curriculum.

Let me be clear: my concern with economic science and its sister social sciences is derivative, not direct; we can readily forgive economists, so to say, as we forgive other social scientists, because we are creatures of our cultures as much as of our consciences and, as Freud urged, especially in *Civilization and Its Discontents*, our superegos are not formed *in vacuo*; the slips 'twixt the cup of metaphor and the truth of honorable lips are so regular that we either (1) become inured to the stains they cause on our intellectual raiments; or (2) periodically act, in casual academic discourse, as if we were not just "Cartesians" or "Newtonians" but feeling citizens, as well, with Adam Smith's moral sentiments that can be mobilized when one or another very clear excess has occurred, as with "price rigging" in the heavy electrical equipment industry from 1935 to 1960; or (3) *here and there*, expose business students not to the palpably problematic quality of metaphor-*cum*-reality across an entire curriculum but only in a course or two in which the application of metaphor to reality is explored and challenged.

The third choice, as Fuchs sees things, can offer only options among which choices may be made. As guidelines, the parameters of options can help us to discuss the effects of policies, but the *hard* answers to tough questions about the costs and benefits attaching to "economic" choices derive from the application of putatively neutral methods to well-constructed files of many subsets of data; so much efficiency costs so much equity and so much unemployment buys us so much reduction in inflation rates. The ethical "oughts" are then juxtaposed with the *measurable* "shoulds" as if these imperatives are orthogonal to each other.

Business school faculties, and economists to an only slightly lesser degree, will of course endorse all three of the foregoing alternatives; they are most unlikely, though, to urge that we give anything like "equal time" to (1) explications of amoral, question-begging qualities attaching to applications of economists' technical apparatus, on one side, and, on the other side, to (2) minorities among students of economic process who do not share the majority's disposition to gainsay the moral imperatives inherent in the conventional model.

Untenured ethicists on business school faculties—there are a few—are especially lonely, for they are often lumped with "antibusiness" types, or worse. Teachers of "business and society" thus become as charms on their deans' (and advisory committees') watchfobs. And the impacts of these courses on the bulk of the curriculum, not to mention the thought process of their students, are about as great as the contributions of watchfob talismans to the time-keeping capacities of the clocks to which they are attached.

Having implicitly imputed a certain ingenuousness rather than intellectual malfeasance among those who massage "user friendly" metaphors among business school professors, we can move to illustrations of the insufficiency of reductionist metaphors without troubling over the sensibilities of those who employ them. We may do so by considering brief examples of the difficulties of doing justice, in intellectual terms, to three current, somewhat related, vexed (and vexing) problems in what A. A. Berle perceptively called the American Economic Republic.

The first example has to do with plant shutdowns; the second with the problem of defining merit and meritocracy in efforts to accommodate economic inequalities to our democratic values; the third with what is called structural unemployment. Limitations on space obligate me to simplify greatly, thereby to be brief; I most assuredly do not, by that expediency, mean to imply that the problems to which I allude are simple ones.

Plant Shutdowns and Declining Areas

There is no need to rehearse the facts about Chapter Eleven bankruptcies and plant shutdowns that have added thousands and thousands of layoffs and discharges in recent years to the numbers left unemployed, otherwise, by economic contractions, in virtually every industry and in all the principal sectors of our national economy; we all know that the numbers are large, unhappily so especially, for those (and their dependents) for whom long years of well-compensated labor, as they knew them, may well be over.

Although only a very few Americans are genuinely happy about these developments, there are some—including a few well-published Harvard Business School professors—who are grateful, in the abstract of course, for the effects of Japanese competition on U.S. business leaders. As they see it, our business leaders have finally been driven by the Japanese to become "lean and mean" and that they may yet take useful pages from Japanese employers' books on "industrial policy," on the care and feeding of "workers' quality circles" and the utility, even, of morning exercises for employees. In business reports, in print and picture tube, Japan's admirers all but rub their hands over prospects that our business leaders may no longer stress short-term conceptions of economic returns at the expense of policies that will yield longer-range, more productive policies and practices. Others, especially among so-called supply side enthusiasts, are also sorry for most of the unemployed, of course. But they pile metaphor on metaphor, nonetheless, in urges that the Republic needs sacrificial soldiers in peacetime battles against inflation just as it must compel sacrifices during wartime conflicts with equally insidious enemies.

Most of the adherents of each of these theorems' champions conveniently recall Schumpeter's bold assertions about the supposed tendencies immanent in free economics toward the "creative destruction" of old economic entities in favor of new and potentially more robust ones. Most of the costs, though, are paid by those who sacrifice in these warlike movements; these patriots receive no combat pay and are obliged to witness the sapping of their communities.

Such "external" costs, furthermore, are best offset over the long term by what are confidently called "trickle down benefits" of the applications of the sapient economic orthodoxy—what the inimitable John Kenneth Galbraith has called "horse and sparrow economics." In the orthodox view, in the short term, before the trickling begins, losers are better aided by (generally insufficient) private acts of *noblesse oblige* than by pooling risks; consider that as of 1985, only a smidgen more than one-third of all involuntarily unemployed Americans were or will become eligible for unemployment insurance. This impurity in the American experiment has appeared even as charitable donations are less valuable in tax terms and as American family ties are attenuated by members' mobility and sky-high divorce rates.

Given that the best that mainstream "economizing" theorists can offer us are purportedly value-free propositions about the dollar costs and benefits of alternatives, there are contending "sociologizing" paradigms about how "externalized costs" might be addressed while worrying over the horrors of inflation—the latter often seen as caused additionally by government deficits and unproductive regulation. Daniel Bell has offered one such "sociologizing mode" of analysis as a complement to the economizing one. His alternative stresses the need to afford communities and larger social systems new ways of dealing with "system imperatives," ranging from needs for costly infrastructures and defense needs to interpersonal trust, social order, reciprocity in human relationships and useful shared hypocrisies in social relationships. Bell thus writes of the needs of the "public household."

To the extent that many "sociologizers" want not only to serve *social system* imperatives per se but also to limit "pure," that is, totally unfettered, economic activities by restrictions (say on mergers and acquisitions among private buyers and sellers, the mobility of capital and on the right to foresake communities where plants will be shut down without any but last minute warnings), they offend economizers because the latter analysts sense that sociologizers seek simply to violate property owners' earned and well-deserved rights.[9]

Another version of Bell's alternative analytic mode would apparently push his initial version's logic a mite further: it urges us to adopt an "income policy" (wage and price controls) and an "industrial policy" for allocating some of our national resources in accord with an economic plan of a greater or lesser detailed character. I would suggest that this version of the sociologizing mode is only apparently extreme; it is informed, after all, by some of the same deep misgivings about *price* competition that haunt many Americans both in and out of business.[10] The differences in many of their effects between private planning by five hundred enormous corporations and a central agency of labor, government, and management representatives, meantime, are believed by many to be more likely quantitative than qualitative in character, an argument Galbraith detailed, in 1967, in *The New Industrial State*.

The sociologizing mode has not been gaining much favor lately, as Mr. Reagan's election victories showed us, though a few Democrats in Congress (including three of his four worthiest Democratic presidential opponents in 1979) have fingered the "industrial policy" rosary; they offer little by way of specifications or elaborations, however.

The more prevalent inclinations of many Americans are to write off (1) declining regions (as in the McGill Commission Report to President Carter) as we do uncollectible debts; (2) northern cities (by real estate and banking "red liners," most Sunbelters and all plant relocators); and (3) communities (by corporate acquirers, diversifiers, divestors, creditors, and deregulators). All act in accord with logics that stress private costs and benefits, abjure novel attempts to calculate social benefits and costs, and, finally, strain to itemize the putative inflationary diseconomies generated by efforts to satisfy "public wants."

Whatever "community" may mean to others, the economizing mode considers the term only at the margins. Thus, some economizers may speak of the needs for guaranteed home loans, highway construction funds, and income tax breaks on mortgage interest payments. Although not intentionally so, however, these politics enabled FHA and VA beneficiaries to undo entire cities by displacing them with suburbs; they clearly served home builders and individual home buyers far better than they did communities, as such.

Indeed the term "community studies" in the post–World War II sociology literature is almost an oxymoron; almost all of them—Herbert Gans's studies the exceptions—are dreary reports on the alienated and alienating character of lives in suburbanized America. Oscar Wilde's cynics, "who know the price of everything and the value of nothing," could readily explain the alleged alienation to social scientists who speak of "market clearing" forces. One can accordingly only hope that most Americans will not be disquieted by urban rioters if we effectively continue to say to inner-city tenants, visited by "land developers," that they should, with apologies to John Donne, "ask not against whom the market clears; it clears against thee."

Poets and novelists have, of course, long argued over whether communities stifle (Sinclair Lewis) or support (Robert Frost) their incumbents, but they apply standards that are anchored implicitly in psychological and in nineteenth-century sociological and anthropological, not in modern economic, terms. The rest of us speak much less of communities than of real estate values, construction jobs, and other variables that lend themselves far better to mensurational treatment than do such variables as community well-being. Indeed, most Americans think of "neighborhood" and "community" essentially only when the matter of school busing comes up; the term "neighborhood" has appeared far more frequently in popular debates over school desegregation than in social discourse otherwise.

It is interesting, in the same vein, to note that we rarely consider judgments about real estate values and their protection against "fair housing" movements, for example, as veiled but thoroughgoing ethical judgments in accord with which we equate segregation with the good life. And, of course, a neighborhood doesn't go downhill because of the impending presence of the "wrong" people moving therein per se—some of our best friends, and all that. No, our neighborhood will change because "others" (not you or I) will sell the homes around us cheap when the fellow up the street puts his place on the market after the first "new people" move in. It is not that we are opposed to black, or Puerto Rican, or other minorities but to the depreciated values of property sold by "panicky bigots" to ruthless "block busters." Americans were not, we are regularly reminded, just buying a home in a friendly place out of town when they moved to the suburbs in such astoundingly high numbers in the fifties and sixties; they were also investing hard-earned dollars in a house and a lot. (For most of us it was the biggest investment we would indeed ever make!) It may take a heap of living to make a house a home, as the old cross-stitched samplers used to urge, but a commission-collecting realtor cannot deposit a 6 percent cut of a seller's sentiments about a home in a bank account. And the homes' sellers cannot use the warm memories imputed to them by romantics as part of the down payment on the new house to which, their putative nostalgia notwithstanding, they conceive they are "trading up."

Chicago, meantime, may have been "the hog butcher to the world" to a fanciful poet in a celebrative mood, but it is, variously, an import-export center, a labor market, urban real estate market, and a Standard Metropolitan Statistical Area in the pages of economics and many sociology texts. "Communitas" and "civitas," in fine, are not very promising variables for inclusion in multivariate analyses. And they slip readily from mind as we pretend that we will reintroduce them as ends, or as means, to the good life, after we make rational economic judgments about reasons for (or against) aid to steel-forsaken Youngstown, arrangements for federal revenue sharing with Detroit, Philadelphia, and Flint, or the sale of "Big Mac" bonds in support of New York City during its fiscal crisis in the mid-1970s. Corporate and personal property can be "priced"; there are, regrettably, no easily recognizable equivalents to "big ticket items" in sentimentalists' and moralists' inventories.

Education, Meritocracy, and the Democratic Demiurge

Americans (and their public and private sponsors otherwise) who made increasing investments in formal education following World War II received ringing endorsements of their actions in the early 1960s. The paeans to education advertised well-publicized findings by smaller groups of economists and sociologists of the robust statistical associations between years of schooling, on one side, and both national economic growth rates and American individuals' income returns, on the other.

In the case of income returns the view has regularly been urged on us that better-educated persons earn more than their less-educated peers because employers, responding rationally to market forces, were in need of the kinds of additional productivity putatively imparted by schooling to those with higher educational achievements.[11]

Note here that we did not measure the differential productivity of differentially educated workers directly—that is a very tough nut to crack, as any observer of tenure committees' efforts and of faculty salaries will surely tell us. Instead, we ignored the innumerable short- and medium-run imperfections of capital, labor and product markets, as well as the folkways and traditions that shape the behavior of employers no less than their employees. With hubris that was shared even by some professors of classics among us, we concluded, as I have noted, that our more-educated citizens earn relatively more because they are proportionally more productive than the rest. But, how did we know that they were more productive? Precisely because they were better paid; we simply elevated *direct* measures of *incomes* into *indirect* measures of *productivity* (as if this were self-evidently reasonable) to prove our point. In the process, however, we dignified a tautology by converting an article of economists' faith (in the marginalist paradigm) into received wisdom.

Professors cheered even as they luxuriated in delusions of adequacy encouraged by their swelling student enrollments. College admissions officers, suddenly armed with new justifications for selling their programs, wallowed in applications. And blacks, with growing alacrity, attended to the advice of (mostly white) antipoverty warriors (who thus conducted many more skirmishes more or less against the poor than against poverty's causes) that they go to school. Young blacks were reminded by video and subway ads in New York City, for example, that their incomes were sadly lower than those of whites because neither their nor our investments in their "human capital formation" were sufficient in a world of changing "job requirements." "Boy. That's what they will call you" if you drop out of school, read New York subway posters.

I questioned the education-productivity-income theorem using *direct*, if admittedly crude, measures in an investigation of the actual productivity of a variety of *differentially educated* blue- and white-collar workers, engineers, scientists, technicians, and civil servants (including air controllers and members of the armed forces), and incumbents of many other occupations *who were performing the same jobs*. I uncovered no support whatever for the position of those who had, in their research designs, confounded their *difiens* (education) with their *difiendum* (income): in data on performance (afforded me by employers, by the way) workers with more education, job for job, did *not* perform better than less-educated ones.[12]

The fact is that though studies of the economics of education raise a good many disquieting questions, we find it difficult to deal with them in our society because most Americans are sanguine about inequality *only if they detect a measure of meritocracy* as the leavening in the democratic loaf; for most Americans "equality of *opportunity*" falls within what Chester Barnard called the zones of acceptance or indifference; "equality of *outcomes*" is quite a different matter! And most of us with many years of schooling conveniently, that is, self-servingly, read meritocracy into the spaces between differential educational achievements and differential earnings. We thus stumble along, on the production side, with questionable readings of correlations because we believe (or want to believe) in the essential validity of the causal arguments they appear to bespeak.[13]

Blacks, in the meantime, have done a heroic job of adding to their educational achievements since 1960, but their incomes still lag well behind whites, in each category of educational achievement, as they did before the promises were made. Axioms about education's productivity, it turns out, are not colorblind. We may well ponder the ethical (never mind the political) issues attaching to broken promises made in accord with parameters generated by Becker's putatively neutral, "relentless," and "unflinching" scientists.

But there has not been much risk that such issues would be very seriously pondered in business schools, one suspects, because the bulk of business schools' curricula would thereby become at least a smidgen suspect: it is not unambiguously easy to defend the neutrality implicitly attributed to "market forces" acting on managers once the genuinely partisan quality of the effects of these forces are acknowledged. The use of income returns as sovereign measures of a person's productive worth in the market is, after all, as suspicious as the use of tests to measure "intelligence," the technical problem being one of the measures' validities in each case.

The private rates of return to schooling, meantime, began to decline in the 1970s. My suspicion is that economists' markets finally did begin, after a long lag period, to force some efficiencies in the uses employers make of education, as Japanese and German producers (who incidentally demand appreciably less education) made markets more nearly competitive. The earlier demand for education, meantime, was financially supported by (1) imperfect competition (enabling producers to "pass on" the costs thereof), and (2) urgent needs for measurable attributes of economic winners and losers; educational achievements afforded us attractive measures of personal worth. We can pursue this suspicion in the final section of this paper.

Structural Unemployment

A review of the lessons we have taught ourselves about the reasons for much of our unemployment, no less than those we have taught ourselves about human capital and meritocracy otherwise, calls to my mind a story about the philosophies of three umpires told by the Honorable Orin Judd, then a federal judge, at a Phi Beta Kappa initiation banquet at Colgate University in late April, 1954, one-third of a century ago: "Some pitches are balls and some are strikes and I call 'em as I see 'em," said the first umpire. "I am a subjectivist." "O.K.," said the second, "some are balls and some are strikes, but I call 'em as they are; I am an objectivist." "Well," said the third, "some are balls and some are strikes, to be sure, but until I call them, they are nothing; I am an existentialist." Followers of the theodicy of innocence treat much unemployment in accord with the third umpire's perspective.

We all know that unemployment, as we measure it, is concentrated among youths, in general, among black youths, in particular, and among women, especially those recently divorced, reentering the labor force, otherwise. Analyses of the attributes of these and other umemployed persons afford us demographic pictures including age profiles. The results are referred to, in the parlance of demographers, as "the structure of unemployment." Armed with these parameters, many economists return to passages in the theodicy's scriptures under the human-capital heading: having already satisfied themselves that we have accounted for the winners in the income race, it follows that we need only be consistent. We accordingly reapply our scriptures' morality-laden lessons to the losers. What could be simpler than to argue that the groups most vulnerable to unemployment suffer this risk because they have deficient human-capital attributes? The indictment follows very logically, by extension as logicians have it, from analyses of the attibutes of the more favored actors in the economic drama sketched in the preceding section. If all the world is a stage, we seem to say, the dress rehearsal takes place in school and the show, after all, must go on.

The unemployed, according to the sapient orthodoxy, are at the bottom of the human-capital apple barrel. Any stimulative or "aggregate demand" policies one might suggest as antidotes to unemployment, moreover, would thus force employers to hire large numbers of inexperienced, lesser-educated workers. The results of the stimulation of demand, in productivity terms, we are told, would in that event clearly be inflationary, especially as so many employers are bound by parameters of the minimum wage law.

The economic structure, the argument continues, has changed, and it has left many workers "structurally unemployable." We then add that the last waves of the "baby boom," especially, suffered because their incontinent parents produced larger numbers—a large age cohort—of inexperienced workers than the economy could absorb. Voilà! The "structure of unemployment"—*a demographic profile*—becomes "structural unemployment"—*a causal explanation for the profile's emergence!* We are accordingly back to confusions between *explanans* and *explanandum*: those of us with apprehensions about tautological reasoning must accordingly suffer when existentialists invite us to assume and simultaneously, as they say in Logic 101, to affirm the consequent.

And the value-neutral conclusions? Place roughly half the blame on the victims, of course, and the other half on their carelessly reproductive parents. And punish them, so to speak, by letting them be the sacrificial shock troops in battles against inflation. Marx may not have been wrong about everything, we seem to say; we need simply to launder his infelicitous metaphor of a "surplus army of labor," neglect real structures (public and private policies and practices), focus on demographic structures *as if* they are economic structures, and, finally, talk in technical (read neutral) language about "Phillips Curve tradeoffs" between unemployment and reduced inflation! It is all really very simple.

Only a very few pay worried attention to the facts (1) that the so-called tradeoff may be epiphenomenal, which is to say that it is a statistical artifact of sorts; (2) that we simply do not have sufficiently long enough time series to prove the "cohort effects" allegedly visited by post–World War II couples on their children; and (3) that the proposed model simply cannot be made to fit the extraordinary facts descriptive of our utilization of human resources during the period of World War II. Anyone over fifty-five knows that although we most assuredly "scraped the bottom" of the proverbial "manpower apple barrel," during those years, we did so to very heartening effects, indeed![14]

It is true, of course, that inflation was *perhaps* less of a worry during the war because we had price and wage controls at the time. But we also had "cost-plus" contracts in the industries most pressed to "scrape and barrel." And we willingly paid whatever the marginal costs of converting ourselves, virtually overnight, into democracy's arsenal. Why social scientists have ignored World War II as a "natural experiment" is a question that has to be addressed with a far better understanding of well-educated scientists' myopia than I possess. It boggles one's mind to contemplate that social scientists could overlook five years of American human resources history. We are, I must emphasize, talking about nearly 20 percent of the period between the ends of the wars in 1918 and in 1945!

There is not a small but a large ethical question inherent in a technical intellectual apparatus in accord with which we can, through artful intellectual dodging, simply assure ourselves that the putatively virtuous among the many owe so little to the blameworthy few. They are hardly rigorous thinkers (1) who proudly plead ethical innocence in accord with a theodicy predicated upon a tautology with moralistic undertones; (2) who ignore the highly relevant "critical experiment"—World War II—as though significant evidence is irrelevant to cogent argument; and (3) who uncritically accept correlations as demonstrating cause and effect relationships.

Conclusion

Business faculties are, of course, not the only members of the academy whose intellectual tergiversations leave one wondering. Nor is the fact that our logics are problematical particularly menacing to more than a lonely ethicist or two. Professor Becker's romantic addition to his metaphor, it turns out, is not inept; the paradigm does have a "heart," that is, an ethical core, however often or articulately the fact is denied; and there is something almost redeeming, after all, about a nearly conscious admission of what is otherwise denied. Consider further that the market paradigm even has an aesthetic, what Michael Piore, in a recent issue of the *Monthly Labor Review* (April, 1983), calls an "aesthetic of continuity."

Thus, almost all economists turned deaf ears when a few liberals suggested, in the sixties, that our economy actually consists of at least *two* labor market sectors: a primary sector, where "good jobs" with considerable protection from the chill winds of the marketplace are found, and a secondary sector—small businesses for example—in which jobs are far less attractive, substantially less protected from competitive forces, and whose incumbents are far less well endowed in terms of either wages or benefits. Beyond taking passing note of them, social scientists also ignored the rather considerable institutional constraints on the intersector movement of workers between the two sectors' boundaries. In fact, more than two in five (44 percent) of the new jobs created between 1979 and 1985 were in the low-wage grouping; highly paid jobs grew by only 10 percent. Bluestone and Harrison point out that in the earlier period 1973 to 1979, "one out of five were low wage and almost half were high wage."[15]

A theory of poverty and income distribution based on the "dual market" approach (or somewhat more differentiated approaches) was simply unattractive to most economists. As Piore notes,

The manner in which segmentation theory was "uncovered" involves approaches [that is, methods like participant observation] to empirical investigation that are excluded from conventional practice. . . . This approach contrasts sharply with the practice of econometric estimation of deductive neoclassical models, which use data gathered from highly structured interviews, the results of which are reduced, before they are introduced into the analysis, into continuous, quantitative variables.[16]

Space does not permit a full description of Piore's intriguing commentary. It must suffice to say, with Piore and a physics colleague of his, that the conventional paradigm is "infused" by an

aesthetic of continuity and homogeneity: the basic tools are applicable only in a continuous, homogeneous world, and the theories which are displayed in the classroom and which constitute the standards of rigor and elegance, against which students learn to judge their own work and that of their colleagues, pertain only to such a world.

He adds parenthetically, that "by convention, perfect competition is the agency by which homogenity is maintained in an economic system."[17]

The paradigm does, of course, sometimes acknowledge troublesome discontinuities with some pain. But the paradigm's devotees do not suffer from an intellectual version of AIDS; their immune systems are hale and, if I may say it, hearty, because they treat rational, instrumental behavior and relate this behavior to competitive markets while, as Piore has shown in his own research (and as I have inferred from my findings on education and work),

> in large territories of the labor market, job allocation and pricing are governed by institutional rules and customs which are only tenuously linked to rational, instrumental behavior or to competitive market forces . . . the process governing allocation and pricing within labor markets [meantime] are social, as *opposed either* to competitive processes *or to* instrumental calculation.[18]

It is not altogether clear that we may infer clear lessons for the teaching of ethics from the agonized reflections in the foregoing pages. Nor is it likely that we can deduce lessons useful to colleagues whose students are being indicted for scandalous floutings of rules against "insider trading" in our capital markets.

One likely possibility is that we simply live with a metaphor "gone real," that we simply live with our "as ifs" treated "as is" and, in doing so, implicitly plead guilty to the charge in La Rochefoucald's wonderful aphorism that "hypocrisy is the homage vice owes to virtue."

We can, in the event, then settle for an occasional lecture to our students, in the social sciences and in business, that will cause some—very few—students, on rare occasions during their working lives, to wake up, late at night, with a sense that their workaday judgments are largely shaped by ethical principles. The forms and contents of the market paradigm that exonerate greed are no less ethically problematical for teachers' question-begging dispositions toward the ethical imperatives built into their paradigm. "Relentless" and "unflinching," indeed.

Another possibility is that we determined that we should *train* our would-be teachers to be more detached in their postures vis-à-vis the market paradigm and urge that they be less relentlessly and unflinchingly disingenuous in their self-exonerating denial that, indeed, they preach when they teach.

One means to such an end might be to have arts and science faculties more directly involved in monitoring professional school programs, as members of overseers and advisory boards. These faculty colleagues, after all, are more likely, by dint of professional urges, to view common and received dogma with a grain of salt; their Muses are less likely to urge two valued logics than do the somewhat less latitudinary guardian angels of business programs. This possibility, interestingly enough, would not likely upset even pure, "straight" economists on business faculties nearly as much as it would their colleagues in accounting, finance, "operations research," and even in business law who, somewhat more often than straight economists, in my experience, resist "those liberal arts types" on the other side of the campus.

A third prospect: a small but growing group of "antireductionists" those who, like many biologists and evolutionary geologists—the brilliant Stephen Jay Gould's name comes to mind, as does Claude Levy-Strauss's—become more influential in the social sciences. These scholars and thinkers, many of them cautiously, postulate the superiority of hierarchical and "interpenetrative" levels of analysis. They urge, in short, that we study our world, natural and social, in "holistic" rather than "reductionist" fashion.[19]

Unfortunately, it is the neo-Marxists in the academy who make the most of the antireductionist sounds in our hallways these days. I say unfortunately because these writers often treat outsiders' critiques as psychoanalysts generally do: if you've not been analyzed, which is to say if you "don't believe," you can't appreciate the model *because* rejection is, by definition, evidence of neurosis, or its functional equivalents, insufficient scientific rigor. Several of my neo-Marxist colleagues thus reduce the debate between themselves and their critics, as the psychoanalysts do, to "paradigm conflict." The implication is that fruitful dialogue between nonbelievers and true believers is essentially impossible. For Marxists, "false consciousness," inevitably, is among the mechanisms that play the roles of "denial," "projection," and the rest for psychoanalysts' assessments of their antagonists. The regrettable result is that their remonstrances are conveniently ignored by those who throw Marxist babies out with their bath water.

My urge would be that we do not continue "to do business as usual," that we not stop with my first alternative but that, instead, we do pursue efforts targeted on the realization of the second and third prospects. Owen D. Young once said, "It is not the crook in modern business we need fear, but the honest businessman who doesn't know what he's doing." I would only add that knowing, truly *knowing*, what we're doing in business education (no less than in business practice) means that we do truly penetrating analyses of our basic paradigms per se.

The fact is that the market paradigm too often becomes law—real law, backed up with enforcement machinery and replete with "perpetrators" and victims, both of which accept the social world, reductionist fashion, as a reasonably well-oiled machine. The basic design and maintenance of this machine, moreover, can be entrusted, as dogmatists view things, only to those of us who actually believe that we can be objective and neutral in the operations of the machines' dials and levers.

For my own part, I'll no longer teach even one ethicslike course for professional students in a curriculum that is otherwise *entirely* organized, in every detail, around a model whose ethical nature is simply denied by "relentless" and "unflinching" colleagues. I have no prescription, in short, for assuring that these colleagues or their students can be helped, in significant ways, either to relent (once in awhile, now and again) or to flinch (even a little bit) because of my efforts to loosen the waist bands on their emperors' robes. Neither my business school colleagues nor social scientists who ultimately give intellectual legitimacy (and a certain elegance) to their strangely whimsical view of man's world, meantime, have any terribly obvious stakes in themselves disrobing their emperor. More's the pity in a world in which the rest of us are obliged to live out the consequences of many of their fanciful dreams.

For my own part, there are other stones I'd rather push up a hill than the philosopher's stone in a professional school. The impending trials of "inside traders" will, I say with regret, prove my point. I do not feel even a tad self-righteous about all this; after one-quarter of a century—something of a misspent youth—I can shake my head and acknowledge only that I have learned a little of Sisyphus's frustration.

Notes

Acknowledgment: This is an edited version of remarks presented in "The Luce Distinguished Lecturer Series" at Wake Forest University, October 1983, sponsored, that year, by the Department of Religious Studies.

1. These reports appeared, ironically, at just about the time that indictments were handed down in the Great Electrical Equipment Price-fixing conspiracy case.

2. Victor R. Fuchs, *How We Live* (Cambridge, Mass.: Harvard University Press, 1983), p. 5, italicized in the original.

3. *Ibid.*, p. 10.

4. *Ibid.*, p. 1.

5. *Ibid.*, p. 12.

6. Charles Rawlings, "The Religious Community and Economic Justice" in John C. Raines, *et al.* (eds.), *Community and Capital in Conflict: Plant Closings and Job Loss* (Philadelphia: Temple University Press, 1982). Rawlings is a moral philosopher and Roman Catholic clergyman.

7. René Descartes, *Les Principes de la Philosophi*, cited by R. C. Lewontin, "The Corpse in the Elevator," *New York Review of Books*, January 20, 1983, p. 34.

8. *Ibid.*

9. The terms *sociologizing* and *economizing* first appeared in a piece by Daniel Bell, "The Corporation and Society in the 1970s," in Ivar Berg (ed.), *Human Resources and Economic Welfare* (New York: Columbia University Press, 1973), pp. 299–338. Similar distinctions have recently been offered by James S. Coleman, *The Asymmetric Society* (Syracuse: Syracuse University Press, 1982). In an earlier version of the distinction, Emile Durkheim compared "mechanical solidarity" with "organic solidarity" in social systems, the first deriving from the division of labor and the second from shared sentiments.

10. Consider testimony, for example, by the then-chief of U.S. Steel, Roger Blough, before the U.S. Senate Subcommittee on Antitrust and Monopoly in 1957 regarding steel industry pricing practices: "My concept is that a price that matches another price is a competitive price. . . . I say that the buyer has more choice when the other fellow's price matches our price." He contended "that if all steel prices are the same then the customer is free to buy from any producer he chooses," but "if prices are different, then the buyer has no real freedom of choice because he must buy from the company that sells the cheapest." See Ivar Berg, "The Confidence Game," in *Columbia University Forum* VI (Winter 1963): 36.

11. I am concerned here with education's "production" side; I leave the innumerable cultural benefits—the so-called consumption benefits—that attach to education entirely aside for present purposes.

12. I was greeted, almost immediately, by a scathing "Op Ed" article in the New York *Times* from a history professor at Washington University, St. Louis. Why, he angrily asked, after learning of my published report and hearing a presentation I made at his university, would the author even dream of *reporting* such findings, findings that would only disabuse members of the Congress, and private donors, of the economic arguments that helped significantly to sustain the education boom of the 1960s? His concern evidently was not with my findings, with honest efforts to discover truths, but with my misjudgment in *publishing* them.

13. Once again, the contributions of educational investments to the consumption of valid cultural activities are not here under review.

14. For a fuller rendering of these three matters see Ivar Berg, "Unemployment, Productivity and Inflation: Misgivings About the Sapient Orthodoxy," in Arthur Brief (ed.), *Productivity Research in the Social Sciences* (New York: Praeger, 1982), pp. 71–90.

15. Barry Bluestone and Bennett Harrison, "The Grim Truth About the Job Miracle," New York *Times*, February 1, 1987, Sec. D, p. 2.

16. Michael Piore, "Labor Market Segmentation Theory: Critics Should Let the Paradigm Evolve," in *Monthly Labor Review* CVI (3):26.

17. *Ibid.*, p. 27.

18. *Ibid.*, p. 28. Emphasis mine.

19. See review articles by Lewontin in the *New York Review of Books*, January 20, 1983, p. 6, entitled "The Corpse in the Elevator," and by Steven Jay Gould, "Utopia Limited," in the same journal, March 3, 1983, p. 10.

I3 | Computers at School?

Israel Scheffler

Introduction

In an essay published a little over twenty years ago, I described American education as then in the throes of a return to formalism. What I referred to was the renewed emphasis of that period on academic values and the rejection of earlier concerns with the child's growth as center of the educational process. The return to formalism also involved what I described as a vast

> emphasis on educational technology, the development of devices, programs, and new curricula for the more efficient packaging and distribution of knowledge. What [had been], in the days of progressivism, a broad concern for scientific inquiry into processes of growth, perception, and socialization, [had] in the name of hardheaded research and development, become more and more a preoccupation with the hard facts comprising educational content, and their optimal ordering for transmission to the student.[1]

Having survived that return to formalism, and the wild swing to the opposite extreme succeeding it in the late sixties and early seventies, we are now heading back in the old formalistic direction, with the insouciant amnesia that has become a hallmark of our educational history. Then, the slogans were "excellence," "mastery," "structure," and "discipline"; and the devices were teaching machines, programmed instruction, and new school curricula prepared by experts in the disciplines. Now, the slogans are "excellence," "basics," "minimum competences," and "standards"; and the devices are television and, more particularly, the computer. Then as now, the rhetoric was couched in broad educational terms, but economic incentives were also at work, and educational motivations were powered by international rivalry. Sputnik was, to be sure, a Soviet achievement, whereas the feared plan for a fifth-generation computer is Japanese. Are we, nevertheless, simply experiencing a déjà vu, watching a return where only the names have been changed to protect the innocent of history?

I think not. There are certainly salient parallels of the sort just outlined—parallels of ideological direction and emphasis, of terminology and motivation. But two differences stand out. First, the progressivism against which the earlier formalism reacted was milder than the antiestablishmentarianism of the sixties and seventies, and it plumbed shallower emotional depths in the nation at large. The antiestablishment trend of the recent period, tied as it was to the upheaval over the Vietnam War, the youth movement, and efforts to improve the status of minorities, had wider ramifications in society at large; it went far beyond the schools. The social, political, and educational reactions it has called forth have been correspondingly stronger and broader.

Second, the earlier formalism was independently narrower in its focus. It addressed the schools primarily, its vanguard composed of disciplinary scholars reforming school curricula, its technologies largely school-based. By contrast, the current technologies are broadly social in their impact; they are transforming society at large, and only secondarily the schools. Our children are living in a world already fundamentally altered by the television environment outside the school. They are growing into a world increasingly computerized in every sphere—industry, commerce, communications, transport, health care, science, government, and the military. Current technology is no mere affair of curriculum scholars. The school is now the tail, the whole world the computerized dog.

Indeed, the feeling that the computer revolution *must* be reflected in the school's basic offerings is widespread. Educators solemnly recommend computer literacy as a basic subject of study, advertisers frighten parents into buying computers so as to avert educational disaster for their children, salesmen present the computer as an instrument of achievement both in school and in life. In 1983, parents spent 110 million dollars on educational software alone, it was reported by Future Computing, Inc., according to the New York *Times* of November 11, 1984.[2] Swept by computer frenzy, the community is urged to express it in home and in classroom no less than in other major institutions. If the general expansion of computerization is in fact here to stay, what are schools and educators to do? What *can* they do?

I suggest three things: First, they can take a critical attitude toward the pressures for computerization being brought to bear on education, recognizing that educational applications of the computer are not given or foreordained. There may indeed be good reasons of an educational sort for putting computers to use in the classroom. But I emphasize "of an educational sort." Mere faddishness, or corporation hype, or status seeking, or parental panic, or widespread social use are not enough. Second, taking an educational point of view respecting the computer, they can raise not only questions of effectiveness but also questions of value, alternatives, and side effects—ends as well as means. Third, they can be alert to the transfer of computer language to education and the consequent hazard that educational ends will be constricted to fit. In the remainder of my remarks, I shall elaborate on each of these three recommendations in turn.

These recommendations, it should be emphasized, are addressed primarily to educators rather than to the computer community. And I make bold to offer them despite my status as an outsider to this community because the use of the computer in education raises basic issues that are *general* rather than *technical* and are of serious concern to all of us.

I. The Illusion of Giveness

My recommendations, you will note, do not imply an antitechnology attitude. They do not urge educators to mount the barricades and fight the marauding technologists under the faded banner of humanism. There is, in fact, a know-nothingism about technology as there is a know-nothingism about pure science, arts, and humanities. Technology is no "evil empire" pitted in ultimate warfare against the realm of humane values. It is, after all, the transformation of the world through thought and, as such, is essential and inescapable. Thought is ineffective without technique, technique impossible without thought. As John Passmore has put it,

Technology, the application of science, is itself an exercise of the human intelligence, the human imagination, the human gift for understanding. The pure mathematician who is reported to have rejoiced: "Well, thank God, no one will ever find a use for *that* piece of mathematics" is as ridiculous a figure as the Philistine depicted by Matthew Arnold, with his monotonous refrain, "What's in it for me?"[3]

The invention and development of the computer, specifically, are triumphs of the creative mind which all can applaud.

Yet it does not follow that the computer must therefore be regarded as a given for education. The illusion of givenness is largely an offshoot of strong independent pressures for computerization. There is, in fact, no necessity that compels an advancing technology to be mirrored in school offerings, nothing fated about it. We do well to note that the Japanese themselves, our primary competitors in the computing field, have not rushed to install computers in the classrooms, relying instead on their traditional culture of schooling coupled with intensive academic work and school and family supports.[4] And Professor Joseph Weizenbaum has reminded us of earlier technological enthusiasms, pointing to the example of home movie cameras gathering dust in thousands of closets across the nation, by contrast with the rosy promise of home computers humming in a swelling crescendo from coast to coast.[5]

I have described the illusion of givenness as largely an offshoot of the pressure for computerization. There is, I suggest, also a deeper source, that is, the absolutizing of the computer as a means. Let me explain. The computer as a symbol-manipulating device for accomplishing various purposes in industry, management, research, and so forth is not *ipso facto* a means for achieving educational purposes. Its instrumental value does not automatically carry over from the former to the latter. To suppose it does is to absolutize its status as a means.

The point deserves some elaboration. To speak of an object as an instrument is to convey some implicit reference to a purpose. In abstraction from purpose, no object is an instrument or, what comes to the same thing, there are no all-purpose means. To describe a hammer as a tool is to imagine some purpose to which it is to be put, some context in which such a purpose is embedded. The concept of a means is a relational rather than a categorical one.

It follows that instrumentality for a designated purpose implies nothing about instrumentality for any other. A hammer's usefulness for driving nails says nothing about its suitability as a soup ladle. Nor, on the other hand, does it follow that driving nails is the only purpose to which it can be put. The stereotype of an object may indeed tend to constrict our thought of it to its standard or conventional use, but the stereotype is itself no more intrinsic to the object than its instrumentality.

If a hammer *cannot* serve as a soup ladle, it *can* serve as a doorstop, or a book end, or a paperweight. Its suitability for such nonconventional uses is neither guaranteed nor precluded by its stereotype but must be independently established for each case.

What holds for the hammer holds for any technology. That an object is described as a technological device bears implicit reference to a purpose; its usefulness for such purpose in itself neither implies nor excludes its fitness for any other. The property of being a piece of technology is not a physical but a teleological property. It is not given but acquired with purpose.

To question the educational usefulness of the computer is thus no denial of its usefulness in all sorts of other ways. Nor does its undoubted value in order of its roles imply anything about its value for education. To put the computer to educational use is in fact to transform it from one sort of instrument to another, to change its character as technology by throwing it into a new combination with human purpose. Its instrumental value for education is not a foregone fact, "out there," decreed by history. *What* our purposes are, *which* of these we choose to implement, *how* we apply our resources to the effort make all the difference—not merely to the application of technology but to its very constitution as such.

II. Educational Ends and Means

What educational purposes might then be served by computers? The answers that have been suggested are numerous and they will no doubt continue to proliferate. I will comment on four of these, not by any means to provide definitive appraisals, but only to illustrate the sorts of questions that should, I believe, be addressed to such proposals.

1. One answer that has been given is that training in computers would provide marketable skills to children growing up in an increasingly computerized world. The computer's role is that of a vocational educator, preparing the masses of our youth for jobs in the future. This answer has been disputed. It has been argued that although some of our youth will obtain employment as computer experts, the promise of such employment to the general student body is empty. Professors Levin and Rumberger, for example, hold that "the proliferation of high technology industries and their products is far more likely to reduce the skill requirements of jobs in the U.S. economy than to upgrade them." An Professor Papert has been quoted as saying that because computer technology is advancing

so rapidly, "what children are learning today [about computers] is going to be irrelevant when they get out of school."[6]

All our youth will of course be affected by the computer in a myriad of ways. They will become familiar with it and its effects in banks, schools, businesses, supermarkets, hospitals, and libraries. But does it follow that, because these effects are widespread, the jobs will be as well? Should the masses of our youth be trained for Hollywood because of the prevalence of the movies, or for Detroit because of the widespread effects of the automobile? The question of future employment possibilities is of course an empirical one. There is, at any rate, no direct inference to be drawn from the social pervasiveness of the computer to the reliable promise of pervasive employment.

Even were such promise true, it would not follow that schools should provide the requisite training. Corporations and businesses have frequently argued, with respect to vocational education generally, that schools can best contribute to the general education of their students and to the development of students' social skills and character, leaving the rest to on-the-job experience. Whatever the truth may be on this issue, such alternatives must at least be explored. Again, it is worth noting the Japanese experience, in which schools have so far retained their traditional orientations, while the youth have acquired familiarity with the computer through informal means.

2. A second answer is more modest. It argues that schools should prepare students in a general way for the computerized world they will inhabit. This answer does not promise the youth employment in programming, for they will, in all likelihood, be consumers of programs rather than producers. However, so the argument runs, any child not prepared to deal generally with computers in the future will be handicapped in a variety of ways, personal, social, and economic, no matter what occupation he or she may follow. For even as a consumer of programs, the child will require facility with computers and at least some understanding of the process of programming. Some such line of thought seems to underlie the notion of "computer literacy," merging as well with the "minimum competency" rhetoric and the "basic skills" idea. The role of the computer is here envisaged not as a species of vocational education but as perhaps akin to driver education in supplying our youth with abilities without which they would be handicapped in life.

Now let us concede that knowledge of the computer will indeed be essential for adequate functioning in the future and, as such, generally desirable. Does it follow that *schools* should invest a significant effort in this direction? Exactly what type and what level of knowledge are, in fact, thought to be required? Do the requisite abilities presuppose a theoretical understanding of computer science or only one or another degree of operational facility? The way in which such questions are answered makes all the difference in the world in determining the school's proper role.

How many drivers understand the theory of the internal combustion engine? How many telephone or television users have analogous theoretical understanding? Driver education, premised on the public interest in traffic safety, leads no one to exalt "driver science" to the level of a new basic skill, along with English and mathematics, as *A Nation at Risk* does for computer science.[7] Yet if only operational facility is involved in either case, why the disparity? It might be suggested that the level of operational understanding required of the computer consumer is significantly higher than that required of the automobile consumer, but a detailed argument would have to be made to this effect. In any case, it would further need to be argued that the school is the preferred locus for acquiring such understanding, rather than out-of-school experience. It is ironic that academic formalists, providing neither argument, often advocate a computer literacy that may require no formal schooling at all, or at best at a level comparable to that of driver education.

3. A third answer is that the computer would enhance the learning of traditional school subjects. Unlike the previous two answers, which urged the importance of learning *about* the computer, the present answer advocates *using* the computer to learn about other things. The idea is to have the computer pick up the rote and repetitive aspects of traditional learning, providing as much individualized drill, practice, feedback, and evaluation as may be needed to reach suitable levels of mastery. The computer is here thought of as a mechanical drill sergeant or, more generally, a mechanical teacher's aide.

As such, the computer has undoubted assets. It can connect with the student's learning process at any level and carry it further, in a manner unhampered by personal biases or social prejudices. It is also enormously patient (so to speak), providing as much practice and response as may be needed by the student to achieve any degree of mastery of school subjects. Behind some of the recent talk of computer literacy lurks perhaps this idea as well: that facility with the computer will enable its use to drill students in the basic skills associated with academic subjects.

Whether such use would indeed be generally effective in developing skills and improving academic learning is an empirical question on which I am glad to defer to educational practitioners and researchers. I consider here only whether an affirmative answer would imply that schools should adopt such use forthwith.

Effectiveness would not in itself, I suggest, warrant such a conclusion. Any means effective in achieving a given end will have costs, side effects, further consequences, and alternatives, all of which require consideration. A recent New York *Times* article reports the insight that flashcards may rival the computer in teaching rote materials.

> Children may initially be more willing to learn their multiplication tables with a computer-graphics program than with flashcards because of the novelty of the learning device. But the motivation often wears off quickly because the process of rote learning is no more creatively addressed on the screen than it is with cards.[8]

In general, one would at least need to consider such questions as the following before moving directly from computer effectiveness to school adoption: What alternative methods might be employed to the same end? What would be the relative social and economic costs? What would be the expected effects on equal access for all children? What consequences might be anticipated for school structure, student motivation, teacher training, school curricula, and the social and moral climate of learning? These questions are not meant to be rhetorical. I list them not as a way of rejecting the proposed use of the computer in the school but only to argue that they require consideration. Such consideration might well sustain the proposal in question. But it would do so on grounds that go beyond the mere effectiveness of the computer in drilling students in basic skills.

One potential side effect is worth special mention. Effective use of the computer in the manner proposed here might encourage complacency with respect to basic skills; such complacency might, in turn, scant other uses of the computer for education in higher level skills. A related effect seems already to have occurred in connection with the general recent emphasis on so-called basics. The New York *Times* of April 14, 1983, thus describes educators as interpreting the recent mathematics survey of the National Assessment for Educational Progress as showing "an emerging trend in the nation's schools: younger students are improving in the basics and older students are doing worse in high-level skills." The report attributed "much of the positive change . . . to improved performance on rather routine items." However, "in general, students made much more modest gains, or no gains at all, on items assessing deep understanding or applications of mathematics."[9]

The president of the National Council of Teachers of Mathematics, Stephen S. Willoughby, was quoted by the *Times* as saying that "the only things we see improvement on—basic calculations—are things that a calculator can do better than a person. There is no way we can survive if kids do well only on trivial skills and don't show an understanding at a high level." In both reading and mathematics, there seems to be a similar pattern, according to Mary M. Lindquist, quoted in the same *Times* report: "In both subjects, we may be concentrating on those skills that are easiest to teach and learn and neglecting the thinking skills that are not so easily taught and learned."[10] The moral seems to be that although basic skills need to be learned, higher skills also require nurture. Putting the computer to work on effective drilling in the basics ought not to fill us with such educational self-righteousness that we forget about developing higher-level capacities.

4. This leads us to the fourth answer to our main question. This answer is that the computer should be used to help develop creative problem-solving abilities. Rather than serving primarily as an adjunct to the traditional academic subjects, the computer is to be used to promote logical, cognitive, and reasoning abilities—what may be called, speaking generally, critical thinking, inclusive of inventive approaches to problems. The computer is to be not a drill sergeant but rather a trainer or coach in developing the student's capacity to solve problems.

This proposal has several of the same advantages as those of the previous one. Its interaction with the student is free of biases, it can be prolonged to any degree necessary for the learning task in question, and it lends itself to individualization of instruction. The question of its effectiveness in promoting critical thinking is, as before, an empirical question. But the setting of suitable criteria of success is here more controversial than in the case of drilling for mastery of basic skills and involves more urgently the question of transfer. And, assuming the method to be effective by any suitable criteria, questions analogous to those raised for the previous case would be relevant here as well, for example, questions of cost, alternatives, side effects, and further consequences.

On one issue, the present idea has an advantage over the last one. It places emphasis upon higher-level, creative capacities, offering a maximal rather than a minimal vision of cognitive competences to be fostered. It tends in this way to counter the image of education as bounded by the familiar academic *subjects*, and to import the notion of *problems* as primary. Thus it moves to break out of the formalist mold that associates the computer with a hard education in the traditional subjects. But empirical evaluation remains to be dealt with, that is, are there determinate criteria of success by which the computer can be shown to offer advantages in promoting creative problem-solving capacities?

Indefinitely many further applications of the computer to education might be devised. Nothing I have said implies that only the above four are possible or that they are the most desirable. I have used these four examples to illustrate the point that no computer use is inevitable and that every such use ought to run the gauntlet of questions ranging beyond considerations of effectiveness.

III. Computer Language

I want now to consider a large-scale side effect of computer use—the impact of computer language on our conception of educational ends. Specifically, I address the potential constriction of such ends through our hypnotic fascination with the computer.

The question to be raised here is not one of efficiency in achieving the ends designated; I concede, for the sake of the present argument, that the computer has been empirically shown to be effective in any or all of the ways previously discussed. Precisely if our means are effective in achieving certain ends are we tempted to lose sight of other and more elusive ends. I have already mentioned the emphasis on basic skills as having encouraged the neglect of higher-level capacities. Similarly, "teaching to the test" is easier than teaching for understanding; teaching facts and habits easier than teaching methods and dispositions. I spoke earlier of the *absolutizing of means*. What concerns me now is the *expansion of means* at the expense of ends.

Nor is this tendency peculiar to education. We naturally tend to shrink our vision of the world to our mode of access to it. As infants, we have to learn that there are objects beyond our field of vision and, as we grow, continually to expand our imaginative construction of the world beyond experience. Throughout life, our perception favors those things assimilable to our categories, rubrics, and models; what does not fit is noted only with difficulty. As researchers, we tend to identify our problems with those questions answerable by our chosen methods. It is no wonder that the phenomenon repeats itself again and again in the field of education.

The general point is this: As the computer's presence grows, the whole array of our educational ends tends to shrink to what is achievable or supposed achievable by computer. Instead of understanding the computer as a means to goals independently sought, we tend to redefine our goals so as to match what computers may do. From its initial status as a technology for promoting independently specified educational values, the computer thus becomes transformed into a general criterion of value. And the whole process is facilitated by language transfer.

Even without hard evidence for the educational efficacy of the computer, the mere promise of such efficacy promotes the transfer of computer language to education. Such transfer tends to filter out ends and values that do not fit the metaphor—for example, ethical sensitivity, social perceptiveness, artistic expressiveness—so that the efficiency of the computer is expanded by definition. For it is the merest tautology that ends achievable by the computer are achievable by the computer. It is, however, far from tautologous that all educational ends are indeed achievable by the computer. Indeed, it is false, and impoverishes education in fundamental ways.

There is a certain irony in this development. Although computer language has promoted a reductive view of the realm of teleological and mental process, teleological language has enriched the view of computer processes. Thus, computer scientists and cyberneticists have increasingly employed teleological and, indeed, anthropomorphic language in working with the computer. They have also tried to simulate certain mental processes with their admittedly partial models, then transferring the unreduced teleological descriptions of such processes to these models. At the same time, researchers and educators have increasingly applied computer terminology to the mind and tried to reduce mental functions to those of the machine, the whole reductive effort threatening to run in a logical circle.[11] How far we now are from a *genuine* reduction of mind may be illustrated by a recent comment of Professor Shimon Ullman, head of the Weizmann Institute's National Center for Artificial Intelligence. According to Ullman,

> The main message of *AI* research seems to be those areas once considered inordinately difficult—such as designing a computer that can play world class chess—have proven relatively simple, whereas teaching a computer elementary tasks such as understanding English or visually discerning shapes, have proved nearly impossible. The main objective is to learn more about the brain through this research. The reason we're not sure just how to make computers intelligent is that we still aren't certain what goes on in the brain.[12]

Looked at from the point of view of research, the transfer of languages from one realm to another exemplifies a creative strategy, often leading to progress. Certain analogies are suggestive enought to justify such transfers in the present case even if computers do not literally think and the mind is not literally a computer. One needs only to avoid making circular reductive claims. But looked at from the point of view of educational practice, the matter is more serious. For the computer metaphor acts to screen out what may be of the first importance, educationally speaking. The challenge confronting educators is to adopt whatever advantages computer uses may be shown to offer, while holding fast to their independent vision of educational values.

"The computer metaphor," as I intend this phrase, is actually a cluster of several related metaphors, operating in different ways and at different levels. Nor—and I emphasize this—is the computer metaphor bound to the strict understanding of the computer by the experts. It generates its force also, or even largely, from public conceptions of the matter, whether accurate or not. I want in what follows to concentrate on one major metaphor belonging to the cluster, that centered on the notion of *information*.

IV. The Notion of Information

A prevalent public image of the computer is, surely, that of an information processor. Information comes in discrete bits, each expressing a factual datum. Data may be entered and stored in the computer's memory, retrieved from memory, and processed in simple or complex ways according to various programs, which instruct the computer exactly what functions to perform. These functions are in the nature of algorithms, specifying determinately how the data are to be transformed. The human operator determines that the solution to his problem might be computed by program from input data, punches in his instructions to the machine to institute the relevant program, and eventually sees the solution displayed on the screen before him.

Now to think of learning, generally, in these terms is undeniably suggestive. But see how much is left out of the picture. Learning takes place not just by computing solutions to problems, nor even just by exchanging words, but by emulation, observation, identification, wonder, supposition, dream, imitation, doubt, action, conflict, ambition, participation, and regret. It is a matter of insight and perception, invention and self-knowledge, intimation and feeling as much as of question and answer. Even the understanding of an answer in everyday life involves catching not just the information literally conveyed by the words but also what is expressed by their overtones and nuances and what is carried between the lines or in the silences. Such understanding is not, in general, reducible to computation.

The activity of the computer operator, in the public's mind, is isolated and cognitive, its vehicles the finger and the eye. But even our cognitive skills are social. They grow in the first instance out of interactions with others more skilled than we, in continuous processes of discussion, demonstration, and exchange. The activity of a learner involves all of his being. It is moral and muscular, visceral and vascular, social and historical, proceeding, in Dewey's words, by trying and by undergoing.

Learning advances not alone when new answers are gained but when old answers are lost, not alone when problems are solved but when solutions turn problematic. Indeed, the categories of question-answering and problem-solving are too meager to contain such educational successes as new competences formed, new attitudes crystallized, new loyalties shaped, new discriminations made, new appraisals formulated, new emotions felt, new insights gained, new challenges undertaken, new purposes assumed. Interactive technology is but the tiniest sliver of interactive life. Unless, indeed, the computer operator had been learning all his life and in multifarious ways before his first approach to the machine, he could hardly learn anything *from* the machine. What questions could he put, what purposes could he have, what significance could he possibly attach to the answers received?

The computer metaphor, as just considered, projects the situation of the computer operator upon the learner generally. Now consider another, and deeper, application of the metaphor, in which the learner is seen not as the operator but as the computer itself. Like the computer, he acquires information, stores it in memory, ready to retrieve and process it in order to solve the problems put to him. But here is the catch: The computer does not pose its own problems to itself but requires an operator to do so, an operator with needs and purposes of his own. Without such needs and purposes, what constitutes a problem? What data require retrieval, and to what end? What functions ought to be activated, what needs fulfilled, what lacks satisfied? What can be the significance of information without appraisal in light of aims? Knowledge of one's enduring aims and purposes is, furthermore, not just another body of information but a form of insight into the patterning of one's chosen problems, the setting of one's life tasks.

To speak of information and memory, not to mention knowledge, in reference to the computer, is itself a metaphorical transfer from the human case. To transfer such terms back from the computer to the mind, now emptied of the connotations of human activity, interpretation, need, and purpose, is an example of the irony I mentioned earlier. This double transfer in the context of practice leads us unwittingly to shrink our initial ideals of education and our conceptions of mind and schooling.

The everyday notion of information refers to material we can understand

and interpret in context. Grasping what is expresses, we can paraphrase it and evaluate its contextual relevance, criticize and reject it or back it up appropriately, respond to it with feeling, sense its metaphorical echoes, appraise its bearing on our purposes, and apply it in our activity. The computer itself cannot be properly described as doing any of these things, in the everyday senses of the terms involved. To characterize the electronic state of computer circuitry in terms of "information" is to employ the word under a different interpretation. Further to construe the mind in terms of "computer information" empties the human notion of virtually all its content.

It is important to emphasize that, even in its full-blooded human sense, the concept of information is far from capable of adequately expressing our educational aims. This is so even if we concentrate on the purely cognitive aims of schooling, as they relate to the enterprise of problem-solving. For although information is certainly essential to education, it is only part of the story. Consider: you can have been given a piece of information but fail to realize its significance either for the problem at hand or for action, more generally. You can accept that such and such is the case but be totally unable to give any good reasons for it, thus disqualifying yourself as really knowing that such and such is the case. You can know it but not recall it at the fitting moment, or recall it but be unable to apply it intelligently to the problem under consideration. You may indeed be *able* to apply it without being in general *disposed* to do so, not having formed the suitable inclination or character trait. The suggestion that at least the cognitive side of education can be fully expressed in terms of information transfer, storage, and retrieval would not be worth a moment's consideration were it not that it is implicitly conveyed by the current formalism, coupled with the public's awe of scientific facts.

To know a fact requires, however, as Gilbert Ryle has put it, "having taken it in, i.e. being able and ready to operate with it, from it, around it and upon it. To possess a piece of information is to be able to mobilize it apart from its rote-neighbors and out of its role-formulation in unhackneyed and *ad hoc* tasks."[13] The Baconian image of science as an increasing accumulation of facts has independently distorted the ideal of education since well before the computer age. With "facts" now translated into "bits of information," the Baconian image is given modern dress. Just see how contemporary Mr. Gradgrind sounds when his little speech in Dickens's *Hard Times* is altered by replacing the word "fact" with "information." He is explaining his educational views to a teacher in the school he manages. I reproduce here the original passage, but you can mentally make the replacement at each occurrence of the word "fact" or "facts": "Now what I want is Fact. Teach these boys and girls nothing but Facts. Facts alone are wanted in life. Plant nothing else, root out everything else. You can form the mind of reasoning animals upon Facts; nothing else will be of any service to them."[14]

The teacher addressed by Mr. Gradgrind agrees. He has learned and proposes to teach his students

> about all the Water Sheds of all the world; and all the histories of all the peoples, and all the names of all the rivers and mountains, and all the productions, manners and customs of all the countries, and all their boundaries and bearings on the two and thirty points of the compass.[15]

Mr. Gradgrind considered the learning of such facts to be hard work. Current formalists think it can be made fun. The educational game selected as the best of 1984 by *Electronic Games* magazine, according to the New York *Times*, is one in which the player "must destroy the Fuzzbomb before it spreads across the entire nation. To confront the Fuzzbomb, the player or agent takes trains from city to city to get to the Fuzzbomb's location, which continually changes."[16] The presumed charm of this game is supposed to facilitate the student's learning to identify the state capitals. The same principle could no doubt be applied to the Water Sheds of all the world, and other such important facts.

Facts are, however, not the sorts of things imagined by Gradgrinds past or present. They are expressed in language, clothed in concepts, organized and transformed by theory, appraised by criteria of value, and intelligently or stupidly employed in the conduct of life. Neither the concepts nor the values we possess are automatically derivable from hard facts or data; they serve rather to mold the forms in which our putative facts are cast. These facts provide tests of our theories through their own credibilities, but they do not generate these theories by any kind of routine processing. They are, in turn, responsive to our theories and tested by them. That we have the theories and facts we do is therefore a reflection not only of our mental capacities or of the "real world" but of our history and our intellectual heritage.

Even the capacity for *intelligent use* of information will not suffice to express our educational aims relative to problem-solving. Drawing on accumulated data is inadequate for accommodation to future change. What is wanted in addition is the generation of new information—information, moreover, that does not result simply from applying old categories to new circumstances. Devising new categories, composing new classifications, postulating new entities, guessing at new connections, inventing new languages and calculi are desiderata of the highest importance.

Problem-solving, further, needs not just the recognition and retention of facts but the recognition and retention of difficulties, incongruities, and anomalies. It does not simply affirm truths but entertains suppositions, rejects the accepted, conceives the possible, elaborates the doubtful or false, questions the familiar, guesses at the imaginable, improvises the unheard of. An intelligence capable only of storing and applying truths would be profoundly incapacitated for the solving of problems.

When we move beyond problem-solving to consider educational aims in general, we find the computer metaphor based on "information" even more clearly inadequate. For we here encounter provinces long cultivated by rival metaphors, alien to the impression or transmission of facts. What I have elsewhere called the *insight model* is one such rival metaphor.[17] It speaks not of information but of insight and perception, vision and illumination, intuition of nuance and pattern, grasp of overtone and undertone.

A second such rival metaphor is that of *equipping*, or the provision of skills and capacities.[18] This is not a matter of storing answers, whether linguistic or numerical, and it cannot be accommodated solely in information-theoretic terms. It concerns rather the forming or strengthening of abilities, the *know-how* commanded by a person, rather than his know *that*, his capability to deal with the tasks and challenges of practice in the various domains of life. Nor is every bit of *know-how* accessible to algorithm, witness the comic's ability to make us laugh, the actor's capacity to make us weep, and the metaphorical ability itself, beyond the regimented interpretation of literal codes.

A third such rival metaphor is represented by what I have called the *rule model*.[19] This metaphor focuses on norms rather than capacities, on the pronenesses, likelihoods, tendencies, and dispositions of a person rather than on his mere abilities and skills—on what he *does* do rather than what he *can* do. In this realm we have again left the notion of information behind. For what is involved here is not the storing or transformation of data but the shaping of habits of mind and feeling, the growth of attitudes and traits, the development of character. Our concern is not with knowing *that* nor even with knowing *how*. For we are dealing not with what people believe, nor with what they are equipped to do, but with what they can reliably be expected to do, with their predictable but typically unarticulated patterns of conduct, taste, and emotion. The inculcation of desirable patterns of this sort, beyond the reach of algorithms, is of the first educational importance, laying the foundation of mutual trust, common feeling, and shared values without which no community can stand, let alone thrive.

These various realms all require to be kept steadfastly in view as we make progress on any educational front. The whole array of ends must serve as the context within which we gauge our educational situation. Rather than cutting this array down to the size of our technology, we should strive to look beyond our technology, to determine the purposes and directions of our further efforts.

The computer has been associated with the recent swing to hard education, with the notion of raising standards, of higher achievement in academic subjects, of increased efficiency in the teaching of fact, of enhanced problem-solving capacity. All these matters are indeed important. There is no positive virtue in low academic achievement, inefficient teaching, or diminished problem-solving capacity. Whatever the computer may be able to accomplish in such areas is all to the good. No such accomplishment, however, should block our vision of equally vital educational goals, or shrink our highest ideals of learning. It is the task of educators to keep both means and ends in view.[20]

Notes

Acknowledgment: Presented April 18, 1985, in the Schumann Distinguished Lecturer Series sponsored by the Interactive Technology in Education Program at the Harvard Graduate School of Education, with the support of the Schumann Foundation, and previously published in the *Teachers College Record* LXXXVII (1986): 513–528. I am very grateful to my colleagues in the Philosophy of Education Research Seminar at Harvard, Catherine Elgin, Kenneth Hawes, Vernon Howard, David Perkins, and Paul Smeyers, for critical discussion of a draft of my paper.

1. I. Scheffler, "Concepts of Education: Reflections on the Current Scene," in Scheffler, *Reason and Teaching* (London: Routledge and Kegan Paul, 1973), p. 59.

2. Peggy Schmidt, "What to Look for in Educational Software," New York *Times*, November 11, 1984, Sec. 12, p. 8.

3. John Passmore, *The Philosophy of Teaching* (Cambridge, Mass.: Harvard University Press, 1980), p. 115.

4. See Merry I. White, "Japanese Education: How Do They Do It?" *The Public Interest* LXXVI (1984): 87–101. White writes, "Computers and other technology do not play a large role in (Japanese) schools. . . . There is no national program to develop high technology skills in children. Americans spend much more money on science and technology in the schools; the Japanese spend more on teacher training and salaries" (p. 90).

5. Address to the Philosophy of Education Research Center, Harvard University, Fall, 1983. I am grateful to Professor Weizenbaum, whose pioneering critical reflections on the computer have taught me much. See especially his book *Computer Power and Human Reason* (San Francisco: W. H. Freeman, 1976).

6. See Henry M. Levin and R. W. Rumberger, "The Educational Implications of High Technology" Project Report No. 83-A4, Institute for Research on Educational Finance and Governance, Stanford University, February, 1983. These authors argue that "the expansion of the lowest skilled jobs in the American economy will vastly outstrip the growth of high technology ones" (Abstract, *ibid.*). See also the Boston *Globe*, November 26, 1984, p. 42, which also quotes Seymour Papert as calling "absurd" the "fear that children will be unprepared for the job market they face on graduation unless they have become 'computer literate.' "

7. *A Nation at Risk*, U.S. Department of Education, Washington, D.C., April 26, 1983.

8. Schmidt, "What to Look for in Educational Software."

9. New York *Times*, April 14, 1983, Sec. A, p. 21.

10. *Ibid.*

11. See the pioneering paper of Arturo Rosenblueth, Norbert Wiener, and Julian Bigelow, "Behavior, Purpose, and Teleology," *Philosophy of Science* X (1943): 18–24, which argues that the concept of "purposefulness" is "necessary for the understanding of certain modes of behavior" and that its importance has been slighted owing to the rejection of final causes as explanatory; the authors then interpret purpose in terms of negative feedback. In my paper "Thoughts on Teleology," *British Journal for the Philosophy of Science* IX (1959): 265–284, and in my book *The Anatomy of Inquiry* (New York: Alfred A. Knopf, 1963; now Hackett Publishing Co., 1981), I argued that if the Rosenblueth, Wiener, and Bigelow paper simply extends teleological language to selected forms of behavior of independent interest, there can be no quarrel with them, "for in such a case, they would not be setting forth an analysis of teleology so much as striving to improve the description of the behavior in question through increased use of teleological language. If, however, as appears to be the case, they intend also to provide an *analysis* of teleological notions, their proposal may properly be judged by seeing how satisfactorily the analysis accounts for acknowledged instances of teleological behavior" (p. 112, *The Anatomy of Inquiry*). My argument was that the authors' reduction of teleology to negative feedback does not succeed. But they thought it did and so, by their lights, weren't arguing in a circle. But in my view, the claim to reduce human purpose to machine purpose by their method can

achieve plausibility only by so enriching the latter as to encompass the former. But the trends I discuss in the text are quite general and go far beyond the above illustrative reference.

12. See *The Forward*, March 8, 1985, p. 33.

13. Gilbert Ryle, "Teaching and Training," in R. S. Peters (ed.), *The Concept of Education* (London: Routledge and Kegan Paul, 1967), P. 111.

14. Charles Dickens, *Hard Times* (New York and Boston: Cleartype Edition Books Inc. [containing the 1854 text and all the author's revisions of 1867 and 1868], n.d.), Chap. I, p. 1.

15. *Ibid.*, Chap. II, p. 7.

16. Schmidt, "What to Look for in Educational Software."

17. Scheffler, *Reason and Teaching*, p. 71.

18. See Gilbert Ryle, *The Concept of Mind* (London: Hutchinson, 1949): "In a word, teaching is deliberate equipping" (p. 310).

19. Scheffler, *Reason and Teaching*, p. 76.

20. See *Teachers College Record* LXXXV (Summer 1984), which is devoted to discussions of the computer and education. Professor Douglas Sloan's editorial introduction to the issue carries the admirable title "On Raising Critical Questions about the Computer in Education." See also Catherine Z. Elgin's critique of computer models of the mind in "Representation, Comprehension, and Competence," *Social Research* LI (Winter 1984): 906–925.

I4 | Dirty Hands

Joseph Margolis

What has now been tagged the "dirty hands" dilemma in the moral philosophy industry is of course literarily and literally linked with the street-wise pronouncements of Hoerderer, the revolutionary leader in Sartre's well-known play *Dirty Hands*. One senses that much of the charm of the puzzle depends on the insinuation that the whole of human existence is tainted in the same way that, either generally or exceptionally, in politics and war, one cannot expect to escape its clutches. And yet, as with so many of the interesting complexities of moral choice and commitment, it is difficult to give the alleged dilemma a suitably uncontroversial formulation. The best-known discussant of the issue, Michael Walzer, clearly fails to sort dirty hands in a conceptually clean way; and we can if we wish indict the entire race simply by ascribing to humans at large, pursuing their quotidian routines unobjectionably and prudently, at least an incipient conviction of the corporate nature of planetary life and of the misery of a large part of the world's population that their own aggregated routines effectively ignore or might relieve.

But we need to do some homework first, if we are to isolate the essential issues from others, however interesting, with which they may be too easily conflated or confused. Furthermore, there are not very many moral theorists who address the dirty hands issue in any way that could be called sustained and penetrating. Walzer is one of the very few in the Anglo-American practice of analysis, with plausible credentials, who has linked the matter to a systematic inquiry into the nature

256

of war. To pursue the issue, therefore, in a way that calls on what there is of a tradition of examination pretty well requires a rather dialectical and argumentative style that may seem otherwise too much focused on quarrel to be worth reading at all. Sometimes, however, a sense of the principal options on an important but nearly neglected question cannot otherwise be supplied, either economically or with sufficient scope or without a distinct impression of idiosyncrasy. So we really must, responsibly, worry Walzer's account—perhaps without mercy—if we mean to get at the essential difficulties the dirty hands question troublesomely force on our attention.

Actually, Walzer addresses the question very briefly in his extended overview of war. He says it is "the hardest question" and concerns "necessity":

> What are we to say about those military commanders (or political leaders) who override the rules of war and kill innocent people as a "supreme emergency"? Surely we want to be led at such a time by men and women ready to do what has to be done—what is *necessary*; for it is only here that necessity, in its true sense, comes into the theory of war. On the other hand, we cannot ignore or forget what it is they do. The deliberate killing of the innocent is murder. Sometimes, in conditions of extremity (which I have tried to define and delimit), commanders must commit murder or they must order others to commit it. And then they are murderers, though in a good cause. In domestic society, and particularly in the context of revolutionary politics, we say of such people that they have dirty hands. . . . Men and women with dirty hands, though it may be the case that they had acted well and done what their office required, must nonetheless bear a burden of responsibility and guilt. They have killed unjustly, let us say, for the sense of justice itself, but justice itself requires that unjust killing be condemned.[1]

Walzer clearly admits that, in a moment of "necessity," murder may (in some morally pertinent sense) be required by a good cause—without thereby ceasing to be murder. He acknowledges, here, the doctrine of *Kriegsraison*, of what, in war, may be "necessary to compel the submission of the enemy with the least possible expenditure of time, life, and money"; but he insists that " 'Reason of war' can only justify the killing of people we already have reason to think are liable to be killed," and he understands this constraint to operate essentially—curiously—in such a way as to segregate soldiers and civilians in the very context of modern war (that is, as an extension of the just war concept).[2] If, however, the just war concept is hopeless to defend in contemporary circumstances—which is not to say that the justification of war and warfare is similarly impossible (in the sense either of *jus ad bellum* or *jus in bello*)—then the conceptual dilemma Walzer takes note of, cannot fail to haunt us in a more troublesome way than Walzer himself is prepared to admit: just consider what, dropping the "just war" interpretation of *Kriegsraison*, would follow (from Walzer's formula) for the whole of World War II.

This is about all Walzer says in this connection, though he mentions the troublesome case of the British Bomber Command, which may well have been the only offensive weapon the British had against the Nazis in the early forties and which deliberately practiced indiscriminate bombing against civilian targets. Walzer himself apparently believes that the command case "isn't really an example of the dirty hands problem"—for either Arthur Harris (who directed the command) or Winston Churchill—since "terror bombing is a criminal activity, and after the immediate threat posed by Hitler's early victories had passed, it was an entirely indefensible activity."[3] He allows it nevertheless, because "it apparently had that form [the form of the dirty hands dilemma] in the minds of British leaders, even of Churchill himself at the end."[4] He also mentions Rolf Hochhuth's *Soldiers* in this context, which of course raises the issue of the necessity and morality of high-altitude bombing. Hochhuth's entire literary career, it may be said, from *The Deputy* to *Soldiers*, is almost completely devoted to examining the dirty hands problem in all its complexity (*and* in historically important settings), although quite serious (unanswered) questions have been raised about Hochhuth's treatment of Churchill's complicity in the death of Wladislaw Sikorski (one of the most celebrated dirty hands charges of our time).[5] In any event, Walzer gives two formulations of the dirty hands dilemma, the first of which he says may be more "realistic," but the second of which he himself favors: (a) "that a nation fighting a just war, when it is desperate and survival itself is at risk, must use unscrupulous or morally ignorant soldiers; and as soon as their usefulness is past, it must disown them"; (b) "that decent men and women, hard-pressed in war, must sometimes do terrible things, and then themselves have to look for some way to reaffirm the values they have overthrown."[6] Notice that (a) is specifically linked to the just war concept and that (b) is not; also, that (a) risks conceptual incoherence but (b) does not—or does not explicitly.

Walzer had written, some years before, an extended analysis of the dirty hands question, occasioned by a number of papers, especially Thomas Nagel's "War and Massacre," that eventually appeared in the second number of the Princeton journal *Philosophy and Public Affairs*. But in some ways, the formulation in *Just and Unjust Wars* is clearer than what is offered in the earlier paper.[7] It is clearer, but its clarity imposes on us the obligation to avoid intellectual and moral scandal or sheer incoherence or barely relevant moral niceties. For the first of Walzer's formulations seems to invite the rankest callousness in the name of a high moral concern; and the second seems to pass over the dilemma itself for the sake of restoring in some way (apparently, acknowledged guilt or contrition) the moral seriousness of those who have dirty hands, now that they no longer face the original or a similar dilemma. Walzer apparently believes that "the world of necessity [the necessity of committing evil acts for just or good causes] is [at least usually] generated by a conflict between collective survival and human rights." Here, it may be said, the very existence of a war (certainly, the existence of those wars that Walzer discusses) automatically entails a presumption of necessity in just those terms in which *Kriegsraison* is pertinently invokable. Walzer himself acknowledges that, under such circumstances, "political leaders can hardly help but choose the utilitarian side of the dilemma": by "utilitarian," Walzer means to follow Nagel's terminology (but not his preference)—although it is frankly not altogether clear whether he means the term primarily in a merely consequentialist sense (actually invoking *Kriegsraison*, which seems not an unreasonable reading) or whether he means it in the technical sense (which, since it would then entail a presumably overriding moral assessment, would compound the threatening incoherence).[8]

The confusion derives in good part from Nagel's original paper. For one thing, it is Nagel who introduces potentially opposed "absolutist" and "utilitarian" reasons or intuitions regarding the conduct of war—and, in doing that, specifically links the "absolutist" view with the advocacy of the just war thesis. An absolutist position, he says, opposes to the utilitarian tolerance of large-scale violence in the name of a just cause or the "more general position that any means can in principle be justified if it leads to a sufficiently worthy end" "the view that certain acts cannot be justified no matter what the consequences. Among these acts is murder—the deliberate killing of the harmless: civilians, prisoners of war, and medical personnel."[9] For a second, Nagel himself conflates the merely consequentialist and technical readings of "utilitarian." He remarks (he is discussing war and massacre, remember) that "utilitarianism says that one should try, either individually or through institutions, to maximize good and minimize evil"; he links quite easily "calculations of utility and national interest," and yet he also considers that "it may even be argued that war [in particular, nuclear war] involves violence on such a scale that it is never justified on utilitarian grounds" (which goes well beyond merely national concerns).[10] And for a third, it is Nagel who formulates the irresolvable dilemma of dirty hands in terms of opposed

2 6 0 | Joseph Margolis

absolutist and utilitarian considerations: "In the final analysis," he says, "I believe that the dilemma cannot always be resolved." It is worth remarking that Walzer and Nagel have, to the present moment, almost monopolized the discussion of the dirty hands issue—within the boundaries of professional philosophy in the United States. It would, therefore, be not entirely unimportant to consider whether their respective solutions are at all viable or coherent. There's good reason to think they are not.

Nagel means to offer "a somewhat qualified defense of absolutism"; and he acknowledges the paradox that, in such a view, where absolutism conflicts with utility, absolutism "can require that one refrain from choosing the lesser of two evils when that is the only choice one has."[11] (The point here of course is that *Kriegsraison* might, on utilitarian grounds [evidently, on Walzer's view], actively favor a dirty hands policy, where absolutism would unconditionally reject *doing anything* in accord with such a policy.) Taken literally, these considerations might lead us to suppose that a utilitarian would override any dirty hands charge precisely by invoking utilitarian principles as sufficient to yield a just verdict; that absolutists would never admit that dirty hands was even a pertinent option, since the dilemma could not arise consistently with absolutist prohibitions; and that Walzer concedes the dilemma because *he* (but not Nagel) concedes the utilitarian principles or values override absolutist principles or values, *in the context of necessity*—as far as choice is concerned, but not as far as reponsibility for acts committed and their consequences are concerned. (This, of course, is the focus of the incoherence of Walzer's position.) But although this would be correct as far as it goes, it is not at all accurate with respect to Nagel's view, because Nagel holds that, in spite of absolutism's giving "primacy to a concern with what one is *doing* [that is, with one's deliberate and intentional acts], there [still] could not . . . without incoherence, be an absolute prohibition against *bringing about* the death of an innocent person."[12]

Hence, Nagel both provides for dirty hands by distinguishing between what people "do" and the "results people bring about" by what they do, and attempts (somehow) to address the dilemma in a way that distinguishes the absolutist position from one that merely invokes the principle of double effect.[13] Nagel's formula, then, is the following: "Absolutism requires that we *avoid* murder at all costs, not that we *prevent* it at all costs."[14] Nevertheless, it is difficult to grasp the sense in which Nagel is *not* committed to a form of the double effect principle. It is true that double effect does not require or entail any commitment to what Nagel calls absolutism; and it is equally true that absolutism does not require or entail any commitment to double effect.[15] For, for one thing, it is certainly clear than an appeal to the principle of double effect could easily be converted into a sly vindication of what might otherwise be a fair instance of dirty hands—say, by an appeal to *Kriegsraison*. The worry with double effect (which Nagel signals an appreciation of) is that even if there were conceded a morally pertinent distinction between intended and merely foreseen consequences, that distinction—particularly when the consequences in question are inevitable, or entailed, or even highly probable or very seriously risked, or the result of merely redescribing what one intends to do (in accord with common practices)—cannot be drawn in a sufficiently strong and principled way that the charge of dirty hands would (for that reason) be precluded as irrelevant to a given case, or that the charge could (for that reason) be mitigated significantly. There may be a relevant distinction between principal and subordinate intentions and between intended and foreseen consequences; but it is certainly not clear that that distinction also serves to divide the culpable and the nonculpable congruently, or even bears directly on the dirty hands issue.

Secondly, there is a straightforward reading of Nagel's formula that accords with the double effect principle, and there is no plausible reading (given a pertinent sense of anticipating consequences, for the serious decisions of war that Nagel has in mind) that would effectively disallow or go contrary to double effect considerations. Nagel's primary concern is to avoid incoherence—in effect, the very incoherence that Walzer's (and the utilitarian's preference) suffers. For he explicitly says that "the notion that one might sacrifice one's moral integrity justifiably, in the service of a sufficiently worthy end, is an incoherent notion."[16] This he offers by way of elucidating the formula given (above), since he wishes to disabuse us of supposing that moral absolutism rests essentially or merely on "moral self-interest" or "moral purity or integrity." So he holds that "if by committing murder one sacrifices one's moral purity or integrity, that can only be because there is *already* something wrong with murder."[17]

Now then, the dilemma that Nagel inadvertently poses for himself is this: *if* we do not invoke the principle of double effect to establish innocence (where a charge of dirty hands obtains), and *if* the concern of absolutism is with what a person *does* (in a robust sense of action), then either: (i) a merely formulaic distinction between what one *does* and what *results* from what one does could never pertinently support the validity of a dirty hands charge; or (ii) all who are correctly so charged must have behaved irrationally or incoherently; or (iii) the dirty hands charge addresses forms of misfortune or evil that are *not* the concern of absolutism at all. In short, on Nagel's grounds, it looks as if the charge of dirty hands cannot even arise or, if it does arise, cannot pertinently bear on the absolutist/utilitarian quarrel. (We have already seen, remember, that, on straight utilitarian grounds—whether merely consequentialist or strict—the charge of dirty hands is bound to be overridden, without remainder; or, if utilitarian considerations override only as far as moral choice is concerned but not as far as moral responsibility is concerned, then we must concede the incoherence of utilitarianism itself.) There appears to be only one conceptual scenario in which dirty hands could be admitted, consistent with what Nagel postulates, and that is this: if one acts conformably with *absolutist* constraints, then one may yet bring about results that are pertinently evil on the *utilitarian* scale. But then, dirty hands logically require a strong disjunction between the scope of absolutist and utilitarian criteria—in spite of the fact that Nagel's entire discussion admits a pertinent contest between the two for jurisdiction in particular cases and in spite of the fact that Nagel is not prepared to invoke the principle of double effect (which would seem to afford the only possible ground for relevantly invoking the required disjunction between actions and foreseen consequences).

The truth, however, is much simpler than we have made out—and, because of it, also much more complex. For Nagel never really comes to terms with the dilemma as here posed—but he poses another, that may well be more interesting. He actually turns instead to (essentially) the same just war application of the dirty hands charge what Walzer champions: "To fight dirty," he says,

> is to direct one's hostility or aggression *not at its proper object*, but at a peripheral target which may be more vulnerable, and through which the proper object can be attacked indirectly. This applies in a fist fight, an election campaign, a duel, or a philosophical argument. If the concept is general enough to apply to all these matters, it should apply to war—both to the conduct of individual soldiers and to the conduct of nations.[18]

But having said this, Nagel *does not* subscribe (as Walzer does) to the doctrine that utility takes precedence, in circumstances of "necessity," over absolute prohibitions. He seems to hold instead that "necessity" may require abandoning absolutism, without abandoning its lexicographical priority over utility (in Rawls's sense) and without denying the evil of what one *does* in such straits. "There may be circumstances," Nagel insists, "so extreme that they render an absolutist position untenable. One may find then that one has no choice but to do something terrible. Nevertheless, even in such cases absolutism retains its force in that one cannot claim *justification* for the violation. It does not become *all right*."[19] Here, presumably, is Nagel's dirty hands concept. We are bound *to do* (it seems we are bound to choose to do) what is absolutely prohibited.

There is a difficulty nevertheless. For one thing, Nagel does not legitimate or explain the sense in which all pertinent moral matters—particularly the dire issues here being raised—can be taken to fall under absolutist or utilitarian principles or both, *and no other*. For a second, it seems conceptually preposterous to hold that the terrible calamities of dirty hands contexts could both *require* "abandoning" action in accord with absolutist prohibitions *and never provide* morally pertinent categories more nearly appropriate than those acknowledged to govern whatever one does *when one is not forced* (in the as yet unexplained sense) to "abandon" absolutism. For a third, it is logically quite simple (as the manipulation of the just war notion itself makes clear) that one *could* be said to adhere to the appropriate absolutist and utilitarian principles without conflict or dilemma, if one merely adjusted or extended the categories and criteria of pertinent moral discrimination suitably: Nagel not only insists on the priority of absolutism, but he defines the scope of what falls under it *absolutely*; but this has nowhere been justified, and (as already strongly suggested) the required distinctions *cannot* convincingly be drawn solely or minimally out of the just war concept. "But one cannot really say," he claims,

> while torturing a prisoner, "You understand, I have to pull out your fingernails because it is absolutely essential that we have the names of your confederates"; nor can one say to the victims of Hiroshima, "you understand, we have to incinerate you to provide the Japanese government with an incentive to surrender."[20]

Here, one might more reasonably say that modern warfare simply *is* evil on absolutist grounds, *not* that one can fight a war (these days) conformably with absolutist (or just war) constraints; for, if (with Nagel and Walzer) one insists that *that is* possible, absolutist prohibitions will be perceived to be suspiciously *ad hoc*, partisan, or implausibly contingent. Also, it would then be quite possible to argue, as Richard Brandt rather neatly shows, that a utilitarian *could generally* accommodate Nagel's constraints—*though not absolutely*—and that where "absolute catastrophe" threatened, it might well be necessary to fall back to considerations of utility (despite what Nagel says).[21] Nevertheless, *on* utilitarian grounds, dirty hands would be *too* easily obviated—except perhaps as a nostalgic memory of an older moral canon or in accord with Walzer's incoherent alternative. Here, one may usefully recall the *Oresteia*. (We shall turn to the tragic theme later.)

The upshot then is this; Walzer and Nagel provide two distinct conceptions of dirty hands; but the first is flatly incoherent, and the second is either incoherent or depends on an essentially incomplete account. In effect, what we may conclude is that the way in which both model dirty hands impoverishes the import of the phenomenon as well as the resources of moral theory by which to accommodate it. Walzer's conception is incoherent, because Walzer maintains that, in contexts of "necessity," utility validly overrides absolutist constraints and yet, in doing so, entails what is plainly to be morally condemned. Nagel's conception is either incoherent or essentially defective, because Nagel maintains that, in contexts of "necessity," absolutist constraints must be "abandoned" even though they are never overridden by utilitarian considerations *or* by whatever moral or prudential considerations rationally oblige us *to* "abandon" absolutist constraints. Furthermore, the principles invoked are insufficiently flexible, for, if utility *overrides* what would be condemned on absolutist grounds, then dirty hands is no dilemma at all but merely an uncomfortably difficult situation in which one must learn to live with more realistic assessments than the "extravagant" absolutist rule would require.[22] And if absolutism *cannot* be overridden, then the only coherent sense in which one must "abandon" absolutist constraints (consistently with the limitations previously imposed on the argument) is the sense in which one acts irrationally or immorally.

In this connection, Nagel offers a very strange and self-defeating maneuver. He says, very plainly,

> If absolutism is to defend its claim to priority over considerations of utility, it must hold that the maintenance of a direct interpersonal response to the people one deals with is a requirement which no advantages can justify one in abandoning. The requirement is absolute only if it rules out any calculation of what would justify its violation.

And yet, in the same breath, he concedes "that there may be circumstances so extreme that they render an absolutist position untenable. One may find then that one has no choice but to do something terrible." He also acknowledges that the Hague and Geneva Conventions do not exhibit "moral immutability," that "modern war" may be "impossible to wage as an acceptable form of interpersonal or even international hostility" (which would then commit us morally to pacifism—though Nagel is doubtful about that), and that "there may exist principles, not yet codified, which would enable us to resolve such dilemmas [as the dirty hands dilemmas]. But then again there may not. . . . The idea of moral blind alley is a perfectly intelligible one."[23]

This is all but preposterous. What is the sense in which we can conduct our lives on moral and rational principles that include what is binding in an absolutist regard, *that would concede a moral blind alley just in the most strenuous and difficult and important situations in which moral guidance is required?* Nagel cannot have it all ways: he cannot claim absolutist constraints, concede that they must be rationally vindicated, and then admit that they do not rationally legitimate *any* behavior in the dirty hands context. This is simply moral and conceptual bankruptcy. Also, it is just the situation in which Brandt reminds us that Oppenheim observes that it is at least coherent (and possibly morally defensible) to release nations facing "absolute catastrophe," or radical threat to their "basic values," from the restrictions normally binding on the conduct of war.[24] At the very least, Brandt's point demonstrates that Nagel has *not* vindicated either the priority of absolutism or the blind alley thesis *or* the moral or rational inadequacy of the utilitarian claim. The trouble with the utilitarian view, however, is simply that, where it obtains, the dilemma disappears.

What we must see, therefore, is that the entire argument calls into question the resolution of the dirty hands dilemma by appeal to *covering principles*. Absolutism is suspect because, *if* it obtains at all, then utilitarianism is at least a reasonable candidate for overriding its constraints in contexts of "necessity," "absolute catastrophe," survival, and the like. But utilitarianism is suspect at least because no one is really convinced that absolutist constraints can always be overridden by utilitarian values or that absolutist values are simply utilitarian values in disguise. At the very least, absolutist values are *not* consequentialist values—which, it seems, utilitarian values always are.[25]

We can, therefore, concede that there *is* a utilitarian solution to the dirty hands problem, but it can be bought only at a price that seems too high: it dissolves what appears to be a profound dilemma and it does this by imposing a very strong consequentialist reading of how to legitimate human behavior. But the point of the dilemma is that *one does what is evil, by way of rational choice, in order to further a good cause*; and that the cause in question arises in a context of "necessity," threat of "absolute catastrophe" or survival or the like, paradigmatically at least (if not necessarily) where corporate societies are thus engaged. This certainly catches up what is involved in high-altitude bombing, the threat of nuclear war, the issues of Sartre's and Hochhuth's plays, and the like. *If*, then, we are to preserve the dilemma, we must acknowledge the hopelessness of capturing the dirty hands case *within the competence of moral principles*—that is, of a principled morality, *whether* of the so-called patterned sort (following Robert Nozick's distinction[26]), as in utilitarianism, *or* of the nonpatterned sort, as in Nagel's (or, further, in Alan Donagan's[27]) account.

There is nothing incoherent in holding that, in certain dire circumstances, it is effectively impossible to do anything that, however intended to further

266 | Joseph Margolis

a good cause and however actually serving or furthering that cause, will not, at the same time, be evil or entail indisputably evil features or aspects of a nonconsequentialist sort (without of course precluding evil of a consequentialist sort). *That is the challenge of the dirty hands dilemma.* It would be incoherent to hold, *if this much were granted,* that rational moral conduct is (or is always, or is in the relevant circumstances) *principled* conduct, of either of the two sorts in question—that is, either by way of some calculative principle regarding benefits or by way of a fixed rule that precludes all calculation. In the dirty hands context, we must proceed rather in terms of exemplary and particular cases, without any prospect of bringing appropriate behavior under fully covering rules or principles. We *might* for instance be rationally driven (for all Nagel insists to the contrary) to practice torture in extreme circumstances: he is of course right to think that we could not be excused from the evil committed, in so acting, even if it were the case that—truly, or at least in our perception—the survival of western civilization depended upon it. (Imagine trying to break in time the code for delaying a first strike using an absolutely devastating new weapon that only the enemy possesses.) But Nagel has offered no reason at all for thinking that acting thus was *not* also right—or even *the* right or the obligatory—thing to do. The simple solution is that *acts committed may, under real-life circumstances, exhibit inextricably good and evil sides*—and that there may not be any alternative available, when "necessity" demands, that could insure the good without the evil. Under conditions of necessity, our choices may then be tragic. But to say that is not to say that they are irrational, immoral, unprincipled, or fall outside the scope of rational and moral considerations. It is only to say that the persistence and seriousness of the dilemma (possibly the likelihood that the modern world will continue to multiply more and more global occasions in which it is bound to arise) signify either or both that the planetary conditions under which men are expected to act rationally and morally exhibit a distinctly irrational and evil cast (maybe becoming increasingly irrational and evil, as a result of human history itself) and/or that the model of what it is to act rationally in a moral way cannot be (comprehensively or in important sectors of application) a *principled* model at all.

To say that, however, is to challenge the thrust of much of recent moral philosophy. A *principled* morality cannot acknowledge *principled dilemmas* regarding the distribution of good and evil: it can only admit, as Sophoclean tragedy long ago perceived, unfortunate collisions, under contingent circumstances, *of* the application of principles that, as principles, form an entirely coherent moral world.[28] Tragedy does not require a collision of principles: Sophoclean tragedy does, in a sense; but tragedy itself, the inextricable intertwining of high good and high evil, may well obtain without being subsumed or subsumable under colliding principles or the colliding application of principles.

If we suppose that moral principles—that are not merely tautological (as, for instance, "promote good over evil")—are themselves generalizations grounded in compelling or exemplary cases, then discerning an instance of the dirty hands phenomenon may well proceed case-by-case, by perceived similarities, rather than by the application of universalized criteria. In that sense, we are hardly logically obliged to construe the phenomenon as morally troublesome because of dilemmas involving principles. Dirty hands may involve dilemmas due to making choices in a morally imperfect and inflexibly imperfectable world rather than to dilemmas of mere choice.

The trouble with Walzer's and Nagel's account is simply that they risk construing moral commitment (in the dirty hands context) as inevitably irrational and incoherent; whereas the truth may well be that moral commitment cannot remain rational and coherent unless we acknowledge, in such a context, that it cannot be (or cannot convincingly be construed as being) a commitment of an essentially principled sort—without thereby being *un*principled. Walzer and Nagel begin with too exalted a notion of moral perfectibility. Walzer sustains it by conceding the initial competence and priority of utilitarian calculation—only to fall back to a grasp of the monstrous consequences of his own concession. So he solves that artifactual difficulty by invoking an absolutist principle *after* first applying the other. The result is a parody of the tragic, since the moral world is made tidy again by a sequence of putatively rational and principled decisions. Presumably, there is no evil that remains within our moral history, for the order is coherently *restored*. Nagel sustains it by conceding the initial irrelevance of moral principles with regard to what is required here and now of human action. We blink at first; then we remember our principles, bring them to bear on acts committed; and so we need never acknowledge that those principles were ever placed in jeopardy by the original occasion. The result is that we insure the present *benefit* of deliberate commitments we choose to judge only *after* that benefit has been secured. There is no order to restore, for there was none ever lost. It was only rationally excused from review—though only episodically and at first. Walzer secures the rationality of a principled moral world by making the application of principles only serially pertinent; and Nagel secures it by making their application only intermittent.

But these are preposterous conceptual maneuvers: ultimately, morally quite irresponsible. They are, however, not unimportant, for what they demonstrate (by example) is the impossibility of construing moral life as systematically explicable in terms only and always of the application of adequate principles to the details of every serious engagement. Tragedy and its cognates—dirty hands, in particular—remain a permanent reminder of the impossibility of ever articulating and defending a purely principled morality.

Notes

1. Michael Walzer, *Just and Unjust Wars* (New York: Basic Books, 1977), p. 323.

2. *Ibid.*, pp. 144–145. He cites Marc Bloch's objection to the demarcation, however, without explaining how "just war" applies to modern states. See Marc Bloch, *Strange Defeat*, trans. Gerard Hopkins (New York: Norton, 1968), p. 130.

3. Walzer, *Just and Unjust Wars*, p. 323.

4. *Ibid.*, p. 324.

5. See, for instance, the extraordinarily detailed rebuttal of Hochhuth's charge against Churchill (which does not directly address the question of whether Sikorski was assassinated or not), in Carlos Thompson, *The Assassination of Winston Churchill* (Gerrards Cross, England: Colin Smithe, 1969). Both the play (*Soldiers*) and Thompson's book are textbook studies of the dirty hands problem. See also Eric Bentley (ed.), *The Storm over the Deputy* (New York: Grove Press, 1964).

6. Walzer, *Just and Unjust Wars*, p. 325.

7. Michael Walzer, "Political Action: The Problem of Dirty Hands," *Philosophy and Public Affairs* II (1973): 160–180. The paper by Nagel and responses by R. B. Brandt and R. M. Hare appeared in *Philosophy and Public Affairs* I (1972).

8. Walzer, *Just and Unjust Wars*, pp. 325–326.

9. Thomas Nagel, "War and Massacre," *Philosophy and Public Affairs* I (1972): 126, 128. Nagel's commitment to the just war concept is strengthened by his favorable opinion of G. E. M. Anscombe's theories. See Anscombe, "War and Murder," in Walter Stein (ed.), *Nuclear Weapons and Christian Conscience* (London: Merlin Press, 1961).

10. Nagel, "War and Massacre," pp. 125, 129.

11. *Ibid.*, pp. 126, 129.

12. *Ibid.*, pp. 124, 129.

13. *Ibid.*, pp. 129–131.

14. *Ibid.*, p. 132.

15. See "Double Effect, Principle of," *New Catholic Encyclopedia*, Vol. 4 (New York: McGraw-Hill Book Co., 1967), pp. 1020–1022.

16. Nagel, "War and Massacre," p. 132.

17. *Ibid.*

18. *Ibid.*, p. 134; emphasis mine.

19. *Ibid.*, pp. 136–137.

20. *Ibid.*, p. 137.

21. R. B. Brandt, "Utilitarianism and the Rules of War," *Philosophy and Public Affairs* I (1972): 146–147, especially n. 3.

22. See also Alan Donagan, *The Theory of Morality* (Chicago: University of Chicago Press, 1977), Chap. 2.

23. *Ibid.*, pp. 136, 141, n. 11, 142, n. 12, 143.

24. *Ibid.*, p. 147, n. 3. See L. F. L. Oppenheim, *International Law*, ed. H. Lauterpacht, 7th ed. (New York: Longmans, Green, and Co., 1948–1952), p. 351; cited by Brandt. See also R. M. Hare, "Rules of War and Moral Reasoning," *Philosophy and Public Affairs* I (1972).

25. See Bernard Williams, "A Critique of Utilitarianism," in J. J. C. Smart and Bernard Williams, *Utilitarianism For and Against* (Cambridge, England: Cambridge University Press, 1973), p. 79 and §2.

26. Robert Nozick, *Anarchy, State, and Utopia* (New York: Basic Books, 1974), pp. 155–160.

27. I find no resolution of the issue in their views; but the thesis here advanced appears to be congruent with the worries acknowledged by Walzer, "Political Action: The Problem of Dirty Hands"; Bernard Williams, "Politics and Moral Character," in Stuart Hampshire (ed.), *Public and Private Morality* (Cambridge, England: Cambridge University Press, 1978), particularly p. 65; and Thomas Nagel, "Ruthlessness in Public Life," also in Hampshire (ed.), *Public and Private Morality*. See also Hannah Arendt, "On Violence," *Crises of the Republic* (New York: Harcourt Brace Jovanovich, 1969); Reinhold Niebuhr, *Moral Man and Immoral Society* (New York: Charles Scribner's Sons, 1960).

28. I take the thesis, here defended, to be congenial to Betty Flower's general caution about easy principles applied without close attention to the actual context of human life—in which alone they both acquire whatever pertinence they have and actually invite responsible assessment. See for instance Elizabeth Flower and Abraham Edel, "What Does Minimal Government Minimize?" *The Personalist* LIX (1978): 386–393.

Elizabeth Flower:
A Biographical and
Bibliographical Note

Elizabeth Flower came to philosophy by way of a degree in chemistry from Wilson College. At the University of Pennsylvania thereafter she was attracted by an unusual seminar conducted by Edgar A. Singer—the first such seminar in the philosophy of science. It brought together not only graduate students but also college teachers (some already famous)—economists, biologists, psychologists—from Temple, Bryn Mawr, Swarthmore, as well as from Penn. Later she was appointed, as E. Flower, to teach at Penn, at a time when women's classes were segregated and female faculty still unimagined. It is not clear whether the trustees were aware that they had appointed a woman (and would have been horrified) or whether they were being socially far-sighted. Whatever the case, generations of students, graduate and undergraduate, remember her classes and seminars, generally conducted (however sizeable) in easy conversational exchange. Flower experimented early with bringing high school students to the university for advanced work, with undergraduate scholars' programs, and with cooperative courses that joined the humanities and sciences from across the university. Her philosophical interests turned from science to ethics at a time when the hard distinction between the normative and the descriptive, the valuative and the factual, was becoming a raging problem. Persuaded that the scientific was value-laden and the genuinely normative grounded in scientific understanding, she dealt with ethics in its relations to psychology and social science, to law and education, and to the larger social and intellectual context. Her courses in the history of ethics preserved historical insights and approaches at a time when American philosphers had largely abandoned historical perspectives.

Although most of her academic life was associated with Penn, Flower has also taught or lectured at Columbia (Barnard), Hamilton College, and Latin American universities from San Marcos (Peru) to the National Universities of Colombia, Chile, and Guatemala. She pioneered intellectual exchanges with Latin America, and worked with the Organization of American States in a series of monographs tracing the history of philosophy in each country. Out of these there came eventually the two-volume *A History of Philosophy in America* (with Murray Murphey), which is today a standard work in that field.

Flower has also engaged in various forms of philosophical practice. Early in her career she worked with the American Friends Service Committee in Mexico—with work camps and with the exiled Spanish Republican intellectuals, especially the philosophers, and with the Indian and Education departments. (Among practical techniques, she recalls helping to bring together two feuding rural villages, by means of a production of Aristophanes' *Lysistrata*, recommending peace by feminine power.) In recent decades she has played an active part in the organization of various professional societies and projects.

Marriage to Abraham Edel was followed by extensive philosophical cooperation. They have taught Exxon-sponsored courses in philosophy and education, and in moral education, have presented joint papers at philosophical meetings, are publishing a voluminous work (with Finbarr O'Connor) in the history of ethics, and recently have been engaged in a work in the theory of applied ethics. As a Fellow of the National Humanities Center in 1978–79, Flower projected a work on the meaning and role of the practical in American philosophy; and as Senior Fellows at the Center for Dewey Studies in 1981–82, she and Abraham Edel have worked on the role of sociohistorical changes and social science development in the maturing of Dewey's ethical theory, a book now in midstream. Her appointment as Professor Emeritus of Philosophy in 1985 has provided the alleged leisure for these labors.

ETHICS

"Comments on the Ethical Theory of Edgar A. Singer," *Philosophy of Science* XXI (January 1954): 1–8.
"Words on Moral Worth," in *The Cultural Heritage of Twentieth Century Man.*

Philadelphia: *Pennsylvania Literary Review* and the Philomathean Society, 1956, pp. 3–14, 1956.

"Edgar A. Singer, Jr., on Contentment," *Journal of Philosophy* LIV (September 1957): 576–584.

"Some Present Day Disagreements in Moral Philosophy," in *Aspects of Value*, ed. Frederick C. Gruber. The Martin G. Brumbaugh Lectures, Third Series. Philadelphia: University of Pennsylvania Press, 1959, pp. 19–37.

"Norms and Induction," in *Philosophy of Knowledge*, ed. Roland Houde and Joseph P. Mullally. Philadelphia: Lippincott, 1960, pp. 280–289.

"Mill and Some Present Concerns about Ethical Judgments," in *Liberty* (Nomos IV), ed. Carl J. Friedrich. New York: Atherton Press, 1962, pp. 140–161.

"Ethics of Peace," in *Dictionary of the History of Ideas*, ed. Philip Wiener. New York: Charles Scribner's Sons, 1973. Vol. 3, pp. 440–447.

Review (coauthor) of Alasdair MacIntyre, *After Virtue, A Study in Moral Theory*, in *Journal of the History of Philosophy* XXI (July 1983): 426–429.

"Introduction" (coauthor) to Dewey and Tufts, *Ethics*, in *The Later Works of John Dewey*, ed. Jo Ann Boydston, Carbondale: Southern Illinois University Press, 1985. Vol. 7, pp. vii–xxxv.

"A Moral Agenda for Ethical Theory," in *Value, Science and Democracy: The Philosophy of Abraham Edel*, ed. Irving Louis Horowitz and H. S. Thayer. New Brunswick, N.J.: Transaction Books, 1987, pp. 239–257.

Morality, Philosophy, and Practice: Studies and Readings, Historical and Contemporary (coauthor). New York: Random House, 1988.

LEGAL AND SOCIAL PHILOSOPHY

"Commitment, Bias, and Tolerance," in *Cultural Pluralism and the American Idea, An Essay in Social Philosophy*, by Horace M. Kallen. Philadelphia: University of Pennsylvania Press, 1956, pp. 116–125.

"Induction and Social Validation," in *Validation of New Forms of Social Organization*, ed. Gray L. Dorsey and Samuel I. Shuman. Wiesbaden, Germany: Franz Steiner Verlag, 1968, pp. 110–119.

"Rights, Strategies, and Strategic Rights," in *Human Rights* (Amintaphil I), ed. Irvin Pollack. Buffalo, N.Y.: Jay Stewart Publications, 1971, pp. 193–197.

"Some Functions of a Functional View: An Historical Glance" (coauthor), in *Anuario de Filosofia Del Derecho*, Tome XVII, Communicaciones al IV

Congresso Mundial de Filosofía Juridica y Social. Madrid: Instituto Nacional de Estudios Juridicos, 1974, pp. 27–35.

"Participatory Equality—An Emerging Model," in *Equality and Freedom*, ed. Gray L. Dorsey. Dobbs Ferry, N.Y.: Oceana Publications Inc. and Leiden: A. W. Sijithoff, 1977. Vol. I, pp. 309–313.

"What Does Minimal Government Minimize?" (coauthor), in *Minimal Government in Theory and Practice* (Amintaphil III), ed. Robert C. L. Moffatt. Issue of *The Personalist*, October 1978, pp. 386–393.

"Some Value Aspects of the Problem of Pollution" (coauthor), in *Law and the Ecological Challenge* (Amintaphil II), ed. Eugene E. Dais. Buffalo, N.Y.: William S. Hein and Co., 1978, pp. 244–259.

"Elitism and Culture" (coauthor), in *The Humanist as Citizen*, ed. John Agresto and Peter Riesenberg. National Humanities Center, 1981, pp. 135–164.

Coeditor, Transaction Book series on Moral and Social Thought: Vol. 1: Morris R. Cohen, *Law and The Social Order*, 1981. Vol. 2: Merle Curti, *Growth of American Thought*, 1982.

"Economic Justice: Notes and Queries" (coauthor), in *The Journal of Value Inquiry* XIX (1985): 251–261.

"Experience and Legal Reasoning," in *Reason and Experience in Contemporary Legal Thought*, ed. Torstein Eckhoff, Lawrence M. Friedman, and Jyrki Uusitalo. Berlin: Duncker and Humblot, 1986, pp. 23–30.

"Discussing Discussing Peace" (coauthor), in *Realism and Morality: International Ethics in a Nuclear Age*, ed. Kenneth Kipnis and Diana Meyers. Boulder, Colorado: Westview Press, 1987, pp. 251–256.

PHILOSOPHY OF EDUCATION

"In Two Keys," *Harvard Educational Review* XXVI (Spring 1956): 99–102.

"On the Language of Education" (exchange with Israel Scheffler), *Studies in Philosophy and Education* IV (Spring 1965): 123–133.

"Comments on Philosophy of Science and Educational Theory," *Studies in Philosophy and Education* VII (Fall 1970): 143–153.

"Fundamental Principles of the Metaphysics of Curriculum," *Philosophy of Education* 1973: Proceedings of the Twenty-ninth Annual Meeting of the Philosophy of Education Society, New Orleans, April 15–18, 1973, ed. Brian Crittenden, pp. 284–291.

"Old Principles and New Pitfalls," *Studies in Philosophy and Education* XI (Winter 1979): 313–324.

HISTORY OF PHILOSOPHY, MAINLY IN THE AMERICAS

"Two Applications of Logic to Biology," in *Philosophical Essays in Honor of Edgar A. Singer*. Philadelphia: University of Pennsylvania Press, 1942, pp. 69–85.

"El 'American Friends Service Committee' en Mexico," in *Boletin Indigenista* (Mexico, D.F.: Instituto Indigenista Interamericana) VI (March 1946): 58–71.

"Panorama de la Filosofia Norteamericana" (some contemporary problems), in Universidad Nacional de Columbia, *Revista Trimestral de Cultura Moderna*, Bogota, 1946, pp. 39–46.

"The Mexican Revolt against Positivism" in *Journal of the History of Ideas* X (January 1949): 115–129.

"Philosophies of History," in *A History of Philosophical Systems*, ed. Vergilius Ferm. New York: The Philosophical Library, 1950. Chap. 45, pp. 574–586.

Review of *Making of the Mexican Mind* by Patrick Romanell, in *The Hispanic American Historical Review* XXXIII (November 1953): 544–546.

Philosophy in Peru, A Historical Study. Translation with interpretive commentary of *La Filosofia en El Peru, Panorama Historico*, by Salazar Bondy. Washington, D.C.: Panamerican Union, 1954; reissued 1961.

Review of *The Vienna Circle: The Origins of Neo-Positivism* by Victor Kraft, in *Scripta Mathematica* XXI (June-September 1955): 169–171.

Principales Tendencias de La Filosofia Norteamericana (with Murray Murphey). Washington, D.C.: Panamerican Union, 1963.

"The Unity of Knowledge and Purpose in James' View of Action," in *The Philosophy of William James*, ed. Walter Corti. Hamburg: Felix Meiner Verlag, 1976, pp. 179–200.

A History of Philosophy in America (coauthor). Two volumes. New York: G. P. Putnam's Sons, 1977. Hackett Publishing Co., 1979.

"Some Interesting Connections Between the Common Sense Realists and the Pragmatists, Especially James," in *Two Centuries of Philosophy In America*, ed. Peter Caws. London: American Philosophical Quarterly Library of Philosophy, Basil Blackwell, 1980, pp. 94–103.

"Der Philosophieunterricht in Amerika in 17. Jahrhundert," in Ueberweg, *Grundriss der Geschichte der Philosophie*. A revised edition of Ueberweg's classic text, edited by Jean-Paul Schobinger. Basel: Verlag Schwabe. In press.

"Philosophy in America." *Encyclopedie Philosophique*. Paris: Presses universitaires de France. In press.

"Classic Themes in American Philosophy." *Revue française d'Etudes Américaines*. In press.

Contributors

Berg, Ivar.
  Associate Dean, College of Arts and Sciences, University of Pennsylvania. Author of *Work and Industry*.

Edel, Abraham.
  Research Professor of Philosophy, University of Pennsylvania, and Distinguished Professor of Philosophy Emeritus, City University of New York. Author of *Science, Ideology, and Value* (3 vols).

Edel, Leon.
  Henry James Professor of English Emeritus, New York University, and Citizens Professor of English Emeritus, University of Hawaii. Pulitzer Prize biographer of Henry James.

Foster, Lawrence.
  Chair, Department of Philosophy, University of Massachusetts (Boston) and Director of the Law and Justice Program. Author of studies on the psychological and cultural aspects of philosophy.

Manicas, Peter.
  Professor of Philosophy, Queens College of City University of New York. Author of *A History and Philosophy of the Social Sciences*.

Margolis, Joseph.
Professor of Philosophy, Temple University. Author of *Pragmatism Without Foundations: Reconciling Realism and Relativism.*

McDermott, John.
Distinguished Professor of Philosophy and Head of Philosophy and Humanities, Texas A & M University. Author of *The Culture of Experience.*

Murphey, Murry.
Professor of American Civilization, University of Pennsylvania. Author of *The Development of Peirce's Philosophy* and coauthor of *A History of Philosophy in America* (2 vols).

O'Connor, Finbarr W.
Chair, Department of Philosophy, Beaver College. Coeditor of *Reading in the Arts and Sciences* and *Deviance and Decency.*

Potok, Chaim.
Author of *The Chosen* and other novels.

Scheffler, Israel.
Victor S. Thomas Professor of Education and Philosophy, Harvard University. Author of *The Language of Education.*

Schwartz, Robert.
Professor of Philosophy, University of Wisconsin, Milwaukee. Author of many studies on the relation of psychology and epistemology.

Simon, Robert.
Professor of Philosophy, Hamilton College. Author of *The Philosophy of Sport.*

Sleeper, Ralph.
Professor of Philosophy Emeritus, Queens College of City University of New York. Author of *The Necessity of Pragmatism: John Dewey's Conception of Philosophy.*

Index

Neighborhood, 225
Neighborhoods, going downhill, 225
Neitzsche, Friedrich, on metaphor, 162
Neo-Marxism and antireductionism, 233
Neo-Marxists and paradigm conflict, 233
Newell, Allen, 7, 87; *Human Problem Solving*, 85; problem-solving language, 88; and Simon, paradigm of inquiry, 93; theory of inquiry, 91; theory of problem-solving, 89
Newman, John Henry, 105
New Republic, 68
Newton, Isaac, 158, 219; and inquiry, 83; and methods of inquiry, 78
Newtonian mechanics, 220
Newtonian metaphysics, 219
New York City, 225, 227; public schools, 103
New York *Times*, 239, 244, 245
NHL hockey players, 217
Nixon, Richard, 46
Noble Savage and Rousseau, 152
Norms as rules, 27
Northern cities, write off, 224
Nozick, Robert, 205, 265
Nuclear Age, 67
Nuclear energy: decisions on, 23; and value conflict, 24
Nuclear war, as unjustifiable, 259
Nuer beliefs, 188

Obligations to other states, 205
O'Connor, Finbarr, 7, 82, 271
Ontological reductions and positivism, 43
OPEC, 219
Operational facility and computer, 243
Oppenheim, Felix, and realist concept of national interest, 198
Oppenheim, L. F. L., 264
Ordinary, potentiality of, 112
Ordinary language analysis, 22
Oresteia, 263
Organization of American States, 271
Orgasm and Rousseau, 151
Osborn v. *The Bank of the United States*, 54
Ought and pronoun, 22

Overpopulation, decisions on, 23
Overproduction and business, 39
Ownership: as animistic and emulative, 141; origin in barbarism, 133, 140; as sign of individual force, 141
Oxford ordinary language analysis, 22

Pacifism, Dewey on, 68
Pain, measurement of, 21
Paine, Thomas, 58
Palmer, A. Mitchell, raids, 75
Papert, Seymour, 241
Parental bent, 127
Pareto, Vilafredo, 21, 220
Parnes, J., creativity model, 96
Passmore, John, 239
Peace, 3, 12; decisions on, 23
Pecuniary culture as animistic, 141
Pecuniary gain and barbarism, 132
Pecuniary manipulation of production and distribution, 133
Pedagogy, 7; and aesthetics, 113; Dewey's relation to his philosophy, 115; and politics, 113; of problem-solving, 97
Peirce, Charles Sanders, 13, 30, 107, 118
Perry, Ralph Barton, 14, 30; Dewey's criticism of, 18; *General Theory of Value*, 14, 16, 22; *The Moral Economy*, 14; *Realms of Value*, 20; spirit and nature, 20; on value, 16, 17, 21
Person, concept of, and rights, 47
Personal factors in science, 178
Personality types, 25
Petition of Rights, 56
Phenomenological influence on value, 22
Philadelphia, 225
Phillips curve tradeoff, 229
Philosopher, role of, 40
Philosophers, Scottish, 5
Philosophical Perspectives on Metaphor (Mark Johnson), 160, 161
Philosophy, 3; academic, 4; American, 5, 11; American political, 46; analytic, 3, 37; economic, 4; of education, 4; of language,

real and teaching, 97; representation, 7, 11, 88; representation and models, 97; representation and solving, 89; representation as outcome of inquiry, 91; representation, Dewey vs. Newell and Simon, 90; situation and consciousness, 30; situation, Dewey on, 18; solving, 4, 5, 88; space and problem representation, 85; space and problematic situation, 88; space, structure of, 85; and thinking, 129; what it is, 249; well defined, 90

Problematic and Dewey, 83

Problems, 7; and computer in education, 245; identification as shared, 70

Problem-solving: as creative, 92; creative, and computer, 245; and Dewey, 82; elements of, 252; as heuristic search, 85; how done, 86; and information, 250; and inquiry, 83, 97; and intelligent use of information, 251; and learning, 299; method, contrast of Dewey and Newell and Simon, 91; as search, 92; theory of, 86

Product hazards, 218

Production: in industrial sense, 138; socialization of, in capitalism, 77

Productivity: differential measurement of, 226; and education, 226, 227; of individuals, 10

Professional schools and arts and science faculties, 232

Program, computer, for problem-solving, 88

Programmed instruction, 238

Programming, employment in, 242

Progress: in evolution, 132; scientific, 5

Progressive education, 117

Progressivism in education, 237, 238

Project method of education, 115

Prolegomena to Ethics (T. H. Green), 19

Propaganda and schools, 70

Property: private, and capital accumulation, 76; protection of, and end of government, 58

Prosperity, 3

Protectorate, 56

Protocol analysis and problem-solving, 88

Psychoanalysts, methods of debate, 233

Psychoanalytic psychology, uses of, 156

Psychological effects: of hybridization, 134; of mutation, 134

Psychological tests of values, 26

Psychology, 22; personality, and value studies, 24; social, and value studies, 24; and value theory, 23

Public and Its Problems, The (John Dewey), 50, 51, 53, 69

Public: capitalism and democracy, 70; democratic and cause of eclipse, 70; origin in transactions, 59; private, line between, 50; wants, 224

Public interest, 9, 51, 196; concept of, 196; as distinct from national interest, 198; as including social, cultural and political factors, 197

Publics, 6; creation of, 79; formation of, 51; as presupposition, 71, 78

Puerto Ricans and segregation, 225

Pufendorf, Samuel, 56; and Wise, 57

Purpose, 4, 14; for which computer is used, 240

Quality in art, 186

Quality of life of ordinary person, 112

Queens College, 104

Quetzalcoatl myth, Aztec revision of, 176

Quine, W. V., 3, 38, 42

Race, Veblen's use of, 134

Racism and value conflict, 24

Radical change and Dewey's views, 74

Rationality, 173; relativistic view, 181; theory of, 189; of traditional thought, 175

Rational mind and Snow, 147

Rational moral action, 266

Rawls, John, 262; justice as fairness, 206; theory of justice, 203, 212

Reaction to predictive failure in traditional thought and science, 175

Reagan, Ronald, 46, 224

Real estate values, 225

Realism, 4; critique of, 209; normative political, 200; Scottish, 4

Realist conception of national interests, 198, 199, 211; implications of, 202;